Praise for
THE BLUE IRIS

"A story of found family, impossible romances, and the ghosts of the past, *The Blue Iris* is a riveting page-turner as stunning as the blooms that fill the shop at the heart of the book. Haunted and haunting, it keeps you guessing even as you cheer for Tessa and the broken but irresistible makeshift family she builds for herself. A story of growing up and deciding who you really are, it's an unforgettable tale of roots in more ways than one."

—Grace O'Connell, Author of *Be Ready for the Lightning*

"Riveting, soul-searching, and full of heart. . . A spectacularly told story. . . . Told in multiple characters' voices, the narrative is riveting, with shocking surprises unraveling at a steady pace. The plot's top-grade tension grows taut as Tessa works herself up to take the hard decision. Readers won't want to put this down."

—The Prairies Book Review

"A gorgeous novel—Stone brilliantly captures the power of optimism, the allure of memory. Readers will fall in love with the Blue Iris Flower Market and the vibrant cast of characters they meet there."

—Stacy Bierlein, Author of *A Vacation on the Island of Ex-Boyfriends*

"This is a special book. Rachel Stone has crafted a narrative that touches both the mind and the heart, carried along by some of the most memorable characters I have encountered—complex, relatable, and very, very human. She writes honestly and clearly, with a delicate lyricism that lingers well after the final page is closed, and in so doing, she shines a light on our common challenge of finding the place where we truly belong. *The Blue Iris* merits a place in the company of books to be read, reread, and cherished."

—Greg Fields, Author of *Through the Waters and the Wild*, Winner of the 2022 Independent Press Award for Literary Fiction

"The lives of five employees of the Blue Iris flower market in Toronto are so tightly intertwined that when one moves, another is impacted, and their story moves forward as well--especially when the handful of outside characters' motivations also come into play. It's truly brilliant plotting and character development."

—Kathleen Basi, Author of *A Song For The Road*

"A fascinating novel that follows a young woman's story as she faces her past and discovers a new future. . . . Rachel Stone has penned an incredible work with complex, unique characters and an absorbing love story. Readers will love its engrossing storyline and unexpected ending."

—Readers' Favorite, 5 Star Review

"In *The Blue Iris*, Rachel Stone shines as a gifted wordsmith. Her narrative is like walking through a lush garden; our senses explode with the beauty in her vivid descriptions. With each chapter, her rich cast of characters take root, grow, and evolve, Tessa most of all. Hers is a difficult journey—to ground herself in truth, she must peel away the facade that has sustained her. Tessa learns a lesson important to each of us: when we let go of dying things, it frees us to hold fast to that which nurtures us. *The Blue Iris* is an engaging, unique novel of love and chosen family—the best kind."   —**Carla Damron**, Author of *The Orchid Tattoo*

"Stone debuts a gorgeous literary novel with a nostalgic aesthetic and themes of complex friendships, family trauma, and healing through self-discovery. . . . Stone's writing is rich and evocative, digging right to the difficult emotions under the surface of the often antagonistic interactions between the characters. She deftly utilizes a multiple-narrator format, offering a deeply intimate look into each character's trauma and how it shapes their interactions . . . (and) real emotional depth for characters of both genders . . . the novel's emotional current, showing broken people whose lives become better when they care for and forgive one another, carries through powerfully.   —**BookLife**, Editor's Pick

"In Stone's novel, a modest Canadian flower shop becomes an arena for romance, heartache, and betrayal . . . it's a pleasure to watch the little community fight for what matters to them—human connection, how to run a flower business and, when the Blue Iris is in danger of being converted into condos, the shop's very existence. A captivating read that's full of humor and heart.   —**Kirkus Reviews**

"Rachel Stone's charming novel, *The Blue Iris*, captures a group of engaging employees working at a Toronto flower market as they come to terms with their individual pasts and as they contemplate their futures. These compelling characters work together steadily, with humour and occasional friction, surrounded by the beauty of the flowers, and they each confront and slowly resolve their own complicated lives. *The Blue Iris* is a joy to read."
—**Michelle Berry**, Author of *The Prisoner and the Chaplain*

"Stone imbues her characters with such depth and personality that by the time readers turn the last page, they feel like they really know all of them. Heightened emotions, palpable romance, and just the right amount of tension keep the pages flying. Stone delivers an intricate exploration of love and friendship with grace, resulting in a story that's as heartfelt as it is poignant. Stone is a writer to watch."
—**BookView Review**, Gold Recommend Review

THE
BLUE IRIS

RACHEL STONE

VIRGINIA BEACH
CAPE CHARLES

The Blue Iris

by Rachel Stone

© Copyright 2023 Rachel Stone

ISBN 979-8-88824-093-9

Published by

köehlerbooks™

3705 Shore Drive
Virginia Beach, VA 23455
800-435-4811

For Leah,
All things are possible.

Iris, Blue / *Iris Versicolor*
(NORTHERN BLUE FLAG, DAGGER FLOWER)

Symbolic Meanings and Uses:
Valour. Purification. Spirit messages.
Believed to increase business when kept by the register.

SAM

New Year's Day

The truth?

He was tired.

Tired of Kinkade cottages fluttering to parquet,

wood spindles lodged in peeling honeysuckle.

Another year of his mother's blue breath

burrowing like a dental drill,

his father's cop-car stare like iron chains.

Just tired.

Tired of sputtering, flailing goodbyes in tides

black as a missing heartbeat.

Hog-tied to a perpetual departure,

to being the one they kept saving instead,

when all he ever wanted was to let go.

Common Spider Orchid / *Dendrobium Tetragonum*

Intuition. Secrets.

◀◯▶

TESSA

T ESSA HELD her breath as Will turned the corner and steered the Porsche south, towards the luncheon she didn't want to attend, on the street she'd avoided for fifteen years.

Her mouth fell open as her gaze stumbled over the boutiques glittering in the late April sun, the cafés with wrought-iron patios. Gone were the fish-and-chips place with the picnic tables, the ice cream store that never changed flavors. Even the old apartment was a two-story Organic Planet.

When she was little, a crisp spring Saturday like this would have seen her skipping beside her mother along this very stretch. Stopping for bagels where that liquor store now stood, the round owner winking as he slipped Tessa a strawberry tart in a box tied with string. They might even have ducked into Toy Town (now a steel-and-stucco Toronto Dominion bank), if only to look.

All this time, Tessa feared returning would be too painful. The Morrow Avenue of memory was a quaint two-kilometer strand between downtown and the suburbs, and home to her earliest, sweetest moments. A place where all was still good and right in the world. In her absence, every inch had been replaced. Every treasure buried with her mother, bulldozed to dust, paved over.

She should have come back years ago.

"Are you sure you're okay with this?" Will asked.

Tessa looked at her hands, her fingernails etching red moons into her palms. Sighing, she nodded. She was twenty-six years old; she couldn't keep skirting the street forever. Besides, Hunter was Will's best friend; missing his engagement luncheon was out of the question.

She'd been dreading this party for days, even before she knew it was being held at the swanky Brunello's up ahead. Airy chitchat waited like an interview scoresheet, Will's friends practically reciting their corporate bios straight off their firms' websites, a growing brood of sleek pumps and pearls moaning about work-wedding balance. Every expression drawing empty as it drifted towards her. *How about you, Tessa? What's next?*

Tessa pulled her dress over her knees. It wasn't like she had no options. Her gleaming transcripts, hard-won internships, and as of a week ago three *summa cum laude* degrees, qualified her for plenty of Big Time Careers; even if she still had no clue what these looked like, or which among them she wanted. Even if she still wasn't entirely sure she wanted any of them at all.

What Tessa *wanted*, more than ever now that she'd finished graduate school, was her mother, Beth's, charmed poise in gliding through any crowd or conversation. Her endearing non-answers for every prying question. When Will turned that corner, a foolish part of Tessa hoped Beth's magic would be here, waiting unclaimed. That in coming back, the way forward might grow clearer.

Beautiful, brilliant-eyed Beth. Killed by a drunk driver on a spotless Tuesday afternoon.

Tessa, eleven and alone. Waiting outside Roseborough Elementary.

Will's hand closed over hers, warm and sure, her ring finger beneath it pointedly bare. Tessa couldn't help smiling as she looked at him, their own news still a private champagne bubble in his eyes. The heat of it fluttering up. Tessa remained uncertain about many things, but Will Westlake had never been one of them.

They turned onto a side street, where the old wartime bungalows had been squashed flat by stone-encrusted mansions sprawling upward and against narrow property lines. They found parking and walked back to Morrow Avenue, where Tessa skidded to a stop, Will's hand dropping from hers as she gaped at the storefront on the corner. The Blue Iris Flower Market. Memories came flooding in a full-color swoosh.

She'd shopped here before. With her mother.

The place was exactly the same; time had weathered it heavily and ignored it completely. Tessa peered through the doorway, age five again, her gaze dancing along the floor: pockmarked cement, green flecks smattered like confetti, water snaking towards a miniature sewer in the middle. A surface so clearly belonging outside but so brazenly indoors.

"Can I help you?" the woman behind the counter called, smiling.

Tessa shook her head, then, on impulse, drew closer. The scent of the place made her gasp—punchy florals, murky soil and standing water, a swirl of traffic exhaust. Her dreams smelled just like this.

Steps inside that very doorway, young Tessa had tugged her mother's hand, eager to resume their walk. With Beth, simple errands often morphed into lengthy meet-and-greets. On this occasion, Beth had smiled reassuringly, indigo eyes aflicker, as they waded deeper into the crowded space, Tessa claustrophobic and her mother glad-handing like a dignitary in Keds.

They must have gone in to buy flowers. *What kind?* Tessa was suddenly desperate to know. *For whom?*

"What is it?" Will asked, glancing at his watch.

They were late for the party. Sadly, there was nothing more to remember. Tessa pulled her eyes from the flowering tufts, the woman. "Nothing," she said, shuffling on.

She fumbled her way through the small talk at the luncheon. Afterwards, Will headed downtown to the firm and Tessa caught an Uber back to her apartment, tucked at the edge of her grandparents' property outside the city. Intent on polishing her CV, she scrolled around on her laptop, typing words but then immediately deleting them. She opened her calendar, staring into the unnerving blank space. No course deadlines, no exams schedule—no job interviews, either.

Tessa couldn't find urgency in any of it. Since walking by that flower market, she couldn't turn her mind to any part of her future without being pulled back to that sunny day lost to the past. She and her mother would have passed by the Blue Iris countless times before moving from the neighborhood to this apartment. How could she have such vivid memories of every other shop, every inch of that street, and only a lone fragmented snippet of the market? It didn't make sense.

That night, winter exhaled as daylight stretched deeper into evening. Tessa lay awake for hours, veins humming. Images of that colorful market swirling. Not since before Beth's death had Tessa felt her mother so alive, so nearly within reach. So *insistent*.

The next morning, she went back.

Charlie, the woman behind the counter, seemed to remember Tessa from the day before. Her sage eyes suggested she remembered, well, everything. "Looking for anything in particular?" she asked.

Tessa stammered. Why hadn't she anticipated such a question? "I guess so. In a way. But I'm not sure it's any specific flower."

Charlie's expression grew distant. "Hardly ever is, is it?" Sunday morning streamed through the window beside her. "Take your time, girlie."

And Tessa did. Under Charlie's guidance, she sniffed every bloom from alstroemeria to zinnia. Still, she couldn't remember more. Couldn't recognize what her mother had carried on the way home.

Over the week that followed, she found reasons to return—Ainsley's cat passing away, neighbor Mrs. Buckley's eighty-second birthday, the mail carrier's husband filing for divorce. And then, the rest sort of just . . . happened.

Tessa traced the bedsheet seam with her thumb as she told Will. Beside her, the patter of his fingers against the laptop fell silent.

He stared through the screen. "You're *working* there? At the flower market?"

Tessa shrugged then switched off the lamp. "Only for the summer. The overtime is no joke. I could pay down my student loans by September and—"

It was only then she realized she'd never actually said *yes* when Charlie introduced her to Rowan, the owner of the Blue Iris, who was looking to hire on short notice. Then again, her new boss never asked the question. It simply hadn't occurred to any of them that she might turn the job down.

Will's voice cut through the dark. "It's not about money, Tess."

He sometimes forgot that for most people it was, always at least a bit, about money.

Tessa tugged gently at his jaw until he looked at her. She held his gaze, her voice soft. "There's more to remember, and my mother wants me to. I just know it." Will gave a disquieted smile. Tessa kissed him, relieved. He pushed his laptop aside and pulled himself closer, her snap decision to work at the market fading from concern.

This morning, in the open refrigerator's chilly glare, it hit her why Will was so thrown by her plans. How could she have forgotten her promise to stick by his side when the time came to take over the firm? If Tessa was headed anyplace this summer, it should be downtown to the spare glass-walled office across the hallway from his, with the high ceilings and hushed carpeting and spotless white furniture. To help the man she adored find footing in his father's big, expensive shoes, like she'd vowed seven years ago to do.

It's incredible, what the human mind is capable of un-remembering.

Tessa glanced at the stove clock. *Tick-tock.* Her shift started in thirty minutes. Groaning, she swung the fridge door shut, predictably unable to stomach the idea of food. First days were always like this; growing up, not even her grandmother's cooking could lure her from the soda crackers and raspberry Jell-O as a new school year approached.

This was a *summer job,* she reminded herself. Casual, completely temporary. Yet, as Tessa merged onto the pink highway towards the city, her knuckles white at the wheel, she understood in a way that was all feeling and zero fact that her mother's visit to the Blue Iris that day was about much more than flowers. With one summer left between now and *what's next,* the old neighborhood taking off faster than a twin-turbo engine, all she could hope for was enough time to figure out why.

Yerba Santa / *Eriodictyon Californicum*

"My grief is unresolved."

CHARLIE

YOU START OUT thinking it's just one. Then, *sure, what's one more summer?* Suddenly, you're forty-goddamn-three, still sweeping the same crack in the cement. Still waiting to be asked to the stupid dance. But the dance was long over, and the only place Charlie belonged now was in bed, alone, killing a pint of pralines and cream.

The scissors hissed as Charlie freed a clump of flesh-colored cymbidium orchids from their plastic. Did Rowan expect her to sell them crammed ten-to-a-bunch like a shoebox full of doll parts? Outside her window by the register, shelves were being stocked for another season, every plant off the truck ironically stealing more of her oxygen.

She thought she could handle it. The start of planting season, her twenty-eighth, without the man under whose command the buds and shoots themselves had always seemed to unfurl.

No, she never truly believed she'd *have* to. No matter how hard Sam tried to self-destruct over the winters, he always made it back, intact and on time, for spring at the Blue Iris.

Back to her.

Screw you, Sam.

The mercury had only a few millimeters more to climb before the local gossips started pouring in. Once they realized their beloved flower frontman was gone, the whole neighborhood would be talking. Six-point-two million souls in this bustling city, yet you couldn't drop a Grande Americano on Morrow Avenue without thirty of them hearing about it. Charlie had none of the sordid details they wanted, but like tuna sandwiches at a wake they'd linger too long anyway, casually riffing on plausible scenarios, as if they were helping. As if she hadn't imagined each soul-curdling one a thousand times already.

When Sam's Chevy was found half-buried in snow up by the cabin, there was still plenty of reason to believe the man who had run this place *wanted* to be gone. January winds had carried him off countless times before, Charlie, too, in the opposite direction, bent on saving the world one off-season at a time. But last week, the spring thaw pushed his trashed snowmobile onto the ice-cluttered shores of Killbear Provincial Park, one hundred and four-point-seven nautical miles downwind from the cabin per Google Maps, and her stomach hit the ground like a rusty anchor.

She poked her head out the open side of the window, as though the glass might be distorting her view of Sam's brother, Darryl, the wrecking ball in black coveralls, hovering over a flat of Marguerite Daisies. The pinch in his wide face confirmed he was trying to figure out whether to shelve them under *M* or *D*. Never, in twenty-seven years, had the outdoor stock been shelved alphabetically; it was the stupidest imaginable way of doing it. Yet, every spring, Darryl tried anyway. And like everything else the miserable oaf touched, his big brother, Sam, had come through afterwards and fixed it.

"Don't even think about it!" she yelled. When Darryl's middle finger flashed above the racks, Charlie pulled her head from the window and stormed outside, prim elbows pumping. She picked up two fluffy trays Darryl had shelved and slammed them back where they belonged.

His arms shot through the air. "Are you fucking kidding me?"

Charlie waved him off like a fruit fly, grabbing more flats.

Darryl followed, the two of them shuttling the plants back and forth between the aisles. At last, he squatted, hands on his knees, and spat his words across the open shelving. "It was alphabetical."

Charlie met his stare, then raised an eyebrow. "Since when?"

Darryl grunted. "Right. Whole place never existed until Queen Charlie showed up."

"Feeling really in charge, aren't you?" she poked. Sam would have been hovering by now, ready to quell another surge in this decades-long storm. "Like you're—" Charlie's voice climbed, forcing her to stomp it. *Like you're him.* "Now, there's a stretch."

In a blink, Darryl hurled a flat of blue hosta through the open shelves. Charlie, long immune to his public displays of volatility, didn't even flinch as it sailed past her head and exploded against the wall in a fireworks of roots and soil. "Go back inside, Spider," he said. "Everything in there's already dead . . . just how you like them."

Too far, even for him. Charlie lunged across the shelving, fists bouncing off his massive body. "It's *my* fault he's gone? Who stepped up when you abandoned that counter in the first place, huh? You made your *own brother* carry all of it!"

"Again, with this shit," he said, spittle flying. "Sam the Saint, everybody's fault but his. Like I didn't clean up my share of the mess? Like you've got one goddamn clue about any of it?"

Their eyes locked. Infuriatingly, Charlie's lip trembled. Darryl backed away, repelled per usual by any emotion besides rage, aiming two thick fingers at her like a Smith and Wesson. "You keep the hell out of the way."

Charlie, already halfway inside, tossed the reply over her shoulder. "Yeah, I'll get right on that."

Back to her cymbidiums. Charlie held a single stem to the light— sixteen meaty blooms, veins the color of a newborn's eyelashes. A creature this majestic demanded to be showcased alone. Charlie would rewrap each orchid in its own sleeve, even if it took all day. Indeed, there were *way* too many here; Sam would've brought in half as many in a month. But did anybody think to ask her?

Pasqueflower / *Pulsatilla hirsutissima*

"Passing Over."

———◄◦►———

TESSA

FROM THE DOORWAY, Tessa surveyed the shop's Monday offering of tattered stems left over from the weekend. The grumbling fridge showcased foggy glass and roses on overturned milk crates, while potted plants claimed the natural light, washing the room in greenish grey. Rowan, the owner, had the phone to his ear, its relic cord twisted through his fingers. A smile flitted before he riffled through a binder, pretending he hadn't seen her.

Charlie clamored into view, her petite frame clenched as she attacked the floor with a broom. She noticed Tessa and uncurled, swiping one cheek with the heel of her palm. "Yo, girlie. Ready to get your hands dirty out there?"

Tessa's eyes pulled wide. She'd assumed she would be working *in here,* at Charlie's practiced elbow, with bouquets and common houseplants, where the margin for error was slim as eight-dollar tulips. Where her mother's laugh lingered like soft perfume. She never dreamed the job would be *out there,* the open-air storefront, where nursery stock was sold by the plastic tray.

Rowan hung up, veering around the counter. "Come on, I'll show you the ropes."

The pilot light of panic flared under Tessa's ribs. It was one thing to shuffle a few stems to fleeting effect, but she knew nothing about gardening. Couldn't tell annual from perennial or tropical from vegetable. The snippets drifting in through the window said it all. *Out there* was an overgrown tangle, powered by forklift exhaust and testosterone.

But she'd followed her gut this far; what choice did she have?

Outside, his hands crammed into his pockets, Rowan delivered the new-hire orientation in one breath followed by a wheezy gasp, almost like he'd written it out ahead of time.

"All set?" he asked. But before she could answer, he hurried off like he'd left his wallet somewhere.

Aisles of sagging plywood stood all around, orange trailing the frames like rust-colored sobs, the stock lean and haphazardly arranged. Tessa busied herself checking the care tags, separating perennials from annuals. Lining sun-lovers along the top, and shade plants underneath. She tackled the clutter under the counter; a garbage bag overflowing with garbage bags, pen after pen that didn't work, half a mouldy sandwich in wax paper.

Darryl's mugshot stare pulled her gaze upwards. The wolf tattooed on his massive forearm glared at her. "Who told you to do that?"

"I just thought—"

He slammed his palm into a shelf, the speed of his rage all but blowing Tessa's hair back. "Who's paying you to think?"

Despite his staggering size, Tessa's own hair-trigger temper reared, which could sometimes be a problem—not least of all because it was inextricably wired through her tear ducts. She stared back, certain her voice would crack if she spoke.

Darryl's mouth turned up at one corner, his eyes dry ice. Tessa couldn't tell if he was amused or itchy.

"He's trying to break you," Charlie shouted from the window. "Do not let him!"

Darryl looked at Charlie. The air between them grew so intense that Tessa stepped back from the line of it, her stomach pumping in time with the vein in Darryl's neck as Rowan, back with trays of coffee, set about biting the skin around his nails.

Yes, *out here* was definitely a mistake.

A tractor trailer pulled up, the diesel engine setting the corner vibrating harder. Without a word, Darryl shuffled off towards the truck and Charlie disappeared from the window.

Rowan turned to Tessa, his thin face a worry line. "The only one who ever could keep those two from killing each other was Sam."

Darryl fired off a loud whistle. Tessa's other two coworkers appeared from the back. Luke and Tony (she wasn't yet sure who was which). Both sidestepped Tessa like she was selling timeshares and joined the scrum forming at the curb. Darryl wanted to offload the metal carts of product from the truck via the forklift. Rowan insisted the forklift couldn't cross the sidewalk. Darryl asked how-the-fuck Rowan thought trucks got unloaded before hydraulic liftgates. Rowan recounted the time a cart fell off the forklift and hit a passing Lexus.

A customer came looking for peat moss. Tessa stared at the woman's blue gardening clogs, flustered because she had no idea what peat moss was. Her entire way forward had been built on knowing the correct answers.

"It's soil, dear." The woman gestured to the wooden fence along the back of the storefront. "They keep it back there? While you're at it, I'll take a bag of sheep manure, too."

The alley behind the fence was lined with many varieties of dirt, all packaged in manageable, pillow-sized bags—except, naturally, the peat moss, sold in cubes the size of a three-drawer filing cabinet. Tessa nudged one; perhaps it was a lighter, fluffier dirt than the rest? She gave it a shove, shifting her weight, ramming until sweat dampened her face. It wouldn't budge.

Fed up with this job, so different than planned and unimpressed by all she *did* know, Tessa slammed her palms into the dirt. Then, angry at it for jarring her wrists, she kicked it, jamming her foot. She was shuffling around the alleyway in a private fit, cursing and shaking out limbs, when the customer and Luke-or-Tony appeared. They looked at each other, eyebrows cocked.

It was the sort of look that had kept Tessa in anonymous lecture halls all these years, reluctant to commit to any environment for longer than an academic term. It was yet another reason she should be helping Will at the firm this summer, where she'd receive no looks of any kind. She was too porous. Everything around her seeped in without permission, while everything inside her refused to be contained. Sooner or later, colleagues noticed. Coworkers talked. Before long, it didn't matter how well she performed; they'd already decided she was *uptight,* or *weird,* or *too intense.* All of which really meant *crazy.*

Luke-or-Tony's face, cloaked in dark sunglasses and even darker stubble, was wary, like she had a ticking timer on her forehead. Like he, too, had already decided. "Chill," he said, "I've got it."

If Tessa did have a timer, the word *chill* would have flipped it straight to flashing zeroes. Did people think *chill* was readily available to her? That it could be scooped up by anyone, in any quantity, like dry-roasted peanuts at Bulk Barn? That given the option, she wouldn't go walking around in a permanent state of *chill?*

He gave a cool shudder, as if reading her thoughts, then slid the peat moss into the customer's Subaru as easily as a bag of marshmallows. Tessa heaved the manure over her shoulder and stalked after him. She had only a few steps to go when the plastic packaging split with a dreadful flutter. Black earth poured like sugar down her side. She gasped as the cold, damp granules wriggled inside her clothes, working their way down her shoes.

It wasn't entirely surprising. Objects around her ruptured sometimes, as if acted by force. Tessa used to imagine she had telekinesis, like in *Matilda,* except she never did learn to control it nor was there ever any gratifying outcome—besides the one, nearly eight years ago, that redeemed all the rest.

Tessa had been at a party, pretending she enjoyed parties. As she approached the screen door to go outside, it popped clean off its track, activating the backyard motion lights. She tumbled over it, vaulting across Ainsley Murphy's midnight lawn like a spot-lit monkey in front of the entire senior class, including the new transfer, a *Westlake,* plus a mob of other guys from school crammed around him, trying to become cooler by proximity. Will marveled later at how unrattled she'd seemed. Tessa assured him she'd been mortified, just not surprised.

Tessa's coworker, expressionless, fetched a new bag of manure. "A little poop never hurt anybody," the customer offered. "Some say it's good luck!" The woman handed him a five-dollar tip before driving off.

"Who?" Tessa muttered, sweeping the mess. "Who says that? The people covered in poop?"

Luke-or-Tony angled the dustpan. Tessa caught the shadow of a smile, and hoped maybe he hadn't decided about her after all. Maybe she could still make a go of this place long enough to figure out why her mother wanted her here.

On their way back to the storefront, he pulled the fiver from his pocket. "Here. She was your customer."

Tessa waved the money away. "Besides acting like a total jackass back there, I cost us a bag of manure."

"Nah, Tony probably went too deep with the box cutter when he unwrapped the skid."

Mystery solved: the dark-stubbled, supremely *chill* one was Luke.

Sniffing herself, Tessa made a face. "It's actual shit, isn't it?"

Luke winced. "Afraid so."

She shook her head in question. *Why?*

"Veggie gardens, mostly. Manure is a natural fertilizer."

"And peat moss?"

"You add it to the manure. Keeps the roots from drying out."

Tessa wondered what sort of mix Pop used at the house. "And the difference between cow and sheep manure?"

Luke's heavy shoulder lifted. "One falls farther?"

Tessa's laugh shot to the sunlight, her stomach starting to uncoil. "So much to learn."

Back at the half-emptied truck, Tony whipped a dead bloom at Luke. Luke returned fire, the bud slapping off Tony's cheek. Everyone chuckled. Tessa lingered awkwardly, wanting to help but feeling strangely like this was invitation only. Cautiously, she transferred two flats from cart to shelf. Darryl ignored her. Luke nodded, so she kept going.

Behind that truck, another waited. Then, another. They all seemed to hold impossible quantities of plants. When the final engine slunk away, the corner fell silent again. Rowan took off up the street. Darryl retreated behind the fence. Tony and Luke bumped fists and fished cigarettes from their pockets, Tony's dangling from his lip, Luke's tucked behind one ear as they, too, disappeared into the alley.

Tessa looked around, tipsy on hue and texture. An overflowing landscape had sprung from the barren concrete like a time-lapse video. Hydrangeas in rustling plastic lined the sidewalk. The boulevard was a meadow of tulips and crocuses, color seeping to each rounded top.

Yellow-orange pansies stretched to the sky like hungry birds' beaks, the purple hyacinths fragrant on the breeze. The morning's haunted expanse had vanished. She stood, entranced, until Rowan reappeared with grilled sandwiches, and her stomach leaped at the smell. Suddenly, she was starving.

Asphodel / *Asphodelus*

"My regrets follow you to the grave."

◄◦►

CHARLIE

SHE WAS SECURING clear plastic to what felt like her thousandth orchid when the elastic snapped. Charlie clenched her teeth, shaking the wet sting from her fingers. *Goddamn you, Sam.* Here, between these ghost-grey walls, her thoughts wouldn't steer clear of him. In this time zone, he still drove her every gesture.

She marched to the staff room, barely bigger than a phone booth with a laundry tub stained the color of cold cappuccino. Rowan was in the walk-in cooler, its vault-like door propped open while he sorted cash for the bank drop. Charlie leaned against it, picking at one of the rust patches. "Give me Tessa in here," she said. "Just for the weekend."

Rowan looked up in alarm. Typically, he would have hired a seasonal worker to assist her with the cut flowers through the summer, but this year Charlie insisted he didn't. If Sam truly hadn't resurfaced by now, keeping frantically busy in here was the minimum penance she deserved and besides, in that case she'd be less likely to dwell on it: the first time in twenty-eight summers that she was here, and he wasn't.

"You do realize it was your idea to put her on the outside counter," Rowan said.

"Actually, now, I say you let her handle the storage yard."

Rowan looked doubtfully at Charlie. Through her humanitarian aid efforts over the winters, she'd seen that same look on benefactors, many of them also well-meaning men with fistfuls of cash who struggled to reconcile her delicate stature with the idea that she did, in fact, know what she was talking about.

"She's still getting her feet wet," Rowan said, apologetic in the usual way. "I need her to hit stride by May two-four, or Darryl's going to pop an aneurysm."

The May 24 long weekend, the shop's most gruelling three-day stretch, marked the official kickoff of planting season. But that was two weeks away, a lifetime in Blue Iris hours. Charlie smashed a woody lilac stem with her mallet, conditioning it to draw water. "Darryl *is* an aneurysm. Come on, it's Mother's Day. I need a buffer."

Rowan's expression softened. While the rest of the world would assign Charlie a level of grief appropriate to any longstanding employee—far below that of Sam's two children, his three ex-wives, hell, even his mistresses— Rowan was the only living soul who knew the truth. Most of it, anyhow. He nodded as Tessa slid into the staff room with more cash from the till.

Charlie smiled at her. "You up for helping me in here with the cuts this weekend?"

Tessa lit up. "Definitely!" She slammed her a high-five. "It'll be such good times."

No, girlie, it won't be anything close. But Tessa would prove a quick study, and already she seemed to have made it her personal mission to make Charlie laugh. Almost like she knew.

A handsy couple who had obviously made it to the bloody dance lined up to pay for some orange parrot tulips. Charlie twirled the feathery stems into a paper cone, ringing it in a touch too vigorously.

"You forgot the flower food," the woman told Charlie.

Charlie forgot nothing. Tulips hated that stuff. Much preferred a daily trim and water change. But as she explained this, the couple stared like judges at a dog show, amused by her show of tricks with zero intention of trying them at home. Sighing, Charlie tossed in the preservative. Since when was the truth enough to sway a woman's mind?

Like every third customer this week, the couple debated whether Mother's Day or Valentine's Day was busiest in a flower shop, and like every customer ever, settled on the latter. Charlie didn't bother correcting them; if decades behind this counter had taught her anything, it was nobody cared about being right when they were trying that hard to sound like it.

She'd worked her first Valentine's Day this past February, when she should have been overseeing the dental outreach in Uganda—*double-goddamn-you, Sam.* It was practically a yoga retreat. The customers, primarily men, didn't stalk in waving some grand floral vision off the internet, to be produced to spec in five minutes, for less than forty bucks. Generally speaking, the men simply wanted out of there. It was one purchase per customer—two or three at most, but discretion was a hallmark of the job—always red roses. Charlie tried suggesting neon Gerberas, a rainbow spray of hybrid teas, but the customers backed away like she was contagious, saying, *"I'd better stick with the red, just to be safe."* Which struck Charlie as much more about fear than love, but what did she know about it?

Mother's Day, by contrast, demanded bouquets for everyone from frail great-grandmothers to disapproving mothers-in-law, the contents of each deliberated at painful, pointless length. The customers, staring down the barrel of brunch with the people who drove them craziest, were harried, resentful, and perpetually running late. There was no topping up displays, no end to the queue. Charlie told herself all of this was why she always ran home afterwards and screamed into a pillow.

Mother's Day was the one weekend Sam spent entirely inside the shop, with her, a butterflies-released-by-the-boxload highlight until it wasn't. By tradition, he kept a pail of blue irises by the counter, presenting one with a flourish and tip of the imaginary hat to every frazzled mom who walked in. Maybe it was Sam's knack for identifying a mother on sight, or how the women always puddled up at his feet, but it made Charlie want to throw up every time.

"Hey Charlie, where do you want these?" Tony held a bucketload of gladiolas to each hip, veins buckling on his forearms, his usual cocksure self. Five seasons here had layered enough grit on his pretty features, legitimizing a satisfaction-guaranteed grin. Striking a resounding note with ladies either too young to realize it couldn't last, or old enough to bank on it. It was a far cry from Sam's universally golden appeal, but having him as floater up front this weekend would assuage the snobby housewives at least.

"In the cooler, please . . . *sweet cheeks.*" Charlie wound up as though she were about to slap him on the bum. Determined to act like herself if it killed her.

Tony dodged out of the way, pails sloshing. "Hey! Watch it!"

Charlie followed him through the staff room, Rowan and Tessa shuffling to accommodate like a car full of clowns. "My gosh, what has you so sensitive in that area today?" she asked in a tone that made it clear she already knew the answer.

Tony dropped the pails with a *clunk* in the cooler and leveled his eyes at Rowan. "Really?"

Rowan lifted his hands in defense. "I just needed a count on Toasted Westerns. Darryl was the one who kept asking where you were."

"Luke is such an asshole," Tony said.

"So, it's true," Charlie said. And there it was, like muscle memory. She was enjoying herself.

"What?" Tessa asked her.

"Nothing," Tony said.

"Bite wound," Charlie said in a stage whisper, "on his *ass cheek!"*

"Would you shut up?" Tony flicked his eyes at Tessa.

"What?" Charlie said. "She's outside, she's going to hear everything."

"They've been tiptoeing around me out there like I'm the Dalai Lama," Tessa said.

Tony eyed her. "If you want the truth, you do have sort of a Sunday school vibe."

Charlie smiled. *It's her aura.* Even as a child skipping down Morrow, Tessa's had shimmered as spectacularly as her mother's—only it wasn't indigo blue, like Beth's, but crystalline white. A pearl lit from within. The untrained eye couldn't see it, but anyone in close proximity would certainly pick up on it, or, in Tony's case, mistake it for a halo and run the other way.

"Well, you can *chill,"* Tessa told him. "If you met my grandfather, you'd know there's nothing I haven't heard."

Tony sighed, relenting. "I caught a live one last night, and now I have sutures to match."

Charlie clapped her hands once, the subject officially tabled. "It was the barista, wasn't it? God, I hope your tetanus is up to date."

Tony snapped the tip off a gladiola and flicked it at her.

Rowan's eyebrows shot up. "Wait, is it? I can't have you off sick on top of—"

"Relax. I'm not missing the MILF season opener. I plan on doing Sam proud this weekend." Tony looked at them. "If you must know, yes, I got a booster at the walk-in."

"I knew that barista was the rainbow of trouble," Charlie said. "Sometimes, when I ask for extra foam, she gets this look in her eyes." She shuddered for emphasis.

"Oh, I've seen it," Tony said, shifting his focus to Tessa. "I knew I recognized you. You parked by here last week, right? Porsche 9-11?"

Tessa lifted her eyebrows. "Wow, good memory. It's my boyfriend's."

"Hard to forget a car like that. Limited edition, right? *So* clutch. Custom rims, trim kit . . ."

Charlie couldn't help puffing like a mother goose. Tony, in platonic conversation with a female besides herself. Now if Luke would just do the opposite, with literally anyone (at this point, the barista would do), she'd lay off worrying about both for a while.

Tessa bounced outside, Tony peppering her with Porsche questions. The girl would be fine out there now, no matter how many times Darryl went Darryl. It pushed the blackout shades in Charlie's head higher, May's tentative rays filtering her dank chest.

She never could have pictured being here without him. Still expected him to waltz through that door any minute, green pail in hand. But staying on this summer was the right move. Even after everything, Sam wouldn't have wanted her anywhere else.

Charlie felt him in here, more strongly than all the years before combined. She hoped it meant wherever he was, he'd finally found peace. For all the spectacular ruin he'd caused, he deserved that much.

For the hundredth time today, she reminded herself that when Sam looked at her through those double-dog-dare eyebrows that first summer, his fervent courtship with death was already underway. She'd expected a tragic ending the whole time. They all had.

What no one saw coming, after spending all her winters do-gooding across the globe, bribing karma on his behalf, was that it would be Charlie herself who finally brought him down.

Honeysuckle / *Lonicera periclymenum*

Permanence.

———◀◉▶———

TESSA

Dusk had settled over the gleaming white Porsche parked at the back of her grandparents' property. Will's trim silhouette leaned against it, his casting-call smile popping like Venus against the purple evening.

"Hey, you," he said, laughing into her mouth when she held his peppermint kiss and pulled him into the car by his tie. "How was day one?"

Tessa traced a finger over his diamond-cut features, stockpiling the feel of him. It was getting as though they didn't even live together anymore. "Oh, it was . . ."

She'd been counting seconds until it was time to flee the tired place. Then, when it closed for the night, it dismayed her to leave. It was possible—likely, even—that Tessa didn't remember much about her childhood visit to the market because she and her mother had been running a mundane errand, nothing more. Yet, all through Tessa's shift today, Beth seemed to rustle every leaf.

Will registered her dirt-smeared cheeks and soiled clothes. His tone hardened, like he was preparing to call out the schoolyard bully. "What happened?"

Tessa stifled a giggle; he loomed far larger in court than on any blacktop. "I'm fine. I just need a shower." The trouble was, having finally sat down to drive, her feet refused to stand her back up. Resigned, she threw her seat back and closed her eyes. "Come get me in ten minutes?"

Will's knuckle grazed her temple. "Babe, Nano's probably been cooking since yesterday. If we're late, and the pasta dries out—"

Tessa sighed. *"The most important ingredient is timing!"*

Laughing, Will pulled her to standing. She slumped against his chest.

"I have an idea," he said. He scooped her sideways and charged the steps to her apartment on the second floor of the coach house.

"Will, no!" she said, elbows tight against the back of his neck as his lean body strained to finish the ascent. "Put me down!"

He thrust open the door, breathing heavy into her ear. "Let me in that shower. You won't have to lift a finger, I promise."

"You just said we can't be late."

Will frowned playfully and set her down. Dirt particles skittered across the entryway tiles as he pulled off her sneakers. "I need to head home straight after dinner. Still have a couple more hours at the office, then squash with Farleigh first thing."

Tessa's gaze fell. More and more, work had been pulling Will downtown, but the penthouse was "home" now? She swallowed her disappointment; he was juggling so much already. "Farleigh, the one who took his shirt off at the holiday party?"

Will nodded, eyes rolling. "Dad needs me to push his caseload up. Family practice's billings are getting to be an embarrassment."

Tessa padded absently into the bathroom, leaving the door ajar. It wasn't like he'd ever formally moved in. But Will was one of so few—certainly the only boy—she'd invited into this cherished space she once shared with her mother. The apartment quickly became Will's haven, too. He'd slept in his childhood mansion maybe three times since high school.

Once Will started law school, and Tessa graduate school, they'd slept often at his parents' penthouse condo in the city, a quick jaunt from both campuses. When he began interning at the firm, Will officially rented the place, and as his hours grew longer still, spent even more nights there. Tessa usually joined him, until a few weeks ago, when Pop's fall changed everything. But she never once stopped thinking of the coach house as home.

She summoned a smile. "I need to get to sleep early, anyway. Rowan offered me an eight-thirty start initially, same as Charlie, but the outdoor crew actually starts at six-thirty."

"That's a thirteen-hour day, outside," he called from the edge of the bed, his gaze fretful as she peeled away her clothes to reveal black rings of earth caked around her waist and ankles. "Isn't that a little . . . extreme?" Will, who could run for a week on coffee alone, knew well the incoherent, weepy mess Tessa became on too little sleep. How her body detested severe temperatures.

"I'll be fine once I get into the routine." She showered quickly, then flipped her head upside down, wringing out her hair. Beyond the walnut tresses, she could still feel him frowning.

"Arbitrary change in employment terms," he said. "On the first day."

"Easy, counselor." Tessa wrapped the towel tight across her body. It was strange not to be pouring out about her day; their relationship nestled comfortably inside the details. But what could she say about her first shift at the Blue Iris that wouldn't leave him even more baffled as to why she was there? How would it improve the situation to mention Darryl the ogre, or her peat moss tantrum, or the exploding bag of manure?

"This was supposed to be a light summer for you," he said.

Weeks ago, her lengthy academic career drawing to a close, her *what's next* anxiety rising, Will suggested one schedule-free summer, a first since Tessa was old enough to dog-walk for the Gilliams next door. She could catch her breath, then turn her mind to next steps in the fall. Tessa had warmed to the idea but preferred to keep busy. Also, she didn't love dipping into her savings.

Signs of collusion followed shortly thereafter at the club, when Peter, Will's father, offered her paid summer placement at his law firm between mouthfuls of Steak Neptune. Peter's political aspirations meant accelerating Will's succession plan, and all agreed Tessa could be of great help through the transition. She could still set her own hours, define her duties however she pleased. Take on as much or as little as she wanted. With the heir to the Westlake empire between your sheets, flexibility came as a given.

Tessa hadn't said no right then; Will's knack for *getting to yes* was an alto to his father's soprano. Instead, she'd thanked Peter, promised to consider it, then reverted to standard Sunday dinner protocol—smile politely, fix your gaze to your plate neatly avoiding that of Eleanor, Will's mother, and defer any real conversation until the Porsche ride home.

Being Will's right hand sidestepped all the palpitations that kept her out of law school. To say they worked well together was an understatement; his transparent office walls would be the biggest snag. But every time Tessa had pictured herself bundled against the office tower air, summer pleading in slits through downtown's concrete canopy, an invisible pair of hands squeezed her lungs.

Will smiled knowingly. "Just promise you won't get pulled under." When Tessa found a void in need of filling, overwork was her idea of work. "At least you'll have Sunday to recharge."

Tessa winced at the mirror. "I'm working Sunday, too, now. And Saturday."

Silence. She'd miss Mother's Day brunch at the club. Though Will's mother would hardly mind, the event was an important opportunity.

Will—Tessa, too—needed to build personal ties with his new clients, and quickly.

Will appeared in the doorway. Tessa searched for signs of irritation, but his face was all compassion. Flying solo at the brunch wasn't ideal, but he'd never take issue with her trying to remember more about her dead mother on Mother's Day.

Tessa apologized anyway. "Charlie asked if I'd help out inside, and I couldn't say no. It sounds like that Sam guy did so much. There were barely any customers today, and already it was crazy, all the care that goes into things."

Will pushed the door the rest of the way open, lavender-scented steam pouring from the bathroom. Tessa laced her fingers in his, folding him over herself. "Speaking of crazy . . ." he said as they stared at their hazy reflection, her head at his cheek, his eyes hungry now across her towel. Slowly, he kissed the length of her neck. "How am I supposed to make it through dinner without losing my mind?"

Tessa sank in as he swelled against her. Between scrambling to complete her thesis and Will getting up to speed at the firm, opportunity lately had been too scarce. His lips found hers, asking softly, then pleading with urgency. She peered over his shoulder at the clock; they were due at the main house for dinner in six minutes.

She slid her fingers inside his collar and up through his fresh haircut, eyes granting their silent blue permission, then let her towel drop. Will grinned as he raced to unbutton his shirt and slung it over the door. When he looked at her like that, she was incapable of saying *no*, no matter the time.

Nano leaned over the Depression-era butterfly leaf, platter high in one hand, her other fist tucked into her hip as a counterweight. "One more, William. Don't make me throw it out. It's a sin!"

Tessa smiled down at her manicotti, bursting with ricotta and spinach and ladled with the incomparable tomato sauce. No one rose from her grandmother's table without the need to unbutton their pants.

Will held up his plate, puffing his cheeks as Nano piled not one, but three pieces of the famous chicken, lightly breaded and baked until golden, then simmered in wild mushroom cream with a hint of lemon. "Thanks, Nano." Ever since Tessa bungled the title *Nonna* as a child, everyone from Pop to the cashiers at Mr. Grocer ended up calling her Nano eventually. Will had taken less than a month. "I've been banking calories all week."

Across the table, Pop threw Tessa a look and pushed down his mouthful of garlic bread. "What the Christ—"

Tessa laughed. "Don't get me started. He thinks he's gaining weight."

Will pinched his stomach, only slightly rounder since his mid-twenties. "People of the jury, the evidence is clear." He sighed. "This Hewson trial isn't helping. You know I overeat when I'm stressed."

"Never mind," Nano said. "Working those hours, you need to keep your strength up. Besides, a belly is nice. It means you're in love. Right, Pop?"

Pop's voice held the same conviction as the first telling. "Saint Paddy's Day, parish hall, 1966. One bite of this woman's tiramisu, and I said, '*This is it, Jimbo. She's the one.*' I still couldn't tell you what she puts in it. But I'm telling you . . . I *knew.*"

Will lifted his wine glass per usual, eyes twinkling at Tessa. "When you know, you know."

Pop followed suit with his beer, a new tremor in his hand. With his emerging health concerns, there hadn't been a right time to tell them.

"You doing okay today, Pop?" Tessa asked.

He lowered his eyebrows. "I'm old, kid. I'm not dead!"

Tessa still shuddered at the memory of that voicemail, waiting for her upon landing three months ago. Pop, wedged between toilet and wall. Nano, clammy and distraught, trying for over an hour to pull him out. Tessa broke in two just looking at her iron-plated grandfather afterwards, hugging the darker side of the hallway, shoulders dejected in his too-big pajamas.

"The shakes are getting worse," Nano told her, easing the cling wrap-toothpick tent from the cherry cheesecake.

"Did you call the doctor back?"

"What for?" Pop interjected. "You know what doctors do? They bury their mistakes, that's what they do! Why do you think they call it a practice?"

"Pop!"

"Pop nothing! It's my arthritis. Don't go making a big deal, and you can quit the night watch, too. I'm fine now. Busier than a one-legged man in an ass-kicking contest around here, eh, Nano? You see me slowing down?"

Tessa glanced out at the wide stretch of lawn, three different lengths because Pop had taken to mowing it in segments. The winding hedge, once maintained to the millimeter using Nano's old nail scissors, still in the winter burlap. Three acres was just too much now.

"What night watch?" she said. "It's just a shorter commute to work from here."

Behind her, the staircase loomed. The main floor powder room, too small to turn a walker in, much less a wheelchair, laughed. This place would have been sold years ago if not for Tessa.

When she and her mother moved here, not long after visiting the market, Tessa had formed an immediate attachment to the property. Nano and Pop's relationship with Beth, historically fractured, had broken off completely when Beth got pregnant by a man she never saw again while traveling Greece. But raising a child alone proved harder than expected, and Beth reluctantly ended up moving with Tessa to the coach house.

The moment Tessa met her grandparents, she understood, even at age five, there was nothing those two wouldn't do for her. But as the Parkinson's progressed, holding onto the home she loved would become impossible.

Pop switched subjects. "Tell me, was the first day worth getting your undies in a bundle?"

Tessa sighed. "I have no clue what I'm doing. And the outdoor department work is so physical." She and Will waved Nano back into her seat, rising to clear the dishes. "As the newbie and the only female, I'm totally the weakest link."

"The only female, huh?" Will said, scraping the plates. "What happened to Charlie?"

Tessa shrugged as she loaded the dishwasher. "She's inside with the cut flowers. I hardly saw her. The guys needed a ton of help unloading."

"I bet they did."

Tessa tilted her head. Will took any chance to downplay the fact that it was he who had girls clawing to stand behind him in the popcorn line at Cinemax. "It's not like that."

Will's knowing smile returned. "It's always like that."

"No, these guys were annoyed on sight. Like I'm cramping their locker room vibe."

"Locker room vibe. Even better."

Tessa swatted him with the tea towel. For as long as she'd known him, a pageant of false lashes had fluttered constantly from the wings. Yet to this day, no matter the room or crowd, whenever she found Will's sea-glass eyes, they were only ever looking back at her. She should be gleefully stuffing invitations this minute, bending her still-tenuous goals around Will's the way water finds space between rocks. Indeed, if her aspirations were wispier, becoming Mrs. William Andrew Westlake would have already solved everything.

Growing up, Tessa panicked when adults asked what she wanted to be. No answer felt right. Pop always saved her, clapping a steady hand on her shoulder, chest proud. "Something *big*," he'd say, "that's for sure." Year after year, loan after loan, Tessa studied harder, expanding her academic disciplines. Preparing for *big*. Waiting for it to reveal itself.

All the while, Will's *big* was proving more than enough for both of them to share. But Tessa hadn't kept her grades up and her grandparents in debt all these years to ride coattails. She needed her own *big*, and her grandparents were never going to sell this property until she found it. How much time did they have left before Pop's illness took over?

This summer had to be her final stall. No longer could her exaggerated need for stability keep her from starting on the path that wasn't mapped out. It was time for a career worthy of all the sacrifice, to start the beautiful life she and Will had been planning for years and let her grandparents enjoy what remained of theirs.

Come September, the future would be her first priority.

Mexican Holly / *Ilex Aquifolium*

"Am I forgotten?"

ELEANOR

ALARM WAS STILL ricocheting through Eleanor Westlake's body, but she kept her tone even. "You'd think we're entitled to know where our own money went," she said, slathering seaweed cream over her chest like drywall mud. In the halo of her makeup mirror, she could have passed for forty. Possibly thirty-eight.

Across their bedroom, her husband, Peter, failed to notice. Eleanor heard him grunting as he pulled on his dress socks. "It's not ours anymore," he said. "He can spend it however he wants."

"That's my whole point, there's no indication he spent it at all!"

The boys were no longer minors, hadn't been for a while, but the quarterly statements for their trust accounts still got mailed to Eleanor, an administrative oversight she'd kept in place. Every set of papers looked the same. Teddy withdrew the maximum weekly amount, Will's remained untouched. When Eleanor got around to opening the latest this morning, she sprayed her coffee all over it.

"Maybe there's finally a ring," Peter said with a grin.

Eleanor glared at him. It was a staggering amount for a diamond, even by Will's standards.

Plus, the withdrawals happened months ago, and Tessa's perky little finger remained empty.

What *had* Will done with so much money?

"It wouldn't be the worst thing," Peter continued. "Working-class roots is exactly what this campaign needs."

"No." Here, Eleanor drew the line. "Peter . . . *no.*"

With her unquestioning support, Peter had turned Westlake into one of those names people recognized without knowing why. His boutique firm catered to clients requiring swift, discreet action that came at a premium. Word of his pulling off the impossible in and out of court quietly spread, until three satellites had sprung up, then a long list of subsidiaries. Now, having reached the loftiest peaks of private-sector success, there was only one apex unconquered—to nobly eschew it all in the name of public service.

After four years on city council, Peter's heavy-hitting network and overt philanthropy all but made him a shoo-in as Toronto's next mayor, if he could gain traction among the low-to-middle income voters. The campaign team suggested weaving a working-class element into the family optics, with Tessa being the most obvious option. But as much as Eleanor wanted—deserved—that mayor's seat, no one was rushing her firstborn into marriage, too. Not even the almighty Peter Westlake.

Peter shrugged. "It's going to happen soon enough, anyway."

"Not this soon."

Yes, the dreaded bells would surely chime, but Tessa had made Will promise straightaway: *careers first.* A brilliant move, dangling her future like forbidden fruit, pretending to have bigger goals than locking him down at full salary; it only set the hook deeper. Eleanor was glad to see Will's ambition sparking, but found it suspicious that Tessa had yet to formulate any coherent career plans of her own.

"There's plenty of campaign left," Eleanor said. "We'll find another way. Promise me."

Peter rubbed her shoulders, tarnished gold cinching his finger in the mirror. "Of course. If you feel that strongly."

"I do." Eleanor's eyes narrowed, dots of foundation framing them like a ceremonial mask. "Something is going on with that boy. I just know it."

But that was all she knew; her son stored his secrets with Tessa now. Eleanor would give anything for one more day of hot chocolate with extra marshmallows, the stool twisting back and forth, navy socks swinging as every schoolyard skirmish poured into her kitchen.

One hand flew to her chest, like she'd spotted a roach. "Could she be pregnant?"

"Okay, now you're being ridiculous."

No, that had to be it. Eleanor ground her fingers into her temples, strangling the very idea. "Peter, I swear to God I will push that little witch down—"

"Jesus, Ellie!" Peter glanced around as if the crown moulding had ears. "He started pulling money in December, right?"

Eleanor nodded. "For ten straight weeks. Right up until winter break."

"Think about it. She'd be showing by now. And, she had wine at the club last week."

Eleanor exhaled. From day one, the girl had a way of driving out all rationality. "What, then? Another animal rescue start-up?" *He always was a sucker for the strays.*

Peter looked as though she'd said it out loud. "He's a sharp kid who knows what he wants. And why not Tessa? Lovely girl, good head on her shoulders." He smirked. "Besides, if she was looking to trap him, wouldn't she have done it right out of the gate?"

Eleanor's gaze bent sharply to his. Peter flashed that look that used to get her into all kinds of trouble, then kissed the top of her head. "Will's never been the one to worry about," he said. "Now, would you forget all this? It's your special day."

Right. Mother's Day. This year, Eleanor had pulled out all the stops—two days at the medi-spa, the latest Dior wrap dress, and an exquisite pair of Choos, the perfect companion to the Louis hobo Peter would be proudly presenting her with in an hour.

Eleanor's favorite associate at Holt's had made sure to flag the handbag for Becca, Peter's favorite office assistant, when Becca was dispatched to choose Eleanor's gift. Limited edition, embossed magnolia calfskin. An absolute must. No doubt the price tag made Peter's eyes bug out, as would the blowjob Becca would surely gift him on Father's Day. The purse, at least, could be counted on to hold up.

Indeed, Eleanor deserved to be spoiled today. She'd sacrificed her pelvic floor and a promising career as a legal secretary to become the most together mom in Hogg's Hollow, a fact she quite enjoyed reminding everyone at the club's annual brunch. Without Tessa wedged between them this time, Will might make the day even more perfect by confiding about the trust money.

Tessa had bewitched everyone; only Eleanor could see it. *Gee Will, I'd love to go to the concert, but I can't handle crowds.* And there was Will, requesting the private box. *Will, the trip sounds amazing, but airports make me a wreck.* And there was Peter, handing Will the private charter's number. Eleanor threw herself an exasperated look before rising to dress. Tessa even managed to piss her off in absentia.

When Eleanor first laid eyes on her through the tinted Range Rover glass, Will and Tessa were on a park bench, eating frozen yogurt and giggling like idiots. Will wore an expression Eleanor hadn't seen since he was three while at Disneyland, sharing pancakes with the Mouse himself. Two blinks later, there he was, eighteen, endlessly capable, painstakingly gorgeous, and drooling like a toddler in broad daylight.

It wasn't his fault. Those Virgin Mary blue eyes, that wispy tank top loose around her teeny waist and snug across those perfect tits Peter still pretends not to notice. Her ponytail hung like melted chocolate, plush and shiny, jolting Eleanor back to when hers did the same. And those legs. How many lunges had Eleanor done trying to recover those after the babies? When she noticed the ratty cut-offs, Eleanor knew; this girl was straight off the clearance rack at Urban Planet. Will wasn't in love, he was fascinated.

Eleanor never bought the perfect couple hype. Will, yes, he was as close as they came. That alone made it all worthwhile. But Little Miss Sensitive could ruin him, and Eleanor would keep tracking her like an ant under a magnifying glass until she found a way to prove it.

In the meantime, Tessa would be accommodated at the family table like a shellfish allergy, because Will had made it very clear she wasn't going anywhere. And if Eleanor wasn't Will's mother, she couldn't be the least bit sure who she was.

Oleander / *Nerium Indicum*

Calculated Risks.

———◀◯▶———

CHARLIE

Twenty-Seven Summers Ago

CHARLIE'S PARENTS made a life of packing up and starting over. Her four brothers would grumble at leaving behind the winning team, or some hopeless crush, as if it all wasn't waiting at the next stop in different wrapping. But by age seven, Charlie wished on every birthday candle for a trip to someplace new. By sixteen, staying in one place felt dangerously restrictive; the world was too big, it had too much to reveal. So far, she'd lived in six cities, two towns, five countries, and three continents. The more she saw, the more she needed to see.

Within an hour of landing at Pearson, she dropped her bags on the twin bed in her aunt's guest room and jumped the subway downtown. On the recommendation of a polite passenger, she took the streetcar to Queen West, poking through a patchwork of indie bookstores and novelty shops spiced with incense. She stumbled bug-eyed through the technicolor tunnels of Graffiti Alley. By the time she crossed the bustling fabric district to the open-air markets of China Town, Charlie decided if she was ever to call anyplace home, Toronto would be it.

Next morning, jet lag had her up early. She strolled her aunt's neighborhood, jonesing for cappuccino and an almond croissant, a morning habit she'd picked up in Salzburg at age nine. The smell of budding gardenia pulled her along the sidewalk to where the sexiest man she had ever seen was unlocking a flower market.

He was older by just enough, his twenty years to her sixteen affording precisely the number of trips around the block required to render boys her own age obsolete. His battered hands worked deftly to untwist the speaker wire connecting the fence panels, a lit cigarette pinched between his lips, the length of ash unnerving. Razor burn streaked the cut of his jaw like a comet, and his damp hair smelled shower-fresh on the breeze. Charlie's face twisted; it physically hurt to look at him.

He caught her staring, his eyes a startling, regal blue. He winked in a way that felt like charity. Charlie jutted her chin. He saw someone's adorable kid sister, and she fiercely resented caring what he saw.

"Someone's up early."

"Couldn't sleep."

"Hah. Story of my life. What's your name?"

"Charlie."

"Nice. Short for Charlotte?"

"Yep."

"It seems to me we have no ordinary spider."

"Huh?"

"E.B. White. *Charlotte's Web?*"

"Oh. Right."

He smiled. "A classic. Still holds up."

Twenty minutes later, Charlie bounced through her aunt's side door, changed clothes, then ran back to the Blue Iris where Sam taught her to deadhead petunias from the base of the arm, not the bloom itself. "It's a pain in the ass," he said, dabbing the droplet of sweat at the tip of his nose, "but do it the other way, and the whole plant looks like shit in a month."

Sand-colored hair brushed his eyes as he demonstrated how to slit sunflower stems five inches up from the bottom, creating a larger surface from which to draw water. "Do you make your linebacker drink from a straw, or do you hand him the whole pitcher?"

He set a houseplant in a shallow dish of water, freeing it to drink what it needed, but no more. His voice dipped low. "The trick here, Spider, is do it regularly. Let it dry out, like this mum here?" His head shook with sorrow. "Drowning's the only way to save it."

Charlie hoped he couldn't feel her pulse clipping as he placed his earth-worn hand over hers. Together, they plunged the full plant into a pail filled with tepid water, holding firm as it struggled to float up. Releasing only when no more bubbles fled through their fingers.

Her blood ran green. She wanted to know everything about the shop's ever-rotating flora. She studied Sam's finger work, rapt, as he dismantled her clumpy attempt at a rose bouquet and started again, baby's breath first, tucking the blooms in and around it, then set the leather fern, shiny side out, much lower than she had. "Fern is the collar, Spider, not a mask." Then, flashing his gut-flipping grin, he made her promise to avoid using both types of filler whenever possible. Charlie decided on the spot that she preferred her roses laced with blue stattice and bear grass, though she'd pick dahlias over roses any day of the week.

Charlie's botanical passions thickened all summer like trumpet vine on a cedar pergola, inextricably entangled with Sam. She worked sunrise until dusk, shoulders peeling, her palms permanently stained by chlorophyll. Sam was dynamic in his instruction, comically encouraging about her mistakes. Playfully affectionate no matter the weary hour or skewering temperature. On days he ambled around, as though towing an oversized load through thick fog, everyone pulled back. But it was on those occasions he drew Charlie closer.

For a while, it was enough to numb the sting of watching him saunter down the back laneway, a new mini skirt trailing every night.

In a too-short moment between retail fray, the leafy aisles a confessional curtain between them, Sam told her his parents had been dead less than six months. They'd given their lives to this shop, raising he and his brother, Darryl, among these pails and flats, as wild and in love as you read about in books. They'd partnered with investor Simon Miller years ago to fund a massive expansion, but it was only now getting off the ground.

"I've got Simon's money and Darryl's muscle. But I'm the only one who knows anything about actually running the place." Charlie heard the weight of his parents' legacy in his voice. The shop held his childhood and his future, along with Darryl's.

Three mornings a week, the white cube truck eased to a stop in front of the shop. Sam bounced from it, belting anything on the radio for all to hear. With him came bucket after bucket of creamy daylilies, roses of every length and hue, puffy snapdragons, rainbow-speckled alstroemeria, and Darryl, lurking like Stonehenge behind him. It was unfathomable to her that they were brothers.

In these hurried spurts, Charlie scurried around the shop floor, topping up displays with the fresh inventory while Sam hauled the overflow into the cooler. Simon rallied to help, as did his teenage son, Rowan. But not once all summer did Darryl cross that threshold. At most, he dumped a pail of cuts or two into the doorway with a clomp.

Darryl's persistent failure to help his brother was appalling. Sam was grieving, too, but it never stopped him from shouldering their family burden. He juggled all of it, without complaint—the cuts and indoor plants, the new wholesale division, the ordering, the staffing. And here was Darryl, acting like Sam owed *him*. Worse, he was outraged whenever Sam leaned on Charlie. As if Darryl preferred Sam to have no help at all.

For the first time, despite ground all over the world begging to be covered, Charlie worried she was missing out by staying on the move. The following summer, Sam asked her to take over the inside counter so he could focus on the rest, and she agreed. Darryl went so ballistic on both of them, Charlie thought for sure the police would be called.

She missed floating between departments. But inside the shop, it was easier to avoid Darryl, who loved to remind her that Sam didn't look at young, willowy Charlie the way he did at other, full-fledged women. He called her Sam's Pet Spider, trapped behind the glass, Sam roaming free.

Charlie fired back; Darryl's temper combusted instantly and it terrified her, but as soon he came charging, Sam dropped everything to defend her. And so, the pattern was set. The more heated the brothers' exchanges, the luckier she secretly felt to have Darryl hate her so much.

By her second August at the shop, it was like Charlie had known Sam all her life. But he still wouldn't say how his parents died. As far as she and Rowan could tell, the brothers had never told anyone.

One slow, hazy Monday, she asked Sam through the window by the register if he was *okay.* If passing along his parents' horticultural knowledge to her was enough, or if, maybe, he needed more. In order to heal properly.

His grin landed like a reflex hammer to her knees. He left the window, then burst inside, cranking the radio in the corner, goof-dancing to the oldies among the casablancas.

"I sell flowers for a living, Spider. How bad can I screw it up?" He pulled her from behind the counter. "Look! Thirty bucks for these, and when you think about it, they're already dead!"

"But what could it hurt to—"

He lifted her hand. Sent her twirling. "Come on, sing with me. You love this one." And just like that, they had sunshine on a cloudy day. The cold outside disappeared into the month of May.

Sam left no choice but to believe him. It would all turn out fine; Charlie only had to wait. Soon, he would look at her in real life the way he did in her mind whenever she flicked off her light. He'd stop denying what they both knew; he didn't need those women anymore. She was right here, she'd be enough.

It might have been the record-breaking heat, or that she was leaving for university the next day and change hung muggy in the air. Whatever the reason, on Labor Day, a measly nine days before she turned eighteen, Sam finally let her follow him. Down the sidewalk. Past the sighing Japanese blood grasses, the feathered Crimson Queens. The vigilant black-eyed Susan. Up the back steps, through the door nobody bothered to lock. Down the hall, to the bedroom on the left, where he took her chin in his rough-sawn hands and pressed his lips to hers like flame to wick, then outright asked if she was on the pill.

Charlie swallowed hard, nodding up at him. Afraid of losing her chance. Starved all over again to learn from Sam everything she didn't know before.

Pennyroyal / *Mentha Pulegium*

Consecration.

————◄◦►————

TESSA

TESSA WHEELED another cart to a stop on the sidewalk, this one flush with Martha Washington geraniums. She lingered over them, the pops of magenta like a melody.

"Sam was right about Mother's Day the whole time," Tony said. "What a legend."

Luke looked doubtful. "I popped my head in, and it seemed kind of painful."

Tony chuckled. "Nah, bro. All you do is run carry-outs, pass out a few irises, and they're all over you. Record tips, no sweat. Right, Tessa?"

Behind her sunglasses, Tessa rolled her eyes. "Yeah, no sweat." Mother's Day weekend at the inside counter saw her ankle-deep in thorny clippings, wet sprigs flying, floral paper clattering in a combined twenty-two-hour sprint through a bramble of cologne and complaining Sunday skirts, infants skipping naps, children mollified with chocolate. Innocent blooms set people unraveling. Tessa was chastised for failing to produce thirty-six *identical* roses, ordered to water eight perfectly happy azaleas *right now,* then screamed at when they were *wet* going into a Mercedes. Yet strangely, she was unbothered by it all, as if that battered counter was an impermeable wall.

It helped that Charlie lulled even the most frenzied retail theatrics with unbending ease. Together, the two women weaved smoothly as pair figure skaters. The air sucked from the shop with every mention of Sam, so Tessa redoubled her efforts to keep Charlie laughing, the booming sound springing forth like a bohemian jack-in-the-box, bouncing off the shop's sweaty windows and filling Tessa with pride in freeing it. Tessa confirmed Charlie was working at the shop the year she and Beth visited—"*every April to September since ninety-five, girlie!*"—but the shop was too busy; Tessa couldn't probe further. Still, somehow, just being in there on Mother's Day did wonders enough.

Now, the crew focused on preparing for the May holiday weekend. Tessa climbed on an overturned bucket beside the exterior wall of the shop with an old hammer and some roofing nails, intent on displaying a soggy collection of gardening accessories she'd found abandoned behind the trilliums. Tony's sharp inhale rang out as he reached for the lower rack, hand flying to his rear where, clearly, his sutures still hadn't healed. Luke laughed.

"Thanks for telling everyone about my ass cheek, by the way. You dick," Tony said.

Luke laughed harder, unwrapping a skid of hibiscus standards to be stacked along the boulevard. "That was your best one in a while."

Tony's bitter expression flipped to a grin. "That's why I wanted to tell it myself."

Luke shook his head, still chuckling. "Charlie holding up okay, though?"

"You know Charlie. But she liked having Tessa around, I think. Me, I could watch her bending over the bachelor buttons all day."

"Dude, she's right there."

"Nah, she's cool." His voice lifted towards Tessa. "I meant that, you know, respectfully. You know that, right?"

Tessa left her eyes on the pruning shears, stifling a smile. "I mean, I'd feel a lot more respected as an Eagle, but sure."

The look between the men was nearly audible. She'd cracked their code for scoping out women; the question "How about those Ravens?" invited a roundtable of sorts, couched in football terms like *tight end room,* while Falcons were inarguably doable, and Eagles warranted a full stop-and-stare. "Speaking of Eagles, there's two at nine o'clock . . . in case you're feeling respectful." Their heads whipped around. Tessa felt a flash of triumph at being the tiniest bit part of the group.

"Damn," Tony said. "She probably could have warned me off that barista."

Rowan appeared with a heavy binder and was about to speak when Luke and Tony's conversation took a noticeable turn. Tessa followed his gaze towards them.

"I could have warned you about the barista," Luke was saying.

"Then why didn't you?" Tony said.

"Would you have listened?"

"Your grenade radar isn't exactly on point, bro."

Luke's jovial tone faded. *"Wasn't.* It's razor sharp now."

"Yeah. Too sharp," Tony muttered. "Like, maybe aim for a butter knife or something."

"What does that even mean?"

"It means get back on the horse already, bro, before you forget how to ride one."

Luke's voice lifted, his *chill* starting to melt. "I told you, I've been busy. That's all!"

Tony's followed suit. "See, now you're making excuses. Nobody's too busy to get laid! Charlie's right, it's a symptom of a bigger problem!"

"And letting some rando go Mike Tyson on your ass cheek doesn't spell bigger problem?"

"For fuck's sake," Darryl barked from the vegetable section. "Give it a rest. You sound like a couple of bitches."

The shop fell silent. Tessa pretended she hadn't heard a thing. "What's up, Uncle Rowan?"

By now, she knew her boss was neither bossy nor anyone's uncle. But he doted on the staff, handing out food or coffee on the hour, pressing extra cash into her palms after those excessively busy shifts, and Tessa was determined to ease his social awkwardness however she could, mostly because she recognized it well. How many times had she peered from behind the velvet rope of Will's arm, feeling like a total interloper?

The wattage in his expression told her she'd chosen exactly the right nickname. He handed her the product catalogue. "For your display," he said. "Thought you might like to do up an order."

Tessa flipped through the glossy pages. "I wouldn't know where to begin."

He shrugged. "Pick whatever you'd want for your own garden."

The west-facing patch by the coach house sprung to mind. Tessa pushed it away, conjuring Pop instead, who always spoke of seeing the world from the deck of a cruise ship, then poured his savings into soccer cleats and orthodontist appointments. Nano, who had hunched over the sewing machine in her magnifiers, altering wedding gowns for extra cash. With the property sold, they could travel to the extent Pop was able, free of worry about lawns or staircases . . . and she and Will could stop living apart.

Tessa never truly imagined moving away for good and not finding Nano and Pop a minute's walk up the driveway, puttering about. Since

Pop's fall in the bathroom, it was all on borrowed time; the oak-strewn lawn, wide enough for exactly thirty-seven cartwheels; the mark on the kitchen counter left by the pizzelle iron; the *pop-pop-pop* exploding from the garage after school as she and Pop ran boxing drills, gloves and pads exorcising what their tears could not.

She moved into the coach house with her mother at age five. The main house, heart shattered, at eleven. Then, back into the coach house by senior year. Her whole history was tied to those grounds. Staying there full-time again only made it harder to leave, even temporarily. But sleeping without Will was equally unbearable. It was unfair making him trek thirty extra minutes to the coach house after finishing work—by which time Tessa was often asleep—then wake even earlier to avoid rush hour back into the city. Tessa felt guilty, but she'd feel even guiltier staying at the penthouse next to Will.

The breeze through the storefront was mild, but prickles rose from her skin. Her mother's voice drifted through her head. *"What's meant for you can't pass you, sweet girl."* Tessa had the whole summer to figure everything out. She smiled at her handwritten order—dainty watering cans, matching mother-daughter gardening gloves in playful patterns, herb stakes labelled in looping cursive—pleased at how easily the choices came, how little the urge to overthink.

The air around the counter darkened. "Shit looks ready for the circular filing bin," Darryl said, eyeing her display.

Tessa remained forcedly unaffected, per Charlie's directive. "It was soaked. But I'm ordering more."

Darryl yanked the paper from her hands. "Fucking Rowan's turning us into a goddamn henhouse." He crumpled it, then lobbed it into the trash. "We sell plants, Princess."

Tessa fished the order out of the bin and smoothed it on the counter.

Darryl squinted through his shadowy sockets, then slammed his palm into the paper. Tessa regretted how it made her eyelids flutter. He tore the order into pieces, scattering them on the ground where the wind obligingly dispersed them. Heat crept through her, incinerating her usual urge to cry. Darryl looked pleased for once, feeding off her reaction like a piranha. He gestured to the trowels she'd hung around Charlie's window.

"You priced those wrong."

"They were already priced. I put fresh tags over top."

"No, you didn't."

"I did." She peeled away a *$9.99* sticker to reveal the weather-beaten original underneath.

Darryl snatched the metal tool, pointing. "What does that say?"

Tessa studied the faded ink. *$9.95.*

"And what does yours say?"

Tessa uncurled the discarded tag. *$9.99.* She frowned.

"Exactly. Redo them."

She gave a short laugh, her face hot, aware now of the others watching. "You're joking."

"Prices here have ended in ninety-five since you were pissing in diapers, Princess."

Tessa was used to blanking out in moments like these, only to conjure the perfect retort in the shower three days later. It took a few seconds to realize her next words had come from her own mouth. "You just said it belonged in the garbage, now you're on my case about five cents? Losing someone you care about sucks, Darryl, but it's no excuse to shit on people. I'm done."

Darryl angled his chin at Rowan. "Told you."

Tessa spun around. "Told him what?"

"You'd quit by May two-four."

"But I didn't quit. I said I was *done*, as in I no longer care that you're a raging, prehistoric psychopath. Stomp around all you want, I'll just redo the order. And feel free to go ahead and change those price tags yourself while I'm at it, if it means that much to you."

At the window, Charlie's eyes curved into valiant crescent moons. Tessa stalked off with two hours left until closing, down the sidewalk to her car without a word or a backwards glance, heads swiveling like weathervanes as she went.

Herb of Circe / *Mandragora*

Demons.

———◄◌►———

LUKE

RAIN PRESSED in a heavy sheet, setting the afternoon on pause. The crew was standing around inside, bantering and cupping hot drinks, except Darryl, who never set foot in here. Instead, he hovered under the awning, droplets smacking against his vinyl-clad bottom half.

Luke stared out the window, avoiding the group. His conversation with Tony by the flats earlier had gotten more heated than necessary, and it was still niggling at him. He knew his friend meant well, but at the end of the day, Tony just didn't get it.

Outside, a young family celebrated every puddle. Mom and Dad each held one squishy toddler hand, swinging in tandem, pulling the boy up just in time to keep the wiggly bum dry. The raincoat had a plastic lion's mane for a hood, and the creases along each sleeve suggested the garment had spent months folded in a nursery drawer, waiting for this day to arrive.

The smiley shark-boots devoured the wet pavement in gleeful bursts. Mom cheered with abandon, wet hair like cling wrap against her face. Dad's glance stole from the boy to his mother and back. Unadulterated happiness on the darkest of afternoons.

Sour heat curdled in Luke's stomach as the word rose to mind all over again, scrawling like bright red graffiti.

BITCH.

His eyelids floated closed.

Maybe Charlie was right. Maybe it was time to go talk to someone.

Hot Water Plant / *Achimenes Cupreata*

"Such worth is rare."

ROWAN

ROWAN WALKED OUT to the corner of Morrow and Cresthaven, jaw slack, phone damp at his cheek, observing his failure in full panorama. He wasn't even listening to the stuffed shirt on the call anymore.

Rowan Simon Miller. A default risk.

The four-hundred-dollar basketball tickets burned in his jeans pocket; payment-in-lieu for six-fifty in inventory. Those would cheer Luke up, at least, while the twelve-hundred-dollar Versace suit from this morning—settlement for a two-thousand-dollar tab—would bring Christmas early to Tony. At this rate, the shop might clear actual profit by Thanksgiving.

Toronto's biggest names strolled past here daily, a stop at the local flower market being every somebody's favorite way to play humble nobody. But as it turned out, approaching the checkout counter was for *actual* nobodies. They all beelined instead for Rowan, looking to swing a deal. Unaccustomed to paying for things, they ran tabs they never settled, bartered goods he had no use for, and were highly insulted by even a roundabout suggestion they owed a dime.

Although Rowan inherited his father Simon's majority stake in the Blue Iris fifteen years ago, and all the coveted midtown frontage it sat on in its entirety, he was still no more a man in charge than a skittish adolescent waiting to be stuffed into a locker. But up to now, it didn't much matter. Even half-rusted out, the place was a license to print money thanks to Simon's expansion in the nineties, and when Rowan passed out the bartered goods, the crews' awestruck appreciation was a direct deposit to his overdrawn ego. What he stupidly failed to acknowledge was none of it was possible without the ticking time bomb named Sam.

Rowan handled the banking, taxes, insurance, the faint-making water bills. But Sam was the lifeblood, despite multiple DUIs and a recent arrest warrant for failing to show for his court-ordered addiction counseling. Rowan should have put a contingency plan in place ages ago. Now, he was officially the pathetic failure his mother had always promised he'd become.

A green Jaguar parked three feet off the curb. Rowan's gut squelched. Another regular, looking for the Rowan Special. *"Go find us some coffee, Browan,"* Sam would have said. *"Keep the hell outta Dodge."* With an easy grin and a firm squeeze of the shoulder, Sam had no trouble taking payment in full, whereas Rowan had a better chance of balancing the till if he stayed out of sight. A stowaway on his own ship.

Truthfully, he wasn't all that worried until April; Sam had holed away plenty of times before, falling dormant with the perennials. Planting season always brought him back, the *only* time he was fully together; but a fully together Sam was pure magic. Propulsive and laidback at once, forever crooning and cracking jokes. Naturally effervescent. Ran the city's largest garden center with all its lightning-speed parts like it was as uncomplicated as a lemonade stand.

Sure, there was some concern Sam would eventually run out of lives, but at the same time it was unfathomable he wouldn't resurface like daffodil shoots after the thaw. The man didn't know how to be anywhere else.

Then, he missed the Easter-Passover rush.

When May hit, Rowan knew. For once, even Darryl and Charlie agreed that if Sam were alive, he'd have been here by now. The only remaining question was, with the business full of holes and his golden bailing bucket lost to the wind, how long Rowan could float this place without him.

Coltsfoot / *Tussilago Farfara*

Stamina.

———◀◉▶———

CHARLIE

Twenty-Six Winters Ago

THE DATE WAS CIRCLED in red on her dorm calendar— *December 19.* The start of the holiday break.

Her boots squawked up the snow-covered sidewalk. Christmas at the shop was more whimsical than she'd pictured, a frosted maze of evergreen corridors and seeded eucalyptus that tickled her sinuses jolly. Inside, the shop was a jewelry box of red poinsettias, the radio jingling over the hum of the space heater.

Sam gave a cordial nod as he passed, nothing more. There were customers everywhere, his head a million places. Charlie got that. She wasn't some needy crush. She'd resisted calling the shop all semester just to prove it.

She had it all planned. On Christmas Eve, after closing, she'd ask him to meet her in the beer garden, which would be strung full of colored lights by then. She hoped it would be snowing when she told him the news. There would be shock at first, she knew. But she and Sam were the best kind of team. Together, they'd figure it all out.

On the twenty-first, Simon, her boss, came by for the bank drop and caught Charlie emerging shakily from the washroom, choking on air freshener. He guessed the father right away and Charlie, confidently clueless as any eighteen-year-old in love with a very bad, very blue-eyed idea, took it as proof that she and Sam were soul mates. The whole world could see it!

That night, Simon showed up at the rental house beside Darryl's, where Charlie was staying (now eighteen, an adult, about to be a *mother*, she was well past sneaking boys into her aunt's guest room). He handed her a drugstore bag full of prenatal vitamins and cash in a fat envelope. "To get you started." He promised her all the time off she needed, with pay. Offered to hire a reputable nanny so she could finish school.

Charlie was taken aback. Like his son, Rowan, Simon was generous to a fault with all the staff, but he'd only known her two summers. "Why are you helping me so much?"

His cheeks puffed as he let out a breath. "This place . . . since Iris died, it's like a model airplane kit without the glue. You keep Sam focused, and Darryl in check. You're kind to my boy. You're the glue, Charlie. Besides, you're carrying her grandchild, and that makes you family."

Simon wasn't technically family himself, but already Charlie understood the shop's capacity to turn anyone who stuck around into blood.

She fell asleep that night thinking of baby names. Would Sam wish for a boy or a girl? Would he go out at midnight to fetch her pralines and cream? There was so much she couldn't wait to talk with him about. *Just a couple more days.* When the holiday crunch was over, they'd have all the time in the world.

On December 23rd, Sam introduced her to Hannah.

Persimmon / *Diospyros*

"Surround me in nature's beauty."

————◄○►————

TESSA

Tessa STOOD with her back to the traffic, head atilt, staring at the tired storefront. A spread in the supplier catalogue had sparked an idea for a display, and she couldn't resist picturing it—even if Darryl wouldn't let anyone so much as adjust the angle of the cash register.

Conjured, Darryl came tearing around the fence, scanning the aisles. He'd ignored Tessa since the price tag faceoff days earlier, a welcome reprieve, but as the big planting weekend drew closer, a charge was accumulating around him like an impending storm. Tessa feared that by standing up to him she'd made things harder for the rest of the crew, who, despite small inroads, remained standoffish overall.

"Where's Flash?" he howled, searching for the part-timer who worked after school.

Tessa didn't turn around. "I thought he was with you."

"Where's Rowan, then?"

She continued squinting into the air. "How should I know?"

"Fuck me, does anybody goddamn work around here?"

She sighed, the sketch in her mind collapsing to dust. "What is it, Darryl?"

"There's a pickup in half an hour, and we never pulled the order. I need Tony for a drop in Forest Hill, Luke's swamped . . . WHERE IS FLASH?"

"Relax. I'll pull it."

Darryl snorted. The storage yard, gated off at the base of the alley, swallowed her coworkers constantly, but his patrolling sniper gaze made it clear that Tessa was to venture no further than the soil skids. He gestured to the now-infamous trowels on display around Charlie's window. "Rowan can put whoever he wants up here, but Suzy Homemaker's not running loose in my yard."

Tessa shrugged. "Your problem, then."

At the curb, Tony tapped the horn and flashed the universal *What the fuck?* hand signal. Darryl tore the list from his notepad and shoved it at her before shuffling off. "Don't touch anything else."

"You're welcome," Tessa called, studying his scribbles. A flicker of triumph; she recognized every plant on the list. But the quantities were too large; they didn't keep that much stock up front. Indeed, she would have to pull them from the storage yard.

With Darryl gone, Flash's beanpole shadow appeared. "Sorry," he said. "I'll go pull that now."

"No. I've got this one. Cover the counter?"

Flash happily trotted over, scrolling through his phone.

In the alley behind the shop, the storage yard gate was propped open by a crumbling cinder block, green shoots sprouting from the holes. Tessa hesitated, half-expecting Darryl to reappear and yell at her for walking through it wrong. An empty cart clattered from the opening, Luke pushing the other end. Ridiculously, Tessa waved Darryl's list like it was some sort of security clearance. "Just pulling an order."

His charcoal eyebrows lifted. "What happened to Flash?"

"He was hiding again."

Luke shook his head. "Whatever. I have three more to pull myself."

"I wonder how he ended up with that name."

Luke looked amused. "They're all Flash. High school kids rarely last a month, Darryl never bothers learning their names."

"Well, somehow, I got stuck with Princess, which couldn't be further from the truth, not that he cares. I meant to ask his real name right away, but now it's been too long and—"

"I'm pretty sure it's just Darryl. Sam called him Brick sometimes, but—"

"Not him." She laughed, eyes bugging in stress of the obvious. "Flash!"

Luke twisted his mouth, straining to recall. He stroked the stubble on his chin, thinking. Finally, he shrugged. "Nope. Just Flash."

At this, Tessa let out an affronted sound, and Luke smiled. It was a completely different version than the one he wore for customers, or the manicured women passing through on their way to the boutiques. "I can be a jackass, too," he said. He sent the cart rolling to a stop among a litter of others. "You want me to look at that order?"

Tessa was still eyeing the space beyond the gate.

"You've seriously never been back there?" Luke asked.

She crossed her arms, tone pointed. "I'm barely welcome up front. Half the time you guys act like I'm about to burn the place down."

Luke winced. "Sorry. It's not you. Really. It's...who you're meant to help replace."

Tessa frowned. She'd assumed the crew felt contempt towards Sam, the irresponsible jerk who left them high-and-dry in peak season. But here, Luke seemed to really miss him.

He ran a hand over his face. "Allow me to give you the royal tour, Princess."

"Don't call me that." Inside the gate, Tessa's breath snagged at the sweeping meadow before her. The city's white noise evaporated into row upon row of color-blocked blooms and hanging baskets hovering overhead like candied cloud cover. She scanned left to right, jaw slack, sunshine filtering through a playful banner of fuschia. *"How is this possible?"*

"Rowan's dad, Simon. He bought in with Iris and Henry, and expanded the retail storefront. But all the rich neighborhoods are within a fifteen-minute radius, and they all have professional landscapers. He wanted that business, too, so he bought up the houses along the back of the block, left three standing, and paved the rest so he could bring in a ton more inventory and sell it wholesale. We call that side of the business *Trucks*, because it sells by the truckload. Pulls in ten times more than the rest combined."

"And I thought all you guys did back here was smoke cigarettes." In the distance, she spotted three faded rooftops. "Does anyone still live in them?"

"Darryl's in the middle, he and Sam grew up there. Charlie's is on the right."

Charlie said she lived nearby, not on the property!

"The one on the left, that's the Lodge," Luke continued. "Sam lived there off and on, but anyone on the crew could crash. Tony moved in five years ago. I've been there almost two."

Tessa envisioned a bachelor's lair befitting of Tony's hookup stories. Stripper pole in the living room, swings in the bedroom. "No wonder everyone's so tight. It's practically a commune!"

Luke's thoughtful expression returned. "There isn't much room for secrets." He pointed to a roped-off section. "Leave your order there until pickup. You sure you're okay to pull it yourself?"

Tessa rolled her eyes. "He was going to let a high school kid do it! I have three—"

"University degrees. You've mentioned. You going to go postal again?"

She narrowed her eyes. "No, *jackass*. But how hard is it to pull a simple order?"

Luke waved a hand over the aisles, inviting her to have at it, then carried on his way.

Frank, the man who had placed the order, followed Tessa into the yard to collect it, steel-toe boots clunking. He looked around the roped-off section. "This is six carts," he said.

Tessa frowned, confused.

Darryl burst into the yard like a heat-seeking missile, then stopped short. "This is six carts."

Bewildered, Tessa rechecked the list. Victoria blue salvia, pink oleander, trailing geraniums in lavender that glowed at dusk. The wide-leafed Montgomery ivy that always sold immediately. "It's all here. Hundred and forty New Guineas, seventy-five white alyssum . . ."

"Bloody hell," Darryl said, saliva beads leaping to their demise. "She pulled a hundred and forty goddamn *pots.*"

Frank pulled a hand through his curls. Tony and Luke found reasons to draw closer.

Tessa thrust the list at Darryl. "I know how to count to a hundred and forty, asshole."

"That's a hundred and forty *flats*, smartass. At fifteen pots PER FLAT, that's a shit-ton more than you've got here. You think Frank's towing a twenty-foot box trailer for the gas mileage?"

Tessa's stomach dropped. She looked at Frank. Had he really ordered *that* many plants?

"It's for a client on Post Road," Frank explained in a South American accent. "Six-hundred-foot driveway, beds on each side. A roundabout bordered by eighteen planters."

Shit. Tessa registered the logo on his shirt: *Frank's Custom Landscaping and More.* He was a professional landscaper. A Trucks customer, not a retail one. This explained why Luke had been skeptical about her pulling the order. She read it out now, praying he and Tony would help her quickly pull the rest.

Tony cringed. "We ran out of salvia this morning."

"I doubt we have enough geraniums," Luke added. "Lavender's hot this year."

Darryl's neck pulsated. He threw his arms in the air. "Un-fucking-believable!"

Tessa was silent.

Frank's tone was kind. "I never imagined a driveway could hold so many plants either." A small chuckle. "And in a country where they only last five months." He turned to Darryl, waving his hand. "I'll shuffle some jobs, start my crew on this and get the rest tomorrow."

Tessa helped him load, then returned to the yard. Darryl was tearing through the aisles, muttering. "You have any idea how much Frank buys from us?" he said when he saw her. "That was *one* front yard. He has three crews on Post Road alone! Starting tomorrow, that man won't have time to take a shit for six weeks, and neither will the other forty-seven landscapers lined up down the block. This isn't housewives shopping for gardening club back here. We don't come through for our Trucks clients, their kids don't eat."

"I didn't know Trucks existed until an hour ago! How was I supposed to know it wasn't a regular retail order? You could've mentioned there was a wholesale operation back here."

"Why, so you can stick your nose in that, too?"

"You get that I took this job thinking it was inside with the cuts, right? I'm doing my best."

Darryl grunted. "By tanking our biggest client's first order of the year."

Tessa stepped forward, studying him. "You wanted me to, didn't you?

You knew there wasn't enough product, so you let me take the hit."

Darryl's silence affirmed it.

"Whatever, Darryl. I'm in this now, so just tell me how we fix it."

"*We* don't. You walk your ass back up to the counter, *stay there,* and I'll handle it tomorrow."

"How?"

"By burning through every one of my brother's favors down at the terminal."

Tessa swallowed. "I'm coming with you."

The look between Tony and Luke made her instantly regret those words.

Darryl snorted. "You want to go to the terminal."

"I don't want to go anywhere with you. But seeing as you set me up in the first place, I don't exactly trust you to make it right on my behalf."

Darryl hissed through his nostrils. "Cube leaves at four-thirty sharp— that's *a.m.,* Princess. Don't be late."

"Tell me everything there is to know about the terminal."

Charlie looked puzzled. "It's the distribution hub, down by the port lands. It's where they settle up with the growers, line up deliveries, fill any special orders."

"What's so awful about it?"

"Besides getting there before dawn?" Charlie shrugged. "I've never been."

Tessa's jaw dropped in horror.

"There's only two seats in the truck," Charlie explained, counting off on her fingers. "Henry and Iris, Henry and Sam, Sam and Darryl. First time stepping outside the bloodline, and Darryl picked *Rowan."* Her lips curled around her coffee cup in contempt. "Tells you how much he really does hate me."

Tessa moaned. "He'll never let up if I back out."

"I won't lie, girlie. I hear it makes this place look like high tea at the King Eddie. But keep your head up, you'll be fine." Charlie looked at her. "*Go.* Then, come back here and tell me all about it."

SAM

The problem?
She was a fresh shoot of morning glory back then,
craning after him like he was the sun.
Did he know better?
She was seventeen, for Christ's sake.

But go find a man on this frost-blighted earth
who swears he doesn't care to be the sun,
and he'll show you the filthiest snake of all.

The sleazebucket truth?
She would have choices by the campus-load.
Bilingual fingernails, soul patches angled with promise,
Byron quotes and pompous North Face backpacks.
It would all be different when she got back.
If she came back.

When the only way he knew to make her stay
wasn't enough,
he had to watch her leave
knowing he got there first.

Foxglove / *Digitalis Purpurea*

"Ambitious only for you."

WILL

A WITNESS AWAITED deposition in the boardroom, the arbitrator on the call was taking her sweet time denying the adjournment request, and his inbox was ablaze with messages from the campaign manager. Will pinched the bridge of his nose, trying to focus. Tessa's smile across the glass hall would have made it all so much more bearable. That smile was the whole reason he ended up here in the first place.

Instead, she was diving headlong into that job, taking on problems that weren't hers to solve. By now, they'd have noticed her impossible radiance and started scrambling after it like candy out of a pinata. Hoarding it, taking advantage. But beyond Tessa's familiar summer employment pattern, Will had no idea what was happening. Crowds, chaos and too little sleep were the things she adamantly retreated from. Her battery drained quicker than most, took longer to recharge. Will worried the long hours, the heat, the physical strain would drive her into the ground. All for a partial memory of running errands with her mother? It didn't make sense.

Beneath the concern, a shallow wound had formed. If Tessa wanted a summer stopgap to keep busy while she decided on a career path, why not here at the firm, with him? She'd have comfortable hours, good pay, as much challenge as she wanted with no stress. They could have spent every day together.

Austin, the associate on the Hewson file, appeared outside Will's fishbowl and sliced the air across his throat. Will nodded. As feared, they'd made a catastrophic oversight during discoveries, and now, the other side knew it. Will would have to settle the case to avoid a trial.

Will's fists clenched. He needed a fat, public win on Hewson. It would have proven beyond all doubt he had what it took to hold down his father's fort. Having to fold this quickly proved he didn't just miss Tessa, he needed her help. Much more than he was comfortable admitting.

In the beginning, whenever Will tried prepping for mocks in law school, Tessa couldn't keep her hands off him. She'd skim his notes, pleading with him to let her play juror, or witness; didn't matter. She always ended up dragging him off to bed. Eventually, recognizing Will did actually have work to do, she forged a strategy conducive to all the needs.

Will shifted in his leather chair now, recalling how she would slowly slide her legs apart on their makeshift stand, a signal that his opening statement was working. How her bra peeled away when he nailed the line of questioning. But if he fumbled, lost composure for even a second, it was over. Tessa kept going only so long as he stayed perfectly on point, training him like Pavlov's dog to be unshakeable. By the time Will hit a real courtroom, nothing could throw off his game. His reputation flourished with impossible speed; bets were placed that he'd prove even better than his father. Legal circles all over Ontario were whispering about the new Winning Westlake, but no one knew the half of how he got there.

Will had long anticipated being a lawyer at his father's firm someday, but he never would have imagined taking over the firm a year out of law school so Peter could run for mayor. Tessa had turbo-charged his ambitions, hardening his fuzzy goals to stone. With her, winning became the most dizzying rush, and he grew insatiably addicted.

Eight years ago, surrounded by fellow trust fund kids at his esteemed private school, Will languished; the world had no more to show him. When a search of his brother Teddy's locker proved thirty thousand a year in tuition had bought him little else but a four-thousand-a-week cocaine habit, both Westlake boys were extracted from the reputational blast zone. While Teddy was shipped to the nearest rehab his father could pay to keep quiet, his parents sparred at length over where to send Will. Peter said public school would offer a more diverse experience. Eleanor feared he'd fall into the wrong crowd—essentially, anyone without an Amex Black. Peter rebutted that Teddy *was* the wrong crowd.

In the end, Peter got his way, and Eleanor got to be right.

Will's first public school party wasn't so different. Puffed-up jocks copying his clothes, cookie-cutter girls pressing into him and acting tipsier than they were. He was about to leave when the motion lighting sent a gold shaft through the yard. Tessa clattered through that screen door like a breakaway banner at the Super Bowl, dark hair trailing in ribbons, lip gloss catching the glare. Will's nose crinkled; where he came from, a social fumble of that magnitude was impossible to bounce back from. But Tessa just laughed it off, high-fiving the onlookers. Zero deference to the repercussions which, sure enough, dissipated on the September breeze. Stunned, Will turned to the pimpled herd behind him without taking his eyes off her and said, *"Boys, that right there is the girl I'm going to marry."*

Naturally, they scoffed and snickered and somebody said, *"Sure, dude, whatever you say."* Because they didn't yet understand Will was a guy who knew—and got—exactly what he wanted. And more than anything else before or since, he wanted Tessa Lewis.

"Yeah? Watch me."

She was beautiful, sure, but Will had known many beautiful girls by then. What struck him most was the near-magical glow, obvious to everyone but herself, the way she commanded every room she entered without even trying. Without even *wanting* to. The other girls had been obsessed with harnessing their sex, wielding phones like weapons of mass destruction, while Tessa had friends at every table in the cafeteria. For the first time in Will's privileged, admittedly pompous life, he was terrified he might not measure up.

Cradling Tessa's hand under Nano's round kitchen table, he was more at home than at the Hogg's Hollow mausoleum he grew up in. The longer he spent in the humble coach house, wanting for nothing but her skin against his, the leftovers in the fridge, and the deadbolt on the door, the emptier life at Peter and Eleanor's became. Suddenly, the extravagance of being a Westlake seemed grotesquely overrated. To be clear, he still *wanted* all of it, if only to share with her. But he was no longer content to have it handed to him by default.

Hearing Will's loose plans to coast through school and become a mid-level, unfireable lawyer at Dad's firm, Tessa had crawled out from under his arm, pinned him in a kiss so slow and smouldering it drove a shiver through his whole body, and dared him to think *bigger*.

"You have opportunity, the means, and if you try, the grades. You could run that firm."

Tessa's lust for *big* was the last quarter turn of the bulb for Will, illuminating the full promise afforded to Peter Westlake's number one son. But even after he'd held her in his arms and felt her whole world tilting, fears of inadequacy still plagued him. She was brilliant and hilarious and eerily attuned. Next-level special. What if she woke up someday and noticed the lineup of men queueing behind him like new Netflix episodes, and decided to take a scroll? What if he wasn't capable of all she believed he could achieve? But Tessa assured him he was, and promised to keep helping him until he could see it for himself.

With her sparkle rubbed all over him, Will really did feel unstoppable. Like he could ensure that whoever came knocking, Tessa would find no man more capable of making her every wish come true than the one already in her bed.

Now, he was on the verge of the biggest possible *big,* and she was off slinging plants. Sleeping a half-hour away. Too busy to prep Hewson, too preoccupied even to ask about it. Will understood why she was sticking close to the coach house, to Pop, but he hated not having her steps away at the penthouse.

The election was still five months out, and already he was losing his footing. It was silly, but he was sure he could handle things at work so much better if she'd at least wear his ring at home, sit down and set a date. But they had yet to even discuss announcing their engagement. Ever since Pop's fall in the bathroom, their glorious future kept getting postponed for reasons he no longer understood.

Tessa was cautious to an extreme, she took longer to process change. That was all. By the time summer was over, she'll have come around, ideally before his mother figured out his trust was empty. Meanwhile, Will simply had to be patient. Keep his eye on the bigger picture as his father carried the Westlake name to the next level, and by helping him do it, Will was guaranteed to push all his worries into the past forever.

Waxplant / *Hoya Astralis*

Broken promise.

———◄○►———

DARRYL

Four Months Ago

IT WAS ICE FISHING week; the cabin was the obvious place to check.

Along the northern shore of Georgian Bay, a licorice vine's length away from the unspoiled town of Killarney, the cabin was the prettiest place Darryl ever saw.

He'd only been there once during summer. Three spotless August days when he was a kid, long before his mother was laid in a pine box and his father locked in a cement one at Metro West Detention Centre. The water was clear as the sky. He and Sam pretended they were shipwrecked on a tropical TV island. They swam into dusk, ate spider dogs and s'mores for dinner. Barefoot the whole time, all four of them—no other shoe to drop.

Darryl's father kept a safe up there. Every January, he took the boys ice fishing and loaded it with his share of the dividends from the shop, claiming he didn't trust banks. Darryl suspected the real reason he kept the family's life savings a four-and-a-half-hour drive away was because he didn't trust himself.

"Half's yours, half's your brother's. Neither of you touches it . . . not ever. Got it?"

"Never?"

"Never."

"Then why bother saving it at all, Da?"

"Because someday, you might run out of never."

"But how will we know if that happens?"

"I hope to God you never do."

By the time Henry died, there must've been a hundred grand in that safe, all bound in neat stacks by the same white bands they used on the dogwood and mag tips. Even after he was gone, both sons feared their father's wrath too much to pull one dollar. Darryl took it as proof his brother couldn't be in *that* bad a shape.

The wind carved snowdrifts in a frenzy, erasing Darryl's footprints as he trudged. Sam's Chevy Tracker was there, by the shoreline, aptly half-buried in the white stuff. Fog poured from Darryl's nostrils; by now, any trace of the snowmobile had spun across the bay in frozen whirlwinds.

With a laborious grunt, Darryl lowered himself into the storm cellar. Yanked the light cord. Spun the dial on the safe. Heart clomping like a blown-out racehorse headed for slaughter.

"Shit."

Charlie must've done a real number on him this time, because the box was emptied straight down the middle.

Sam's half of the cash was gone.

Kantuta / *Cantua buxifolia*

"Let's start again."

———◀◯▶———

TESSA

4:27 A.M. Her usual parking spot sat pooled in darkness, the houses along Cresthaven stuck in the unclaimed void between porchlight timers and sunrise. Tessa walked briskly towards the shop, unnerved by the stillness, Will's words last night looping through her head.

He'd called at ten, proudly done at work and on his way over. Tessa, hard asleep when the phone buzzed, ordered him to turn around. As the grogginess cleared, she apologized. After botching Frank's order, she wanted nothing more than his arms around her, but she was meeting Darryl in six hours to go to the terminal.

Will, voice tinny with disbelief, dove headlong into the worst-case scenarios of four-thirty in the morning. Tessa, bone-tired, insisted she was *going,* but before she could explain why she had to, after what Darryl pulled, Will apologized for disturbing her with the detached politeness of a telemarketer and hung up, all the while insisting everything was fine.

Tessa was pretty sure it wasn't fine, and now, thanks to him spooking her, neither was she. She pushed her keys through her knuckles, wishing she'd parked closer as she clipped along in the dark. Steps ahead, Darryl was undoubtedly waiting to catch her late. She came up on the shop just as Darryl started the cube truck, the headlights illuminating a figure standing directly in her path. Male build, something long and thick in his hand. Tessa screamed, sprinting to the cube truck and vaulting herself into the passenger seat beside Darryl. Darryl gave her a strange look as he rolled down the window, nodding a greeting at the stranger whose eyebrows, she saw now, were bushy and white like Pop's. Beside him was a collapsible buggy, same as the one in Nano's Buick. Tessa felt the sweeping relief of her own stupidity. The object in his hand was a *newspaper.* Darryl took it, then drove off.

Morrow Avenue was an abandoned bowling alley, the downtown skyscrapers stacked like pins in the distance. Tessa rubbed her arms; she could see her breath. Darryl eyed her cropped leggings and long-sleeved tee. "No jacket?" There was rust in his voice, like he hadn't used it since yesterday.

Tessa glanced at him. "They were calling for hot and sunny today."

"Yeah, well, it's not today for a few hours yet." He fumbled with the knobs until heat poured from the vents. "We're twenty minutes out. Sleep if you want."

Tessa would sooner prop her eyelids open with toothpicks than fail to keep pace. They rode in silence, neighborhoods whipping past. The only other person they saw was a string-haired woman in torn lace, who flipped her skirt as they passed, a slash of red thong through rippling grey flesh, her middle finger sinking in the rear view.

4:57 a.m. The terminal gate lifted, unveiling a pulsing chaos. Scooters and forklifts zig-zagged. A myriad of languages, horns, and backup alarms.

Exotic trees like slices of Amazonian rainforest. *PERISHABLE* splattered everywhere in red ink.

Tessa stepped from the truck into a mini-shockwave of low whistles and the wet innuendo of tongues pulling at teeth. The male ratio was so high here, none were at all shy as their concentrated gazes began peeling her skin away. For the second time that morning, Tessa tucked in next to Darryl for protection.

Darryl pulled off his windbreaker and tossed it at her. "Stick behind me, and try not to get run over."

Tessa drafted him through the makeshift aisles, sidestepping extension cords, garden hoses, milk crates. A blue lizard with yellow spots. None of the vendors were of help in supplying Frank's missing plants; everything was sold ahead of the planting weekend. Darryl had said he'd call in Sam's favors, but so far, he hadn't.

She darted in front of him. "Do they know?" she asked. "About Sam?"

Reluctantly, he met her eyes. Tessa could see telling people his brother was gone, likely dead, was still too much. She broke away from him. Immediately, a forklift stacked with raspberries grazed her nose, forcing her back with what Will affectionately referred to as her "man yell." The driver leaned out, ogling her while lobbing mucous into a passing skid of lettuce.

Tessa ran back to the first vendor they'd seen. *Carlo's Greenhouses,* the name on nearly every truck unloaded at the Blue Iris. Carlo's low-set glasses were a caveat. *You may speak, but it better be good.* She explained all she knew from Luke. Sam went missing without a trace since New Year's Day, his snowmobile recovered from the icy shores of Georgian Bay last month.

Carlo's round face softened. The clipboard in his liver-spotted hand dropped to his side. "I knew him when he was strapped to his mother's chest." He jerked his chin at Darryl, now panting a few feet away with his hands on his knees. "I wondered why he passed me off to that miserable shit." Carlo agreed to make some calls.

Vendors began clearing out, their day drawing to a close as the rest of the city's was beginning. Someone in checkered flannel urinated against a truck tire, gold mist sifting through the early light and settling on a skid of basil. Tessa would forever scrub her produce with vinegar.

Fifteen minutes later, Carlo had pulled together the missing product. On impulse, Tessa threw her arms around him. "You're a savior!" He pulled back, staring. Tessa cringed; the hug was too much, too soon.

Carlo gave a slow, wistful smile. "I haven't met a soul so shiny in all this filth since Iris. Your spunk . . . it reminds me of her." He handed her his card. "My direct line. Call if you need anything else, okay?"

Walking away, Tessa flashed Darryl a peacock grin. "What else you got, asshole?"

By the time the cube truck was loaded, it was full daylight. Darryl beelined for the barbecue stand Tessa had been smelling since they arrived. "Double sausage on a bun, extra-large Mountain Dew." He turned to her. "Want anything?"

"It's barely six!"

Shrugging, he heaped sauerkraut and hot peppers onto the bun, shoving one end in his mouth as the other emptied onto his shoe. It must have been tough for such a clunky brute to grow up in the wake of Sam, whose name seemed to linger in people's mouths like fresh-baked bread. "You sure? Nothing open between here and Mississauga."

She looked at him. Mississauga was twenty minutes west, and nowhere near the shop.

Darryl crammed the remaining food into his cheek. *"Clock,"* he said through wet crumbs.

Tessa waited, sighing when he failed to elaborate. "More words, please, Darryl."

More chewing. "Notice we haven't loaded any cuts, Princess? Next stop is the grower's auction, *aka* the Clock."

"Fine. Was that so difficult?"

They rode in silence, the highway filling in around them. Tessa's eyelids were lead. Unbelievably, she longed for a burger from the terminal. After awhile, she said, "Hey, Darryl?" He eyed her across the cab, arm slung like cured meat over the wheel. "I'm sorry about your brother."

He looked away, tracking something far beyond the windshield. "Me too, Princess. Me too."

6:45 a.m. The theatre-style gallery was well-lit and buffed to a shine, and no one paid Tessa any attention. Trolleys loaded with product rolled past on metal tracks. Overhead monitors tracked the bidding. Two auctions ran simultaneously with lot prices fluctuating between cents and dollars and quantity counts varying by stem, bunch, or pail. Still, the wide room was quiet as a confessional.

Tessa, the sort of numbers geek who once took advanced calculus as an elective, studied the screens keenly. Beside her, Darryl looked like he was having a root canal. He pecked at the keypad, robotically bidding on every third lot, but it wasn't clear he was following the right auction. She winced as he won a full trolley of anthurium, a plant with waxy heart-shaped blooms and a long, yellow rod poking from the center of each.

"What's Charlie supposed to do with sixty red wiener-flowers?" she whispered.

He shushed her.

"Darryl. You just paid *six-fifty* a pot. We'll be lucky to sell them two-for-seven!"

His army tank body twisted in the too-small plastic seat, eyes shrinking to wrinkled prunes.

"Do you even know which auction you're bidding on?" she asked. A few lots went by. "There, the cornflower. On the A-clock. Buy those."

He stared at the keypad, considering.

"That weekend I worked inside," she offered, "anything blue sold immediately."

"All right, smarty-pants, how much? If we can't sell for double our cost, this field trip isn't worth it."

Tessa did the mental math and poked him when it came time to press the button. The screens lit up; bid successful. Triumph rose to her chest. She punched his arm. *"Nice!"*

He looked at her like snakes were about to come out of his follicles. She drew her hand back, then led him through four more lots. All flowers Charlie could sell at a premium, all clearing the profit margin.

His spine pulled straighter. "How about those?"

Tessa nodded. Gerbera daisies had been popular on Mother's Day. "But not that lot."

"Why not? I'm on a roll."

"Because it's mostly red again. The next one is assorted, get that."

"What's with you and red?"

Tessa shrugged. "It didn't seem to sell."

8:03 a.m. The cube truck was stuffed to the roof. Delphiniums stood like bejeweled soldiers between them, but the vibe in the cab had lightened. Tessa balanced three trays of the dreaded red anthurium across her lap, plastic sleeves brushing her cheeks. Darryl shoved a handful of ibuprofen from the glove box into his mouth.

Tessa's eyes widened. "It's one or two pills every six hours!"

Darryl gulped the mouthful down with the last of his Mountain Dew. "My right knee's slipping out of its socket, my rotator cuff feels like pulled pork, and I've still got eleven hours to go. If two pills work on someone your size, you think they'll make a dent on me?"

Against the shop's fluffy backdrop, Darryl seemed carved from titanium. But here, at arm's length, he looked haggard and worn. The physicality of this job was no joke at Tessa's age; Darryl had to be pushing forty-five. "It's not even June," she said. "How are you going to manage?"

"Don't have much choice, do I? Another human sandbag like Tony or Luke would've been nice to have around. No offense."

"Maybe Rowan can hire more people?"

"Tweety Bird's tweaking out as it is. Thinks we can't get by without Sam."

Tessa hesitated. "Can we?"

Darryl considered. "We're about to turn a profit on cuts for the first time in months. With Don Carlo eating out of your hand, we'll probably have first dibs on product again. Could be a game changer for Trucks."

Tessa smiled, then frowned. "Wait! What were you doing before today?"

Darryl scoffed. "Me and Rowan were two monkeys trying to fuck a football. Buying was Sam's gig. My job was to get him there on time and stand there with my thumb up my ass until it was time to load. Rowan made sure he sent enough cash. The rest . . . haven't got a goddamn clue."

"Why not ask Charlie?"

"Fuck. That."

"Bidding top dollar on the wrong clock is better?"

Darryl's shoulder lifted. "We really thought my train wreck of a brother was coming back. Rowan's been fronting his own money to cover the losses until Trucks starts ramping up."

Tessa picked at a plastic sleeve. "I could go with you again. Until you get the hang of it."

Darryl set his jaw. "Tuesdays, Thursdays and Fridays. Same time."

She smirked. "What do you know? A *broad,* sitting in this seat. Helping *you.*"

"My mother sat in that seat. She's the one who really ran things, I know that."

"Ah, so it's not all women, then. Just me?"

His shoulder lifted. "I didn't want you up front." He looked out the window. "Still don't."

Tessa made a strangled sound. "You're impossible!"

"Ask me, Flash can handle kissing retail ass all day just to sell ten lousy flats of begonias."

"I'm not quitting, Darryl." Tessa meant it. It wasn't even about her mother anymore—not entirely. As soon as this job ended, she'd have to face the uncertainty surrounding her next one.

"You ever let anybody finish? *Two hundred* flats from yard to road in under a minute. No sidewalk vultures swiping your colors. Another eight grand worth of orders being shouted at you from all sides. That's not for everybody."

"Is there a point somewhere in this story?"

"Point is, you can handle it. If you want to."

Tessa stared into the road. Pulling orders was better than standing at the counter while customers whined and waffled. Plus, she *loved* that storage yard. "I'm game."

Darryl nodded. "Welcome to Trucks, Princess. Try not to fuck it up again."

Tessa grinned out her window. Moments later, she heard a rumbling and looked around the cab. *Laughter?* She lowered her eyebrows at Darryl. "What's so funny?"

He gestured to the anthurium, a slew of phallic red-and-yellow wands bobbing about her head. "Those things really are ugly as sin." The laughter escalated into roars, littered by the odd wheeze. "It's like a whack of gonorrhea-dicks flapping off your face!" He wiped his eyes with his mammoth wrist.

"You're disgusting!" But he was yipping so hard, Tessa couldn't help laughing, too.

Back in front of the shop, he made no move to get out. He just sat there, exhaling one long breath that sounded like it had been locked in a dungeon for a thousand years.

Rattlesnake Root / *Polygala Senega*

Hermitage.

---◀◯▶---

DARRYL

THE LITTLE BALL BUSTERS were clucking away as they unloaded the cube truck, their mocking voices clear as a gong through the cab wall.

"Hey, Darryl, is this truck a mirage?"

"Does anybody goddamn WORK around here?"

Darryl stayed where he was, at the wheel his father, and then Sam, had gripped before him. Willing the damn pills to kick in.

Tessa's voice: "Guys, give him a minute."

Carlo wasn't wrong; in a bass-ackwards way, she'd reminded Darryl of his mother this morning, too. Iris wouldn't have thought twice about milking some dead stranger's memory to get the job done. And then, at Clock, calculating a dozen variables while the seconds ticked money away like some psychotic game show, like it came as naturally to her as breathing. It was reminiscent of Sam, who once set price on every lot in the place on a speedball and a twenty-sixer of Jameson. For the first time in weeks, Darryl didn't feel entirely alone.

It didn't change the fact he was barreling towards a cliff with no brakes, or that he was too goddamn pissed at Sam to mourn the guy. Darryl's tenth-grade finish and winning personality left few options outside the Blue Iris, though it burned like hell to see his parents' ghost-flirting behind every shelf, hear his mother's wisecracks on every jasmine gust of wind. It was just, all this time later, the shop was still *all* there was. And he was getting too old for this shit.

The shop in high season, with its now-or-never earnings window and back-to-back double shifts, was all-consuming enough. But buying for the shop was a different orbit altogether. Darryl went to bed while it was light, woke in the dark. Spring was sweaty hibernation while the rest of the city threw open their doors.

And those were the easy months.

Darryl spent his winters available twenty-four seven, dragging an uprooted Sam out of ditches, scraping him off glass-strewn floors. In between, he managed to eat, sleep and fuck, but not on anything resembling a schedule. He never imagined it would be forever. If anyone could wriggle back to normal after what went down that night in their parents' kitchen, it was Sam. Especially with Charlie behind him.

She was the first to stand behind that counter who wasn't his mother. Darryl, his whole world flipped and shaken like a snow globe full of rocks, loathed Charlie's little bird-palms, wiping Iris's fingerprints off the stapler. Her crushed gravel laugh replacing his mother's soft morning hum. He resented her trampling their time-tested routines, how effortlessly she rendered Darryl redundant. But the worst of it was how she was always *there,* forcing him to face everything he didn't feel when looking down at her feathery collar bone in a tank top.

Darryl had been so determined to un-gay himself, *gay* having triggered the whole bloody mess in the first place. It wasn't like he couldn't get off on girls; he'd slammed six beers and banged one in Timmy Butler's garage after winning divisionals.

It didn't matter in the end. Gay, straight, men, women—Darryl was too damn angry all the time. He hated pretty much everyone, and anyone who sparked real feeling got ghosted immediately for fear it might go down the same way.

He was no tall, golden jar of honey like his brother, whose demons settled to the bottom as soon as the sun came out. Instead, Darryl was a sack full of hammers. Sam had skimmed all the best genes in the pool, leaving Darryl with the rest—Iris's gaslighting fetish; Henry's blinding temper. How long before he dragged one matchstick too many? How soon after letting himself fall into some barf-worthy romance would it be his own fat fingers in some poor fucker's throat? Better all around if Darryl just . . . didn't.

Common Myrtle / *Myrtus Communis*

Souvenir from Eden's garden.

◄○►

TESSA

PLANTING WEEKEND seemed like one long, blurry shift. Trays lay overturned, portulaca and cilantro swaying like seaweed. SUVs idled in the street as screaming matches broke out over parking spots, the last cherry tomato plant. Tessa climbed up the back of a *Carlo's* truck, ready to offload the premium assortment. A customer in head-to-toe Chanel pointed a finger at the citrus-scented lantana on board, so laden with blooms its branches were sagging, and shrieked, prompting a horde to form. From the bumper, Tessa rationed out the plants until, minutes later, the truck was empty, its contents sold and carted away without ever touching the ground.

When at last the shop was caged in snow fencing for the night, the crew dispersed. Tessa, lagging tiredly, heard a voice calling and spotted a bucket hat in the enclosure, surrounded by the shrubs they'd stuffed up the aisles.

"Is this woolly thyme?" the customer asked, the beaded string of her glasses swaying, unfazed at having nearly spent the night barricaded among the flats.

Rowan, back from the bank drop, cursed under his breath. He and Tessa unfastened the fencing and cleared a path, hands outstretched search-and-rescue style until the customer and her four-inch pot of woolly thyme were safely on the sidewalk.

"How much?" she asked, as if this was a perfectly ordinary shopping experience.

Rowan glanced at the counter, now buried behind potted fruit trees and devoid of a register. "It's okay, Mrs. B. This one's on the house."

"How *kind!*" She then requested a second freebie, which Rowan re-opened the fence to fetch. Tessa shook her head. *No Good Deed Went Unpunished* would be etched on his headstone. The woman gave her a funny look. "Sorry to keep you, Iris, dear."

"Oh, I'm not—"

"*Shh!*" Rowan hissed, steering Tessa stiffly into the laneway, out of view. "I swear, that woman must have two acres of woolly thyme by now."

Tessa pointed back towards the street. "My car's on Cresthaven…"

Rowan frowned. "Park at the Lodge and cut through the yard from now on, especially if you're doing buying runs. Safer than walking up here alone."

"Thanks, Uncle Row." She eyed the sidewalk again. "You think she's gone?"

"Are you in a hurry?"

After the last three days, did he expect her not to be? She shrugged. Rowan beckoned her towards the yard, where the blooms, colors indistinguishable at twilight, stretched into one sleepy mass. He kept walking, all the way to the the scraggly swamp cedars way at the back, then . . . marched headlong into them? Tessa regarded the hedge with alarm; the weekend had left him delirious.

His copper head poked from a gap in the trees, visible now that she knew it was there. "You coming?"

Tessa hesitated. This was exactly what Will meant when he said she was too trusting. Then, remembering Rowan's moral compass had just prevented him from taking three dollars off a senile old lady who legitimately owed six, she ducked through the hole. The ground turned soft, couching her achy feet. She heard the timbre of male laughter, the clinking of beer glass. An orange speck lifted off beyond the greenery. Rowan pushed aside yet another section of tree with a proud flourish, like it was a false bookcase, and for the second time since passing through that storage yard gate a few days ago, Tessa was transported to another world entirely.

Auricula / *Primula Auricular*

Pride.

◄◦►

ELEANOR

FIRST, MOTHER'S DAY brunch, and now a no-show at weekly family dinner? What was Tessa thinking?

Against the ivory tablecloth, Teddy's phone seized defiantly. Will stabbed at his plate of microgreens; the poor boy struggled to keep his figure ever since the Lewises got hold of him. Eleanor didn't have the heart to tell him it only got harder with age. Sometimes, she felt like throwing in the napkin altogether, shock every starched collar in this country club by ordering a nice gooey chunk of lasagna.

"Such a shame Tessa couldn't fit us in again this week," she said, motioning for a server to remove the empty chair. Across this room, dried-up debutantes would be salivating at the sight of Will untethered. Just imagine if they knew Tessa's car hadn't sat overnight at the penthouse for weeks.

"Mom, I told you. She's working. It's a big weekend at the Blue Iris, apparently."

Eleanor drew the crystal globe to her lips, making a conscious effort not to stiffen in her chair. "The Blue Iris? On Morrow?"

Will huffed. "Yes. Do you even listen when she talks?"

Eleanor inhaled for a count of . . . six? No, it was supposed to be seven. Wait, no. It was *hold* for six, exhale for eight . . . or was it *exhale* for seven? Her head about to explode, she blew all the air out at once. The Blue Iris wouldn't be a problem, she was fairly certain. With Peter's help, she could make sure, but no way that was an option.

Will waved his fork dismissively. "It's only a few weeks. I'm working around the clock anyway."

Peter clapped Will on the shoulder, and Will beamed. Their first born was adamant he could handle Peter's portfolio, and indeed, there was no better candidate for the job. Voters needed to see Peter confidently divested of private sector responsibilities, fully committed to the fine people of this world-class city. At the same time, the firm's clients needed assurances their files remained in close, capable hands. Will had the name, the charisma, the drive and the mind. Still, it was a *lot* of pressure; Eleanor wasn't convinced he had the stomach.

Teddy scoffed. "Will Westlake, Douchebag at Law. Didn't think you had it in you, bro."

Will sneered at his brother. "At least I'm not mooching off Mom and Dad."

"No, you're *becoming* Mom and Dad."

"This from the kid living in their pool house."

"Dude, you live in their penthouse. You're driving their car!"

"First of all, the car was a gift. Maybe if you got into law school . . . or kept a driver's licence for ten minutes. And, I pay rent on that penthouse. You know, because I have a job."

Teddy snorted. "Peter's Bitch is not a real job title, FYI. I'm building my own brand."

"Pumping teens full of booze and drugs on camera isn't a brand, idiot, it's an indictment. Ever heard of Joe Francis?"

"Enough," Peter said. Teddy snatched up his phone, still twitching like roadkill.

"Is it too much to ask that you put that away while we're eating?" Eleanor asked.

Teddy replied on beat. "Is it too much to ask that you're not a raging bitch?"

Eleanor downed her wine with a tiny hiccup. Even in boyhood, Teddy's angular face had been the sort that set one's hand itching to slap it; she was beginning to wish someone had.

Now, Teddy had a glowing discharge report from rehab, and a thriving, if unusual business venture hosting exclusive parties in exotic locales and posting footage under a social media alias. So long as it suited him, he could walk the line perfectly well. Across the table, Peter gave Eleanor a look acknowledging that despite all this, their youngest was still very much a liability. They'd managed to keep Teddy's escapades off the radar, but a mayoral race invited a much broader scope of scrutiny. Scandal on the home front could derail the campaign overnight.

Eleanor caught herself wishing Tessa *was* here. The girl pulled Will from his funk, his wattage increasing a hundredfold with her beside him, effectively banishing Teddy into the wallpaper. Indeed, when that couple walked in a room, they were like co-stars in a rom-com; people couldn't look anywhere else.

Eleanor's eyes sparked wide. *They couldn't look anywhere else.*

If they kept the family lens trained on Will and Tessa through the campaign, Teddy would be all but guaranteed to go unnoticed. It gave her heartburn to agree with Peter here, but a fat diamond was the foolproof way; fairytale weddings were society column kryptonite. It would take only a few well-timed leaks: the dress (custom, the more expensive the better), the guest list (high profile, minimum five hundred heads), a candid of the happy couple cooing at somebody's baby. As a bonus, they'd glue down the low-to-middle income voters, while cementing Will in the clients' minds as a mature, well-settled, responsible successor for the firm.

Eleanor grinned, wondering why they paid that campaign manager at all.

The marriage was a foregone conclusion. Eleanor gave it two years, tops, but why not start the clock? The slightest nudge from Peter, and Will would make the engagement happen by breakfast, Tessa's so-called career still pending or not. He'd stop at nothing to please his father.

But was that even more reason to avoid putting him in such a position to begin with?

Something about Tessa remained deeply unsettling. Will insisted she was painfully introverted, that being *on* in social settings wore her to the point of physical depletion. Yet Eleanor had watched her draw entire cocktail lounges into her orbit with infuriating ease, smiling at everyone from CEO to waitstaff, bewitching them in less time than it took to circulate the satay. It didn't matter that she constantly humiliated herself, toppling welcome displays, shattering water glasses, losing an earring in the gazpacho. The same people Eleanor took years to win over found Tessa abso-fucking delightful on sight. It was off-putting. Downright weird.

But now, it could prove helpful.

Given the stakes, would it be so awful to watch Tessa become a full-fledged Westlake, unraveling that *cum laude* mind, motherhood ravaging that taut figure, deflating and swelling her in all the wrong places until

Will's well-groomed hands grew as nomadic as his father's? Then, at least, there would be two women at this table with nothing to show for any of it besides children who will never understand the sacrifices, a husband who has long forgotten, and a big, sparkling house with no speaking role at all.

China Rose / *Rosa Chinensis*

"Your smile I aspire to."

TESSA

ON THE OTHER SIDE of the cedar hedge, multicolored lights cast a jovial glow against trees that had been competing for sun their whole lives. Luke and Tony sat on overturned Clock pails, tipping beer to their lips. Charlie had one leg tucked on a lawn chair, hair wet and clothes fresh.

Darryl stooped inside a mini fridge, passing beer backwards. "What took so long?" he asked Rowan, who claimed the pail beside Tony. "We were locked up tighter than a nun's—" Spotting Tessa, he straightened.

Tessa froze. Did her presence back here violate an unwritten rule? Would it set off another fit of rage, ruining the festivities for everyone?

Darryl held up a bottle. "Want a beer?"

Tessa hesitated, the same question having punted her from many a low-lit circle before.

As far back as grade-school birthday parties, she was the child helping moms plate cupcakes in the kitchen, avoiding the gory video games and intense blockbuster films that gave her nightmares. When spinning bottles began sending her peers into closets together for seven airless minutes, she stopped going altogether.

Then, her mother died. Eventually, Tessa tried being social again, to appease Nano and Pop. But the loud music commandeered her pulse, her thoughts thrashing along with the bass. The smell of weed made her gag. Alcohol afforded zero lubricant value; a few sips and she was being dragged through Willy Wonka's tunnel of hell. Which meant that, although fairly well-liked by every social subset at school, Tessa came off as too goody-goody to be fully embraced by any of them.

These days, she only drank while at dinner with the Westlakes, who automatically filled her glass with the most expensive red on the menu, or at firm events, where sipping said wine was easier than being constantly asked why she *wasn't* drinking it. Having Will beside her, knowing he understood, proved enough to temper the adverse effects. One after the other, Will turned once-harrowing experiences into euphoria. His mouth on hers in a small, dark space was fire. Concerts through the buffer of a private box, twenty-thousand strong holding the same note, were out of body. Tessa realized she could have fun anywhere; she just needed to feel safe first.

She glanced around the circle. The only available seat was on the other side of the fridge, opposite Darryl—a peeling Adirondack that matched his own. Sam's, obviously. Tessa declined the beer, turning to head home.

Darryl called after her. "Somebody might as well sit in it."

Tessa looked to Charlie, whose expression was a wrenching mix of pain and affection.

"Go ahead, girlie. Your feet are killing you."

Tessa sat, relief flooding her soles. She took a long sip of water, thighs growing heavy against the wooden slats.

Everyone raised their drinks. "Let the games begin," Rowan said.

"*Begin?*" Tessa said.

Luke chuckled. "That was just the kickoff."

"Landscapers will be lined up again by seven tomorrow," Darryl said.

"How do you do it?" Tessa said.

"We drink," Tony said.

Luke sent a chain of smoke rings into the breeze. "And smoke."

Surprisingly, Tessa didn't mind cigarettes, but it had been years since she'd tried one. Will abhorred them. Tonight, her system struggling to gear down, the urge was undeniable. "Can I bum one?"

Luke tossed the pack her way. "Sorry, didn't realize you smoked."

"I don't."

"Ah." He smiled. "Retail."

A few drags in, Tessa's shoulders unrolled. She leaned back in Sam's chair. Overhead, the rugged tree line curved, the sky a deep orange porthole.

"Sam and I used to play back here," Darryl said, pointing. "There was a treehouse up there."

"Now, it's the one place Tony's hookups can't find him," Rowan said. Laughter tumbled into the breeze.

"Speaking of," Tony said with a sly grin. "Flashy landed his first housewife today."

Tessa's eyes grew wide. "No!"

He nodded. "Slipped her number right down his pants."

"Was he . . . okay?"

"Couldn't stop grinning. Said she hired him to walk her dog."

Darryl snorted. "More like pound the pooch."

"Definitely," Charlie said.

"You guys are messing with me." Tessa looked around. "He's barely out of high school!"

"And come September," Tony said, "he'll be the most educated frosh on campus."

"Women around here love a guy in work boots," Luke explained. "They know we don't run in any of their circles."

Tony gazed into the sky. "I'll never forget my first delivery. She asked me in to open the pickle jar, and I really thought she meant the one in the fridge."

The others' laughter egged Luke on. "Mine asked me to help her move a couch . . . in her bedroom. Next thing, her tennis skirt is on the floor. That one did *not* like hearing no."

Tony feigned confusion. "We're supposed to say no? I thought it was part of our benefits package!"

The two of them were in hysterics now. Luke tapped one finger to his temple. "Just once, I'd like to be noticed for what's *up here.*"

Tessa turned, intent on swatting him with her water bottle, but stopped short. Two beers in, ball cap turned backwards and sunglasses hanging from the lip of his shirt, Luke was jarringly different. For the first time, she saw how the unreserved grin emanated from his eyes, like honey spilled over. She steered her thoughts back to the conversation. "I'll be sure to remember how rough you two have it next time I'm walking through the terminal."

All of Darryl jiggled all at once. "Princess here got eye-fucked so hard, *my* ass was sore."

"You two made quite the team, though." Charlie smirked. "Nothing like a woman's touch, huh Brickie?"

"Bite me, Spider."

"Told you, girlie."

"Told her what?"

"You go out of your way to make people hate you, until they bite back."

"I do not."

"Uh, yeah you do."

"Because I don't sing Kumbaya and talk about my period and shit?"

"You were so awful to me that first spring, Sam came at you with a shovel."

"You tried to run me over with the forklift," Tony added.

"You threw pruning shears at my head," Luke said.

"You shot gravel at me with your slingshot," Rowan said.

Tessa lifted one eyebrow. Darryl twisted the cap off another beer with his palm, plugging his face with the bottle like a giant baby. Apology issued. She shifted gears. "What's the deal with vinca?" The group looked at her. "I showed a landscaper where it was, but he shook his head. Came back with periwinkle, like, *see, idiot? VINCA.*"

Luke laughed, the smile taking over again. "I saw that. One of Marco's guys," he told Tony. Then, to Tessa, "it goes by both names."

Tessa's mouth twisted. "But then another landscaper asked me to add his *vinca* to the tab, and it wasn't either one of those. It was a completely different plant." She upturned her palms, questioning. Her academic brain couldn't move past this; she needed a clear-cut answer.

Charlie began counting on her fingers, her eyes reflecting the colored lights like polished onyx. "There's annual vinca, which we stock in white or hot pink. Upright, full sun, looks a bit like impatiens?"

Tessa nodded. "That's the one I showed him. With the tag that says *vinca.*"

"Always a smartass, this one," Darryl interjected.

Charlie moved to her second finger. "There's also a trailing variety, without flowers."

"Looks kind of like licorice vine?" Tessa asked.

Charlie nodded, onto finger three. "Then there's perennial myrtle, which also goes by vinca. Dark green vine, purple or white flowers, likes shade."

Luke pointed his bottle for emphasis. "Commonly known as periwinkle."

Now Rowan looked confused. "Is that the same myrtle we use inside?"

Charlie shook her head. "Nope. That's Holy myrtle."

"So, to recap," Tessa said, "annual vinca comes in upright and trailing varieties, no flowers on the trailing. Perennial vinca is periwinkle, *aka* myrtle, but not the same myrtle as in the cut arrangements?"

Charlie slapped her hands together. "Exactly!"

"And I'm supposed to figure all this out in one summer?"

Everyone laughed. "Plants go by tons of different names," Luke said. "If you're not sure, just help the customer search."

"They'll know what they want when they see it," Charlie said.

"Fake it 'til you make it," Darryl said.

"I'll drink to that," Rowan said, tipping his bottle.

Tessa wasn't sure how much time passed before empties were rounded up and cigarettes stubbed out. Everyone creaked to their feet, carried away on the bleary promise of doing it all again tomorrow.

Tethered to the wall by her phone charger, Tessa strained to coil her wet hair into a bun.

Will picked up on half a ring. "Sorry," she said. "My phone died."

Silence.

"Tessa, it's nine-thirty."

"Ugh, seriously? How am I still conscious?" The microwave beeped. Another pause as she shoveled food into her mouth.

"I texted. Finally called the house. Nano said your car wasn't back. I thought something was wrong."

"We closed two hours late. And like I said, my phone died."

"We missed you at dinner."

Tessa stopped chewing. Sunday dinner, moved to the holiday Monday this week, had slipped her mind. But hadn't she told Will days ago she'd likely miss it? "I never would have made it. The lineup was never ending."

"Two hours past closing puts you at eight o'clock."

Tessa frowned into her bowl. It wasn't a question, but he was clearly asking for an account of the missing ninety minutes. "Some of us hung out afterwards."

"You see these people all day. What's left to talk about?"

She bristled at his tone. "We needed to . . . regroup, I guess. Go over everything."

Will scoffed. "Heavy agenda, I'll bet. *Did we water the pink tulips first, or the white?*"

Tessa had never heard him speak this way. "What's up with you tonight?"

"What's *up* is I've been worried sick! We haven't talked since Thursday, when you yelled at me not to come over because you were exhausted. Now, you've got all this time and energy for a bunch of strangers?"

Tessa sighed. "I'm sorry. I *am* exhausted. By closing today, I was practically cross-eyed. I figured it might be good to rest a bit before driving home."

"I texted about dinner this morning. You went all day without checking your phone?"

Tessa forgot she owned a phone. She felt terrible, given how their last conversation about the terminal had ended. She'd meant to call him since, but then he was in meetings until late, then she didn't want to wake him on her way to work, and then the shop got so busy she'd lost all sense of time. "It was in the cooler."

"May I ask why your phone suddenly requires refrigeration?"

Tessa pinched her eyes shut. "Because, counselor, I'm climbing in and out of trucks all day. There's dirt and water and mud everywhere. The cooler is dry, and customers aren't allowed in. We all keep our stuff in there."

"You don't get a lunch break?"

"We end up working through. Rowan brings in tons of food, anyway."

"So, you're just unreachable?"

"It's a job, Will! Do you monitor your phone when you're in court?"

"That's not the same."

Tessa's defenses reared like a rodeo horse. "Why? Because it doesn't pay as much? Because I don't have a corner office with my name on the door?"

"Because it's a summer job that means nothing! Your hours keep getting longer, your responsibilities heavier. You're running yourself ragged for a bunch of plants!"

"You and Hunter grab drinks after work all the time. What's the big deal?"

"You were *drinking?*"

Tessa sighed. "Let the record show, I had water." She held off mentioning the cigarette. "Now, if the Crown is through cross-examining, I really need to sleep."

"By all means. It's all about you."

"What does that mean?"

"It means Hewson wrapped on Friday."

Tessa's mouth fell open. "Already?"

"I killed it. Open and shut. I was dying to take you out to celebrate with the team, or better yet, skip the whole thing and stay in to celebrate. But you've been completely off grid for four days!"

Tessa's gut performed an odd twist. Not long ago, she'd have been more intimately involved with the Hewson trial than anyone knew. She could have claimed a private piece of that win for herself. Will's first major corporate litigation, and she hadn't played any part. She hadn't even remembered it was happening.

In the beginning, Tessa was uncontrollably aroused by Will's targeted ambition, the easy confidence that came from knowing his place in the world. Yet, over time, a shameful envy had also taken root. The closer Will's professional plans came to fruition, the further behind she felt at having no plan at all, apart from being with him.

On one hand, she wanted to dance on the spot over Hewson. That trial was expected to take weeks, and Winning Westlake brought it home in two days! At the same time, everything she wanted to tell him about her own week—turning things around with Carlo, cracking the Clock, advancing to Trucks—shriveled like a dead leaf in comparison.

Will sighed. "I'm sorry. I'm being a brat. Who am I to lay a guilt trip, after all the times I've bailed on you for work? I just miss you, baby. The days feel empty without you."

She flopped backwards onto the bed. "I'm sorry, too. I've logged eighty-two hours since Mother's Day, and the days are bleeding together. But I miss you, too. Every second. Now, I want to hear everything about Hewson."

"Later. Right now, we need to talk about you. Remember that time we had six parties in two weekends? It took you a month to recharge. There's nothing wrong with needing down time. Tell them you need to scale back. They'll figure it out. And if it's about money, I can—"

"You can't. But thank you." Will spoiled her with lavish gifts and surprises, but Tessa paid her own bills and carried her own debt. She wanted, *needed*, to manage on her own, not to mention, Eagle-Eye Eleanor would be all over him if he lent her a dime. "It's only a few weeks, then I'll have enough banked to carry me through the job hunt. And, crazy as it sounds, I like it there. In between the chaos and the exhaustion, I can feel my mother right behind me. I have to figure out her connection to that place."

Will's voice was gentle. "Then that's where you need to be. But can we at least make a point of talking before you go to bed, even if it's only for a minute?"

Tessa smiled. "Deal. And tomorrow, we'll figure out which nights you have the best shot at staying over and I have the best shot at staying awake."

Will laughed. "Can't wait. But just for Friday, I was hoping we could stay here? Nano and Pop could call for anything."

Friday? Tessa did a quick memory scan. No milestones in June.

"Tell me you didn't forget about the gala."

Shit. The firm's annual fundraiser was a big deal, but never more than this year, with the mayoral campaign approaching. She'd talk to Rowan first thing about leaving early. "Of course not. I wouldn't miss it for the world."

SAM

If he could have been your typical, run-of-the-mill brand of asshole,
fucked up, then fucked off,
he would have.

It wasn't in the genes.

Was it flowers the people lined up for,
or a surging slice of the Iris and Henry Show to go?
We're talking Lucy-Desi interplay, right there on the sidewalk.
Heat so high, everyone left a little hotter,
walked through their own door a little bit sad.

Love in their house was red space on the gage,
a quarter turn of the dial from rage.
A trembling pinky finger,
hooked on someone else's trigger.

Then she came along, quiet as a spider.
He kept searching for the gas, a match,
the kill switch to flip.
But things with her were just too simple.

Too easy to qualify as real.

Milkvetch / *Astralagus*

"Your presence softens my pain."

———◄○►———

LUKE

T HE RAIN was back.

Rowan ducked inside the shop, doling out breakfast sandwiches with the gusto of a soup kitchen volunteer. Tessa inhaled hers, complaining about the lack of morning food at the terminal while viciously rubbing at her ear. "What's up with your ear?" the boss asked.

"Bug bites, I think."

Luke frowned. "Mosquitoes aren't out yet."

"There's three little bumps. Super annoying."

Luke bent her ear, examining the back. "I don't see anything."

"It's really red," Rowan offered.

"Because she keeps rubbing it," Luke said.

She elbowed his hand away. "I keep rubbing it because it hurts, jackass!"

Luke's eyebrow lifted. *Game on, then.* "What if—" He lowered his voice. "Oh, man, and they don't have the right antivenoms up here yet, either."

Tessa stopped chewing.

"Those tropicals coming into the terminal," he continued. "Foreign spiders hide in them. If you were carrying trees around, would you even have noticed? It could've just felt like leaves."

Her stuffed cheeks held perfectly still.

Luke choked back laughter; Sam the Prank King would've had a field day with this one. "Or, maybe, it's a fungus. All those banned pesticides—" He feigned disgust and backed away.

Tessa, catching on, lunged at Luke in mock indignance, attempting to wipe invisible ear-cooties on his shoulder. He held her off, laughing.

From the doorway, Darryl called above the ruckus. "Let me see it."

They stopped. Tessa looked over at him but didn't move.

Darryl rolled his eyes. "For fuck's sake, would you just show it to me?"

"Exactly what it says on his dating profile," Charlie said. Beside her, Rowan snickered like a schoolboy.

"Fine, I don't give two shits either way. Just trying to help."

Tessa swallowed and set down her food. "All right. Come take a look."

The room froze. Darryl mumbled into the distance, then lumbered half-sideways through the door. The building, already near capacity, could barely contain him. Charlie and Rowan swapped looks. Darryl stooped over Tessa, nodded, then pinched her ear between his sourdough thumbs so hard his own face puckered.

"OW!" Tessa screamed. "*What the fuck?*"

Everyone burst out laughing; even Darryl surrendered a half-grin. Watching the profanity that came standard with working outdoors take its hold over straightlaced, uptight Tessa was like watching the Queen of England hawk chewing tobacco.

Tessa touched her ear. "The lumps are gone!"

Darryl held out his hand, wet with clear liquid. "Sun blisters. I used to get them way back, before I turned to leather. Little heavier on the sunscreen next time, eh Princess?" He wiped his hand on his pants, chin down, then disappeared into the rain. Luke looked at Charlie, who was looking at Rowan. Nobody said a word.

With the rain easing to mist, Luke resumed pulling orders with Tessa in the yard. "I can't believe you got him inside! The guy hasn't set foot in there since he was seventeen!"

Tessa strained to unhook a soaked basket of Million Bells overhead, drawing a breath as the cold, black runoff gushed over the lip and down the inside of her sleeve. "That's not possible."

Luke nodded. "Charlie said he refused to go in after his mom died."

"Now I feel bad. I thought it was just Darryl being an asshole."

"You gave him a way out, and he took it. He's probably relieved."

Tessa chewed at her lip. "You think he'd let me change up the corner display? I have this idea that would look way better, and deal with that bottleneck by the counter when it's busy."

"You've gotten further than anyone. Who knows?"

Tessa nodded. "Hey, what do you know about his dad? I only ever hear about Iris."

The sun broke through, the air instantly humid. Luke peeled off his raincoat and hung it from one of the racks. "They both died young, but nobody talks about that. Sam had a few good stories, like when Henry took them ice fishing as kids. He said when his parents were getting along, it was off the charts, and when they weren't, all bets were off."

"What does that mean?"

"Once, after one of Darryl's blow-ups, I asked Sam why he never stood up to him. He said, 'Lukey-boy, shit went down in our house growing up.

The kind of shit you don't come back from. No point trying to fix each other now.'"

"You two were pretty tight."

"He *was* this place, you know?"

Tessa's blue eyes rested patiently on him. "Tell me about him."

Luke drew a long breath. "Hah, let's see. A born lead singer, for one. You always heard him coming way before you saw him. Legit crossword puzzle genius, sports trivia legend, the greatest prankster ever. When he was on his game, he was...I don't know. A campfire. Everyone just . . . gathered around."

"And when he wasn't?"

He sighed. "There was another side he couldn't shake. Like he had this uncontrollable need to self-destruct that kicked in the second life got too good. Drove Charlie crazy."

"I knew it! So those two—?"

"If you came right out and asked? No. But, yeah, we caught him coming out of her place a few mornings. He was with Harper though, so it wasn't like . . . you want a hand?"

Tessa, tripping over Rowan's too-big rainsuit, was dragging five-foot passion flower standards to the sold area one at a time, each pot wider than her and heavy as cement from the rain. Luke hoisted one plant on each hip, cold rivers forming down his vinyl pants and his legs *swish-swishing* as he cut across the yard.

"Show-off," she said as he passed.

"You know," Luke said when she caught up to him, shaking the wet from his hands, "you two would've gotten along great. Sam loved a smartass."

Tessa wiped soil from her cheek with the back of her hand. "You really miss him."

Luke's jaw tightened like a vise grip. He tucked his chin, a wall of tears rising, and shifted away from her. They were both silent for a few beats. He heard her wiping her hands against her rain pants, then a gentle squeeze landed on his forearm. She held it there, then slipped from the yard without a word.

The clammy handprint lingered on his skin long after; the only condolence he'd received. He wasn't entitled to the same grief as Darryl or Charlie, even Rowan, but losing Sam burned all the same. It drove him crazy how nobody said his name anymore. For weeks, he'd longed to remember his mentor, his incredible friend, out loud.

Darryl's whistle rang out, signaling an incoming delivery. The crew reported to the curb, where the sun was full, setting off a greenhouse effect inside their waterproof layers. The guys stripped down to their cargo shorts and tees—except Rowan, who wore jeans no matter the weather. Tessa, waddling like a vinyl-clad penguin all morning, took it down to a black tank and grey running shorts. Tony looked straight from her to Luke, one eyebrow cocked.

Luke knew what was expected of him. He watched her tug at her messy ponytail and shake out her long, wet hair, then lock it up again in one of those twisty knots.

Nothing.

He watched her plant one foot against a skid and lather sunblock all the way up her smooth, sculpted leg, expecting at least a generic, hardwired urge.

Nope. Still nothing.

Luke often faked being back in the game so the guys would quit busting his balls, but all he felt anymore was numb. Like a blight of Dutch Elm disease, one woman's betrayal had felled the whole lot. And the worst part? He didn't care. He preferred the company of plants, anyway. Sam would have sat him down on that very skid and said, *Lukey-boy, you are totally FUBARed.*

Or was he all the wiser now? That mother, in the rain with her young son, and Tessa, too, were both gushingly coupled off. Platinum seats in the Happily-Ever-After Lounge. Why did guys like Tony find it so unsettling that Luke wasn't interested in checking out women who were firmly attached to other men? You'd think *not* fantasizing about being a lying, cheating douchebag was just good moral character. Yet somehow, Luke was the one in therapy.

Carlo's longstanding driver, Doug, threw open the truck box. "No carts today, just trees." He held out a well-worn hand to Tessa. "Let's do the high work, shall we? Leave the heavy lifting to these lads."

"Unbelievable," Luke said.

"So much for *treat me like one of the guys*," Tony agreed.

Tessa poked her tongue at them and hoisted herself up the truck's side ladder. Tony, never one to miss an opportunity, glanced appreciatively up the back of her shorts as she went.

Darryl shook his head. "A cock-doctor in a locker room, this guy."

Tessa and Doug slid dozens of fruit trees to the bumper's edge, where the others offloaded them. They were nearly finished when Flash called frantically from the sidewalk, something about the card reader. Tessa, three feet off the ground inside the truck and bent at the waist, halted mid-handoff, straining to make out what he was saying. Which left Luke innocently waiting for her to let go of the five-foot Chanticleer pear, and no other place to look besides directly down her shirt.

Fortunately, Tessa was able to address whatever Flash was after; Luke didn't hear a word the kid said. His vision telescoped to the mounds threatening to tumble from her bra and smack him in the face. Holding his gaze above all else was a beauty mark on the left one, a whisper from where her nipple surely hid. Hand to God, it was shaped exactly like the thumbs-up emoji.

Less fortunately, Tony turned around in time to catch Luke's expression, which he was now imitating with gleeful exaggeration in the alley by the skids.

"Fuck off, before she sees you," Luke said, pulling on his cigarette.

"I can't believe she didn't see *you*," Tony said.

"I told you, it was the birthmark. It looked exactly like—"

"Yeah," he roared, "a *thumbs-up!*" He slapped Luke's shoulder. "But seriously, dude, this is progress. Didn't I tell you she had a tight rack?"

"Whatever, man. She's practically married to whatshisname."

"So? You can't look? Have a little fun for once? Two years is way too long, bro."

Tony kept insisting the cure was to go full random mode. Luke had opportunities, hot girls in a mad hurry who didn't care if he knew their names, but unlike Tony, he couldn't get a handle on the mechanics of staying uninvested and, ironically, the Brittney debacle seemed to have nuked his chances at learning how. The rush brought on by those months, that incomparable scent that had you willingly tanking your credit score—now that Luke knew love could feel like *that,* how was he supposed to be satisfied with less?

Hours later, as people with office jobs settled in front of their televisions, the Lodge sat in darkness. Luke tossed fitfully in bed, stuck in the void between sleep and consciousness where there's no telling if two minutes or two hours have passed.

Some time later, there are cries erupting in the house—the jagged, grating wails produced by tiny lungs. Luke's head jerks, trying to dodge the sound. He flinches as someone slides under the thin sheet next to him. He tries lifting his head, but slumber has paralyzed him; he can't see her, only the ceiling. She's warm and smooth against him, long, fragrant sections of her hair licking his bare chest. His nerve endings ignite. Above him, her face moves into view, but her features remain lost to the moonlight as her lips part, searching for his in hungry silhouette. Over and over, she falls shy of reaching them.

Meanwhile, the crying grows louder. The baby, too, is now somewhere in the bed. Desire and panic collide. Luke is desperate to locate the child, equally eager for these strange, tender hips to blanket the firestorm across his groin. He rails against invisible restraints, commanding his hands to touch her skin, find some way to soothe the screaming. *Anything.* Again, his body betrays him.

Luke lurched upwards, awake now, the bedroom silent. He looked around, heart jackhammering as emptiness settled in like meandering pillow feathers. Outside, dawn faintly bloomed, and with it, a realization that made him groan as he squeezed his eyes shut against it: he'd known the temptress in his dream the whole time.

It was Tessa.

Kudzu / *Pueraria Montana*

Overtakes all in its path.

———◀◉▶———

TESSA

I N THE SHOP'S tiny washroom, between the pink pedestal sink and the door that didn't lock, Tessa's best friend Ainsley dunked an old toothbrush in bleach and attacked Tessa's earth-caked fingernails with it.

"What are you wearing?" Ainsley asked, brow set in concentration. With two hours to go until the gala, she had to work fast. As Tessa described her dress, her friend frowned. "Skinny straps? With this farmer tan?"

Tessa peeled back her sleeve to reveal a neon-pale shoulder, then let out the kind of shriek that only surfaced around Ainsley. She had to make a good impression tonight, for Will.

"Relax, I've got you." Ainsley proudly pulled two foil squares from her purse.

Tessa made a face. *"Condoms?"* What these had to do with tan lines, she had no clue, but Ainsley knew perfectly well birth control was not something Tessa left to chance. The only children she intended to parent would have fur and four legs. Will had a huge soft spot for rescue animals, and Tessa would take in a hundred of them—but no kids. To become a mother would be to live each day with the possibility of being torn from her child forever. It was just too much.

Ainsley rolled her eyes. "Self-tanning towels. Exfoliate, then rub in little circles, like this." She pretend-scrubbed herself.

Tessa gazed at her friend like a full-color billboard. Ainsley worked hair and makeup at the pretentious-on-purpose Veronica Randall's salon in Yorkville to supplement her artist's income, and was a work of art herself. Hand-stenciled jeans, impeccable eyeliner, hair coiled into perfect-messy mounds at the crown of her head. Inconceivably cool, just like when they were kids.

The girls shared a classroom since sixth grade, but Tessa had only studied Ainsley from afar, awestruck, until halfway through eighth. Tessa spotted Ainsley in the waiting room after her weekly grief counseling session, her amber-gold eyes in a pamphlet. When Ainsley looked up, Tessa noticed tears among the glittery shadow.

"What are you doing here?"

"My parents are getting divorced. What are *you* doing here?"

"My . . . uh . . . I don't have parents."

Pain being a powerful common dialect, the unlikeliest of friendships was forged. Ainsley got a B in algebra, and a new iPhone. Tessa found her perfect shade of lip gloss. Tessa was Ainsley's faithful wing-woman all through high school, while Ainsley offered safe escort through Tessa's social misgivings.

"What color are you feeling tonight?" Ainsley's purse also held a felt-lined case of mini-nail polishes.

"Your call. I just want it over." The pressures of this evening were starting to build. So many Westlake colleagues and high-profile clients. So much empty small talk.

Luke appeared in the staff room, face flushed, veins protruding along his thick arms. He gestured to the moons of sweat soaking his shirt. "Time for a costume change." He popped into the cooler, swinging the door shut behind him.

"There's *two* of them?" Ainsley whispered. "How do you get any work done?"

Tessa chuckled. Ainsley never had boyfriends, only exes-in-the-making, and like a twirling lipstick tower, she was constantly assessing her options. Last week, on passing through after her shift at Veronica's, she'd swapped glances with Tony, then planted a smooch squarely on Tessa's mouth in goodbye, cementing his place in her lineup.

"Sorry I bailed early," Tessa said when Luke emerged in a fresh shirt.

Luke bit into a protein bar and winked. "You should be. What's this party, anyway?"

"A charity gala. Will's dad's firm puts it on every year. It's kind of a big deal."

"It's a huge deal." Ainsley knew all about the gala through Veronica's. "It's at the Royal York, for one thing. Sixteen thousand a table! Eleanor Westlake is chair, and she's ruthless about who's even allowed to buy tickets."

"Eleanor's ruthless, period. She'll be smiles and air kisses tonight in front of Will, then freeze me out the second he's not looking."

"Whatever," Ainsley said. "She can't handle the golden ticket going to someone likeable."

Tessa threw her a *cut-it-out* look. Ainsley had affectionately referred to Will as Tessa's golden ticket since the night he asked her out within seconds of seeing her, but Tessa was uncomfortable gushing in front of Luke, given his clearly awful breakup.

Oblivious, Ainsley straightened to admire Tessa's nails, now flawlessly dipped in a rich pink. "Please. He's brilliant, filthy rich, looks like a movie star and his entire goal in life is to make you happy." She shooed a hand in Tessa's direction. "No biggie, just the luckiest girl alive."

Tessa snorted. "Yeah. I get to plaster on a smile while his mother and her Botox blondes fire shots at my back, and their skanky daughters flirt with him to my face."

"Sounds like a blast." Luke balled up the bar wrapper and pitched it in the trash. "I'm out."

"I'd better run, too." Tessa hugged Ainsley, then slung her backpack over her shoulder.

"Nails!" Ainsley barked.

Tessa winced, checked for damage, then flashed a thumbs-up. "Oh, Ains? The tan towel thing."

"Already texting the instructions."

"You're the best." She slid past Luke and blew a kiss to Charlie, arranging a hand-tied bouquet at the counter. "See you guys in the morning."

"Have fun, Tessa."

"Knock 'em dead, girlie!"

A large gold box waited on her bed. Tessa pulled the ribbon and gasped at the black, full-length Alexander McQueen, no doubt the inspiration for the knockoff she'd bought at the mall weeks ago. The column silhouette and simple V-neck were exactly her style, but the weightier fabric and rich detailing elevated the gown into the stratosphere of luxury. She held it to the light, the late sun trickling down the crystal-beaded sweep train like a million tiny flashbulbs. Briefly, she worried the hem would be too long, but the strappy four-inch Gianvito Rossi heels beneath solved that—even if they set her sore feet throbbing on sight.

Next to the shoes lay a smaller box, its signature turquoise a piercing reminder of the one in her underwear drawer, pleading like a lovesick puppy under the jumble of cotton and lace. But there was no time to dwell on that; *this* box held a pair of sparkling diamond-and-platinum drop earrings that could have been custom made for the dress. How did Will do it?

Thirty minutes later, she gave herself a once-over, glad to have done a reasonable job hiding the dark eye circles. At the bottom of the steps, Will was a cologne ad sprung to life in an immaculate tuxedo, his green gaze a cool whisper in the heat. If Nano was in the yard, she would have said he looked like a young Paul Newman.

"Wow." He kissed the back of her hand, not without glancing at her empty finger, then pulled his face into a grin again and helped gather her train. "You look incredible."

"Thanks to you." Tessa introduced herself to the driver, then slid into the backseat. "Will, it's all so beautiful. Too beautiful. You didn't have to."

Will slid his arm around her. "First of all, there's no such thing as *too beautiful* when it comes to you. And second, I wanted to. Thanks for being my date tonight. I bet you're tired."

Tessa had been on her feet since four-thirty; tired was an understatement. But at least they were finally together for a whole night. She kissed him, then smeared away her glassy imprint.

"Oh, I almost forgot—" Will pulled out yet another turquoise box; the diamond bracelet match to her new earrings.

Tessa stared, stunned, as he clasped the shimmering strand. Her wrist dipped under the weight. A dress fit for royalty, these shoes, the earrings. Now this? It was over the top, even for Will. "I don't know what to say."

Will winked. "It's no designer watch."

They exchanged knowing smiles. He was referring to the one he gave her after she delivered the valedictory speech at high school graduation. Minutes after putting the watch on, the second hand stalled, ticking erratically. Refusing to keep time. Tessa watched Will, her cheeks growing hot as he gaped at her wrist, insisting she loved it anyway. The watch was perfect; the problem was her. She had weirdo magnets in her blood or something, because she'd never had one that worked properly. Will looked up at her, mouth parted, with a wonder she'd never forgotten. *"Don't you dare apologize. I knew you were magic the second I saw you."*

In the back of the limo, she laced her hand with his. Will's gaze lingered over her ring finger once more, then drifted out the window. She studied the pale crescents of his nails in her lap, each as familiar as her own. Affection and apprehension rose to her throat in complicated measure.

She wanted so badly to tell him what he'd been aching to hear since February, that she was finally ready to tell her grandparents, then the world, about their engagement. But Pop's prognosis was still uncertain, and truthfully, Tessa wasn't ready to put that ring back on. The hoopla it was sure to unleash would pull her along, distract her from putting her own plans in place. It would be too easy to get absorbed by Will's career, the wedding plans. Her *big* would fall by the wayside. She'd worked too hard to be a tagalong. She and her grandparents had invested too much.

Tessa turned from Will, looking out her own window and willing her focus towards the skyscrapers twinkling all around the limo, instead of the landmines now glowing inside it.

Spanish Moss / *Tillandsia Usneoides*

Voodoo doll stuffing.

———◀◯▶———

CHARLIE

Twenty-Six Winters Ago, December 23

H ANNAH WAS TALL, Sun-In blonde, smile straight off an orthodontics brochure. She walked into the shop wearing one of those cutesy, impractical holiday getups: plaid red sweater dress, cropped faux-fur jacket, gleaming white boots with dangling pom-poms. She introduced herself like it was redundant. Like she'd known Charlie for *years*. But Charlie had never served her before.

Sam told Hannah to pick whatever flowers she wanted, and Charlie would whip them into a gorgeous bouquet. "Charlie here's a wizard with the cuts. She should be at one of those high-end florists in Yorkville. But we'd fold in a week without our Spider."

Hannah giggled, and Charlie beamed. Both of them idiots.

Half an hour later, Charlie was running a carry-out. She spotted Hannah's furry whiteness among the holiday throng, leaning against a sporty Mercedes with her tongue down someone's throat. Her fingers groped at his shaggy hair. His hand moved inside the hem of her dress, her ass a pomegranate in his fist.

Charlie recognized the flannel sleeve.

When Sam waltzed back inside, he announced he was asking Hannah to marry him.

Tomorrow, on Christmas Eve.

After two whole weeks of dating.

Charlie retched in the bathroom until closing. Back at the house, she sank to the floor inside the door, sobbing. She was still there when Simon showed up with pizza, a tub of Ben & Jerry's and a file folder. He dropped to the parquet and held her for a long time. Then, he explained the paperwork in the folder—a permanent lease agreement, at a fixed rate easily covered by her seasonal wage. "This is your home, Charlie. You and the baby."

Charlie looked at the address typed on the documents. It was *this* house, the one she'd been renting. Before this afternoon, she'd assumed that going forward, she'd be living at the Lodge with Sam. Her fury poured out. She was keeping the baby, but no way she was staying. She *hated* Sam. She'd never set foot on this block again.

Calmly, Simon reminded her the child was going to need a home. Why not a few steps from a stable, well-paying job and a family who lived in one place?

Charlie ended up signing the papers. For all her rage, she still carried a nucleus of hope where Sam was concerned. What if the sight of her swelling belly in the coming weeks changed everything—for both of them?

Meanwhile, she needed far away from here. She faked a family emergency, asked Rowan to cover inside, then caught a flight back to the deserted halls of student residence.

This time, it was a caretaker who joined her on the floor, after prying open the bathroom stall to find Charlie curled half-conscious around the toilet, soaked from the waist up in bile, her bottom half a staggering shade of crimson.

The doctor called her lucky and sterile all in the same sentence.

Begonia / *Begonia*

"We are watched."

———◀◯▶———

TESSA

GOWNS AND TUXEDOS funneled into the storied brass-and-marble hotel, where the gala's cocktail hour was underway. Functions like these wore heavily on Tessa, but Will said he only survived them because she was at his side, whispering wisecracks in his ear. Inside, she fixed her gaze a few inches above everyone's heads; she could grin and bear anything for a few hours, knowing it would soon be the two of them again.

Food was top priority; Tessa hadn't eaten since lunch. She was reaching for a passing tray when a cluster of reporters began firing questions assault-rifle style.

Will's hand flew to her back. "Dad said to expect media attention, but this—" He spun her gently by the shoulders to face him. "You okay if we give them a few minutes?"

Speculation was feverish that Peter would formally announce his bid for mayor tonight, which, of course, he was, and why his team leaked the rumor in the first place. The gala had to go off without a hitch, and not just for Peter. If Will's father got elected, Will would get his hard-earned chance to run the law firm when he took office. Tessa nodded, coaxing her smile bigger.

Will led the reporters to an ornate black and gold clock tower at the center of the lobby. A few minutes in, a tuxedo-clad Teddy strolled over from the men's room, dabbing his nose with the heel of his hand. Will dismissed the reporters, shuffling Tessa and his brother behind a pillar.

Teddy slapped Will's lapel with unnecessary force. "What's up, Ken doll? Nice threads." Tessa held her breath as he pulled her into an embrace. When it came to hugging, there were two types of men—those who carefully avoided a lady's chest, and those like Teddy, who pressed with mammogram force. Will glared at him.

"No date tonight, Ted?" he asked.

Teddy shrugged. "No randos at the head table, Mom's orders. God, I hate that bitch." He eyed Tessa from top to bottom, head cocked. "We could go hit up a real party." He winked. "Ditch the heir, test drive the spare?"

Tessa ignored him, looking to Will in horror. *Head table?*

Will winced. "The campaign team wanted the family front and center."

"And you're just telling me now?"

"We haven't talked much lately, have we?"

Tessa's eyes darkened. How many times did she have to apologize for *working?* Not far behind that thought, an uglier one; did this explain the gown, the shoes, the jewelry? Was her original outfit not *head table* enough?

Her thoughts were swimming, heels unsteady. She needed to *eat*. She needed out of here.

Will touched her elbow, pumping the brakes. "There's an extra seat at Hunter's table if you want. But I'll be miserable up there without you. Please?"

Yet again, Will was caught between the man he truly was under the lapels, and the one his surname demanded him to be. Tessa sighed. No use making a fuss now, here. There was no one she'd rather sit with, and certainly not Hunter and his Barbie fiancée, Portia. "All right." Will grinned and swung her into the open again, discharging another round of flashbulbs.

The Casino Royale-themed ballroom was a kaleidoscope of black, white, and red against arched windows and gold chandeliers. Tessa's eyes went straight to the centerpieces: crystal candelabras exploding with poufy hydrangeas, dyed ostrich feathers, velvety flames of red celosia and Black Magic roses. Spectacular, and a bit tragic. Cut hydrangeas had been priced through the roof this week; these ones would wither to burnt lace by midnight in so little water. Tessa sighed. She may never look at cut flowers the same way again.

Peter waved them over, photographers in tow. Tessa did a double take; the tuxedo had trimmed years from his face, and the resemblance to Will was uncanny. Eleanor stood at arm's length in mermaid taffeta the color of fresh blood, showering Will in gooey overtones. In the dim light—and because she seldom smiled in earnest—one could hardly detect the fillers packed into her face. When Eleanor's gaze finally wafted over Tessa, colder than the air conditioning, a wry grin pulled at her mouth. "*So* glad you could join us this time, sweetie. New dress?"

At first, Eleanor had explicitly objected to Will dating Tessa; he spent too much time at the coach house. His extra-curriculars were suffering. *Tessa* was teaching him irresponsible spending habits! When Will sided repeatedly with his new love, Eleanor pretended to be accepting, but only he was fooled. His mother stonewalled Tessa at every turn, without saying or doing anything, leaving Tessa with no factual basis for proving Eleanor detested her besides the unshakeable instinct it was true. In the end, Tessa opted to keep quiet; Eleanor's love for Will was her only sincerity. How could she of all people come between mother and child?

"You've done it again, Eleanor," Tessa said. "This room belongs on television."

Eleanor trilled, then set about working the crowd. Tessa helped Will do the same—schmoozing clients, reintroducing herself to women who pretended never to have met her, posing for photos until her face hurt. Hunger built towards rage, which she longed to aim at these sadistic heels. She slipped to the ladies' room, the marble counter cool against her palms. A chaise she did not dare to sit on mocked from the corner.

When she emerged, Will was waiting. Not surprisingly, Portia Taylor was planted in front of him like a point guard in a push-up bra.

Tessa hung back, scrolling through her phone. Portia's father, Philip Taylor, was the surgeon whose malpractice suit put Peter on the litigative map. Her mother Moira sat on all the same auxiliaries and book clubs as Eleanor. They also shared a cosmetic surgeon, housekeeper and personal trainer. Indeed, they were close as two wealthy, narcissistic housewives could be. And so, wherever there were Westlakes, Taylors weren't far behind. Portia had known Will since preschool, and despite being engaged to Hunter—Will's best friend, now coworker—her aptitude for homing in on Tessa's man remained shamelessly intact.

Will extracted himself, rushing over. "Why didn't you save me?"

Tessa didn't look up. "You know she has to get her Will fix."

He slid his hands over her hips, then laid a strand of kisses in her mouth like delicate pearls, tongue teasing. "Well, I'm way overdue for a Tessa fix, so I told her to kick rocks."

Tessa wanted to walk him straight back to that stiff-looking chaise in the ladies' room, but they'd been missing from the ballroom long enough. "Speaking of Portia," she said as they walked, "her dad came by work the other day. He didn't recognize me."

Will looked surprised; Tessa had met the man countless times. She told him how Phil, curt and condescending, had stuffed his Audi with their most expensive mixed planters, then drove off without paying.

"He said to put it on his tab! No wonder Uncle Rowan's always hiding. They spot him and pounce, acting like they're his *best friends* and shouldn't be expected to pay."

Will frowned. "Phil Taylor has more money than God . . . wait, *Uncle* Rowan?"

Tessa shrugged. "I nicknamed him. He's always buying us sandwiches, coffee, smoothies. Between all that and the freebies customers give themselves, plus what I found in the binder, I'm surprised he makes any money at all."

Will looked at her, piqued. Tessa felt a flutter of pleasure. This was the part she missed most—dishing with him, sharing confidences they wouldn't dream of saying aloud in front of anyone else. She related how, after Darryl told her Rowan was fronting his own money to cover the shop's losses, she went through the accounts' binder. "There's a ton of balances owing. Some people haven't paid in years. I guess it wasn't a problem before, but with Sam gone, he's in real trouble."

"This Sam guy was that big a deal around there?"

Tessa nodded, grateful he was finally starting to understand. "He ran the whole operation."

"They can't get him back? Offer more money or something?"

Tessa lowered her voice. "It's not exactly public knowledge. Sam's *dead.* Snowmobile accident."

Will's lips pulled into a silent whistle.

"Rowan's hanging on by a thread. He's not the type to demand payment, but he's running a business! Why should people like *Phil Taylor* expect him to float that kind of cash? They can well afford their flowers!"

Will stopped short in the ballroom's arched entry. Tessa glanced around, worried she'd spoken too loudly. When she looked back at Will, his expression held such ache, she felt the twist in her own chest. She touched his cheek. "What? What is it?"

"Tessa Catherine Lewis, you're the realest person I know." His voice broke. "I can't do this without you, baby. I'm serious. I can't."

Tessa wrapped her arms around his tuxedo collar and pulled him in tight. "Then it's a good thing you won't have to." She kissed him then, a kiss she felt all the way to her toes. Every neuron fired at once, a rush so slurry and consuming she forgot to care whether anyone was taking pictures while she did it.

It was a curse, sometimes, to feel too much. But it made the good parts so much better.

"I told you." She cupped his jaw with her palm. "I'm with you all the way. And so we're clear . . . I'm the lucky one."

It was true. Sharing her life with a Westlake brought its challenges, but every second in Will's arms was completely and utterly worth it.

Wood Sorrel / *Oxalis Acetosella*

Maternal Tenderness.

———◀○▶———

ROWAN

FOR A FRIDAY NIGHT, his phone was pinging excessively. Rowan powered it down, kicking off his sneakers as he sank into the leather couch. Developers had been circling the Blue Iris site like sharks for forty years, but tonight was different. Like they could taste Sam's blood in the water.

Rowan pulled the air in his father's study deep into his nostrils. Somewhere in these cherry bookshelves, a trace of cigar smoke lingered. The creak of those wooden doors once transformed this room into their secret bunker, a safe place to wait out his mother's moods. The credenza held board games and model airplanes, a true-to-scale replica of the solar system. He used to sit right here, feet dangling, eyeballs inflamed. Riveted. His father spoke unreservedly about economic inflation and free trade agreements, the Holocaust, the Civil Rights Movement, like the boy was already a man. And in the years that followed, if the conversation went past his third vermouth, Simon would broach the subject of the Blue Iris.

On Sundays, Rowan was charged with holding the zippered bank envelope and the sweating paper bag full of bagels. It didn't matter how busy that corner was when Simon's regal blue Cadillac drove up; Iris, a blush cloud of freckles and wildflowers, dropped everything to pull young Rowan into a hug befitting a soldier back from war, slipping caramels from her apron into his palm before floating back to the counter.

Rowan had one memory of his own mother touching him. In the looping driveway, by the waiting Town Car. Rebecca was in head-to-toe white, earlobes winking. Rowan abandoned his grassy fistfuls, pudgy legs pumping after her like a driver steering into the very deer he's meant to avoid. Rowan got close enough to smell his mother's perfume, then her pearl-rimmed eyes snapped into abhorrence. Her hand landed across his cheek with such force that the diaper he was too old to be wearing exploded with a *splat* against the asphalt.

His grubby hands never dared soil her again.

But on Sundays growing up, there was always Iris. Simon ran carry-outs, gabbing with neighborhood fixtures as Rowan rubbed petunias between his fingers, marveling at the sticky scent. He gave biscuits to passing dogs, secretly hoping Sam and Darryl would invite him to play hide-and-seek among the shelves. They didn't, but with Iris's golden wrappers crinkling in his pocket and her eyes watching over him with affection, the same royal purple-blue as her namesake flower, Rowan felt part of a real family nonetheless.

Iris's death, so tragic and sudden, broke Rowan in two. He stepped up, covering shifts as needed, willing to do whatever it took to keep her store thriving. By age twenty-eight, he'd inherited his father's majority stake in the business, and the prime real estate it sat on. His mother tried her damnedest to force a sale, but Simon's will had been carefully worded with her resentment in mind.

Rowan took over as the shop's business manager on top of his day job in the financial district. The living backdrop of plants, the bustle of Morrow Avenue, the gritty soap opera that was Darryl and Charlie and Sam, it was all so vivid compared to Rowan's robotic existence. Jockeying numbers all day. Being jockeyed at home by the woman he married because she'd ordered him to.

Simon's wholesale expansion proved a huge hit; for the landscapers servicing the mansions of Forest Hill and Hogg's Hollow, the famed Bridle Path estates, there was no better place to buy product than the Blue Iris. Rowan's thirst for the snap of cash between his fingers grew insatiable, but it wasn't greed that drove him; it was finally feeling like a somebody. He traded cufflinks for blue jeans, the decision sending his wife straight into the arms of an orthodontist and unleashing his mother's serrated cackle. But, he was certain, his father would have approved.

As the neighborhood evolved into one of Toronto's most coveted pockets, purchase offers began pouring in. Rowan's answer was unchanged; the Blue Iris was not for sale. For him, the place had come to hold everything that couldn't be bought.

But the offer floating through his phone tonight carried significantly more favorable terms than ever before. Unprecedented zeroes, a long-term leaseback that would let him keep the shop open another five years, plus three luxury condos in the new development to replace the aging bungalows. With Sam gone, Rowan was slipping deeper into the red every day. Striking a deal while he still had some leverage left was the responsible thing to do.

It's what his father would have done. Or was it?

On any other investment, Simon would have injected some capital to see a healthy return, then moved on. But to his wife Rebecca's grating annoyance, he entered a lasting partnership with Iris and Henry, doubling down on the Blue Iris time and again, as spellbound by the flowers as he was by the couple's chemistry. Later, Simon would question if he'd pushed them too far. If the extra pressure of the expansion is what did it.

Whatever the case, Rowan couldn't let the place fall on his watch. Over time, the storefront needed improvements, upgrades. But Darryl, a cauterized vein since his mother died, wouldn't let anyone so much as adjust one shelf, least of all Rowan, whom he still regarded as the interloper, stripes bought rather than earned.

Then and now, Rowan was terrified of Darryl. The deadness in his eyes made it impossible to predict whether he was about to twist Rowan's neck until his head popped off, or change radio stations. On the rare occasions Rowan worked up the nerve to suggest a cosmetic overhaul of the aisles, computerized checkouts to plug revenue holes and better manage inventory, Darryl became a rhino preparing to charge. Typically, Sam and Charlie would have backed Rowan up, but on this subject they silently retreated.

Darryl's mother died in their kitchen, his father arrested, then dead himself not a week later. Nobody had the heart to push. Anyone with an introductory psych class under their belt could see Darryl was holding onto happier times. Rowan backed down; with business skyrocketing, where was the harm in status quo?

Until now, with Sam gone and the profits running dry.

Tessa's help with the buying had the numbers inching towards the black again, but there was barely enough to cover Rowan's overhead, never mind keep his creditors at bay. Selling was the only option.

Sam's snowmobile had been recovered; how much longer before his body washed up, and prospective buyers figured out the Blue Iris didn't have a leg to stand on? Once word got out, the offer price would plummet. Rowan couldn't afford to wait much longer.

Leopard's Bane / *Aconitum Napellus*

"A foe is near."

———◄○►———

TESSA

ESSA COLLAPSED into her seat at the head table, hungry and worn out by reporters and cameras and phony small talk, her grip on the evening rapidly loosening. She had to hold it together; Bradley Thornton, tonight's keynote speaker and attorney general for the province, was seated beside her.

"Thornton's the youngest AG ever," Will whispered as the man approached. "He was Dad's protégé out of law school, made partner in *two years.*" The prickly tone suggested Will felt outranked. "He's our clincher in this election."

"Why haven't I met him?" Peter's colleagues often blurred together, but Tessa would have remembered this one—early forties, gym physique, green eyes that saw right through your clothes.

"He was heading up the Calgary office, then the Winnipeg merger. Now that he's back, we'll be seeing a lot more of him."

Thornton took her hand in his, insisting with the practiced smile of a politician that she call him Bradley. His watch, a monstrous chunk of yellow gold and steel, so over-the-top it was almost cartoonish, sparked to life like a snake in her periphery. Tessa really needed to eat.

At last, the first course was served. At the podium, Peter's welcome address was building towards the big announcement. It was all white noise to Tessa, until the room erupted at the word *mayor,* and he called the family over for a photo op. She brightened, hoping to sneak a piece of brie from outside the spotlight. Instead, her name boomed from the microphone.

"You too, Tessa! Don't be shy!"

She froze, doubtful she'd heard correctly. Eleanor subtly ensured candid family snapshots were taken with Tessa outside the viewfinder; she'd never allow her to pose with the Westlakes at her gala, in front of major news outlets. But Peter beckoned again, then Will's hand stretched before her. Tessa abandoned her plate to cut across the stage. Eleanor's expression was vacant, but Tessa nearly smelled smoke coming from her ears on the way by.

Tessa's composure was fizzling, too. She'd agreed to accompany *Will* tonight, not to be some cog in his parents' propaganda machine. After the photo, they returned to their seats, where her salad had been cleared away untouched. Will rubbed her back, his breath a welcome warmth in her ear amid the chilly air conditioning.

"The rest of the night is all ours, I promise."

Did he know this? Or was he merely hoping, like she was?

"You belonged in that photo, babe," he said. "You're part of this family. It won't be much longer before that's official, right?"

And there it was. The topic they'd been dancing around for months. Will had chosen now, while she was near-delirious and on display before six hundred people, to confront it directly. Worse, just as a mouthwatering plate of agnolotti in truffled cream landed in front of her, Bradley interjected on her other side.

"So, Tessa, what do you do?"

Fabulous. An interrogation sandwich. Tessa pinned her fork to the table, the gesture nearly sparking tears. She'd fumbled through this subject far too many times tonight already. "I finished up my doctorate a few weeks ago."

Bradley chewed slowly, taking time to dab his napkin to his mouth. "Very impressive, congratulations. What's next?"

"There are a few different paths from here," she began to say. Indeed, a liberal arts degree, an applied statistics degree, and now a social sciences degree could lead in any number of directions. The more subjects she knocked off, the wider her options. But while Tessa excelled at student life, where all requisites for success came outlined on a tidy syllabus in advance, no field of study called to her the way law did for Will, or mixed-media art did for Ainsley. She was highly trained in how to *think,* to reason and use logic, but had no idea how to apply it. Loads of ambition, no clue where to direct it.

Tessa reached for the parmesan cheese, layering it over her pasta. She could keep plenty occupied—and well-compensated—helping Will indefinitely, forging a full career out of being Mrs. Westlake, like Eleanor— except, totally unlike Eleanor. But her 4.1 GPA proved Tessa had what it took to be successful in her own right, and she still wanted to be. She'd just hoped that by now, given that choosing what donut to get at the Timmie's drive-thru often sparked panic, she'd have some sort of blueprint for going about it.

Lost in thought, the crystal bowl erupted in Tessa's hand, sending cheese petals flying as the spoon clanged against her plate and sliced through the dinner music. She squeezed her eyes shut, cursing inwardly until she smelled Bradley's lemony aftershave.

"Forgive me, I seem to have forgotten my manners." He eased the dish from her and finished sprinkling the pasta with cheese on her behalf. "Please go on. I want to hear more about this promising future you've lined up."

Something about having the AG in her personal space set her insides quaking. His charm and good looks suggested it was simple attraction, perhaps flattery, but strangely, Tessa's physiology signaled fear. That watch, with its piercing ridges, began taunting her again. Tessa couldn't understand her odd fixation with it; Will had a Rolex, too, though it was nothing like this one. She probably had watches on the brain after reminiscing in the limo about the one he bought her at graduation.

Tessa forced her focus back to the conversation. "I'm working at a flower market while I weigh my options."

Down the table, Bradley's wife, Olivia, perked up for the first time. Decidedly understated in champagne satin, her strawberry hair in a simple ponytail, she was a stark contrast to her husband. "Oh, I love gardening! Which place?"

"The Blue Iris? Up on Morrow Avenue."

"We live a few blocks away. I jog past every morning."

Tessa placed her instantly. Olivia stopped by the hydro pole on the boulevard around nine-thirty daily to check her activity tracker. Toned arms, flat abs, never in the same athletic outfit twice. *Eagle,* hands down, everyone at the shop agreed. "I thought you looked familiar!" An uncomfortable pause. Tessa was sure it was her. "It's me . . . stocking the trays. When you're on your run?"

Olivia shook her head, uncertain.

Surely Tessa didn't look that different because of a designer dress and some makeup? Or was Olivia, like Phil Taylor and everyone else in this overstuffed room, truly only just noticing her now, *because* of these things? Because she was here, tonight, on this hollow, black-skirted, pointlessly elevated stage?

Compass Flower / *Silphium Laciniatum*

"Finding North."

———◄○►———

CHARLIE

Twenty-Five Summers Ago

SAM WAS STILL MARRIED, and Darryl was still an asshole. But the shop's expansion was rapidly underway, gradually overtaking the whole block, and Simon was counting on her to be the glue.

Besides, Charlie had earned her place behind that counter. Planting season coincided with university break, the wage was beyond fair, and she loved the work. If Darryl hadn't driven her out by now, why should Sam? The whole mess was ages ago. History.

At least, these were the lies she told herself.

Sam breezed into the shop, half-singing, half-nattering about some glitch at auction. Work boots traipsing across the ruts in her heart created by himself, and their family that would never be.

An hour ago, she'd arrived at work wondering if today might be the day he finally offered some acknowledgment—a lingering look, a loaded grin—of that afternoon spent in his bed last summer. Charlie stabbed at the crack in the cement with her broom when he sailed past, willing her cells not to respond.

She'd dated a few guys from campus since Christmas, trying to move on but mostly trying to discern if it could be the same with others. These past months had turned her harder than she suspected a nineteen-year-old should be, more cutting with her tongue than was attractive. Sam was changing too, with bullet speed. His tone was shakier, his moods more volatile, the space around him a blaring dog whistle only Charlie seemed to be able to hear. But that was Hannah's concern now.

This new Sam was much easier to step away from. And step away Charlie did, all summer long as men older and better looking than him pulled up after work in cars he could see his reflection in, brought her to dinner instead of a rickety back porch. She and Rowan grew closer than black-sheep cousins. Customers requested her by name. It wasn't clear whether Sam noticed, but Charlie came impressively close to not caring whether he did.

Until her last shift of the season.

She arrived to find cappuccino and an almond croissant, still warm, in the staff room; the same things she'd carried three summers ago, when Sam winked at her and everything else went dark. The shop was empty. Finally, she noticed him through the window by the register, sprinkling the hose over a sweeping mass of bleeding hearts.

He held her gaze, not for as long as her own heart now wanted all over again, but long enough to acknowledge that today was Labor Day.

One year exactly since she'd followed him into the Lodge.

And so began a lifelong apology Sam couldn't manage to say aloud, and Charlie couldn't bring herself to fully reject.

One morning, still dark, she rolled over in bed and screamed so loud every window in the bungalow rattled. Perched on the bed at her feet, solemn as Holy Communion, was Sam.

"Sorry, Spider. Didn't mean to scare you."

"How the hell did you get in here?"

Sam lifted one weary shoulder. "It's keyed the same as the Lodge."

He looked so broken, so unlike the ball of charisma the neighborhood adored. Charlie sat up, bunching the covers to her chest.

"What do you want?"

He flopped down beside her, arms behind his head, staring through the ceiling. Charlie waited, pulse climbing. Sam was finally about to tell her about that night in his parents' kitchen, how they died, the heaviness that reared each night with the fence panels.

"My marriage sucks."

Hannah ran her course. Then came Lena, Sam's NA sponsor, with whom he eloped in Vegas against the stern advice of Larry, his AA sponsor. They lasted four years, but neither were lucid for much of it. Sam stayed infamously single for eight years thereafter, women and bottles churning through the Lodge like it was Union Station.

Meanwhile, Charlie's carry-on bag bounced up her bungalow steps every April, as though summer wouldn't show up without her. In the off seasons, she traveled to anyplace she hadn't yet been, intent on checking off every landmark and postcard beach in the guidebook, until she found herself seeking out the nearest soup kitchen instead. No matter the city, town or village, there were always people in need, and Charlie felt a near-physical need to be helpful. Probably because she couldn't help Sam.

She signed up with as many aid organizations as she could juggle. Filled her winters building schools in Peru, handing out water filtration tablets to First Nations communities in northern Canada, making education more accessible for adolescent girls in sub-Saharan Africa. All the while, where signal allowed, she wiped her inbox clean of Sam, wind-chilled and completely foreign, drunk-dialing from one neon-lit curbside to the next. Slurring at her to fly home. Which Charlie might have, except every time she *was* home, the summer version of him—the one she knew like the alphabet—never bothered to call.

The shop was both fuel for her wanderlust as well as the cure, providing reliable income and a fixed address without infringing on the freedom she'd come to hold above all else. International relations degree in hand, she aimed for unwavering focus as there was important work to be done. But too often Morrow Avenue lingered in her mind. Gradually, she established her own non-profit, partnering with like-minded souls all over the world to facilitate outreaches in ever-expanding capacities—flying eye hospitals, prosthodontic treatment blitzes.

Charlie and Sam's perennial strain persisted, greening anew for a few weeks each year. She stopped flinching when she rolled over to find him on her bed, or on the floor beside it, the still-unspoken tragedy in his parents' kitchen next door pressing down like lead. Sometimes, she slipped from her covers into the dark alongside him. Other times, her judgment groggy but her desire as alert as a third cup of coffee, she lifted them in invitation. In these faint-lit mornings, conversation and silence and sex poured like ballads in the shower. Clear-ringing, unashamed. Confined to four walls.

Outside, they continued on as though they were still on opposite sides of that scorching equator. Charlie convinced herself it was feasible to remain whole while splitting herself across hemispheres; it was all the commitment she had room for, anyway.

Then came Harper.

In very short time, Charlie didn't sing in the shower anymore.

Emu Bush / *Eremophila Duttonii*

Answers needed.

WILL

GROWING UP, his father used to gush at length about Bradley Thornton in a tone Will's blue participation ribbons never managed to elicit. Tonight, the jerk was more intolerable than ever. Openly holding Tessa in his crosshairs was a bird-flipping reminder that as attorney general, Will's entire career now fell within his purview. That kiss she gave him on the way into dinner was the only thing keeping Will's smile in check.

Next to Will, Peter set down his fork. The way he pressed his napkin to his lips reminded Will that even during a party, business was always top of mind, and there was no opportunity more private than while on full display.

"Excellent call on the dress," Peter said. "You two made a bigger splash than I'd hoped."

At what cost? Will scraped the gravy from his prime rib. Tessa hated the spotlight; all the extra attention tonight nearly made her bolt, he could tell.

"You know," Peter continued, "I was half-hoping you two would make your own announcement tonight."

Will stopped chewing. His smile was meant to convince onlookers they were sharing some mildly inappropriate anecdote. "You mean, get engaged?"

Peter nodded. "Surely you've discussed timing by now."

Will drew a breath. If his father only knew the lengths to which they'd discussed it . . . and then stopped discussing it altogether.

"So? When are you popping the question?"

Will forced an airy tone. "Soon, I guess, when the moment is right. Why does it matter?"

Peter sipped his wine. "Tessa lends a certain . . . accessibility to the family optics. Could prove helpful at the polls. Not to mention, we need to distract from your brother."

They glanced down the table towards Teddy, rising to go to the rest room again, as he had been doing roughly every thirty minutes all night.

Peter leaned in. "I'm sure you bought all the time you could with the trust money, but we need a new plan. We're one bathroom trip away from scandal."

Will frowned. *The trust money?*

"Ah." Peter squeezed Will's knee in approval. "Plausible deniability, the only thing more important than optics, especially in an election year. That you understand so well already, it blows me away. More like the old man every day, huh?"

Peter knew about Will's empty trust account and thought Will used the funds to clean up one of Teddy's messes? That worked out well, actually. But Will couldn't care less about his brother right now. He glanced over at Tessa, breezily keeping Thornton under hypnosis in front of the entire room, including the guy's *wife*. She really could hold her own with anyone. Her knack for cracking people open, gaining trust, getting an immediate read was otherworldly.

It was the difference between Will winning the hands he was dealt, and taking the goddamn house.

He turned to his father. "You're saying I should marry Tessa to help get you elected?"

"I'm saying if you were planning to propose anyway, because it's what you *want,* now would be an ideal time, for all of us."

Will's forehead creased. "Does Mom know?"

"Son, the first lesson in marriage is knowing when to seek forgiveness over permission. It's not like she doesn't know it's coming. No rush on the ceremony itself, of course, but frankly, I can't think of a reason to hold off on the ring."

As usual, Peter Westlake advanced an irrefutable argument. Indeed, Will himself couldn't quite understand why he and Tessa weren't publicly engaged. Pop's fall, followed by the word *Parkinson's*, came as a terrible shock, but months had passed. He was stable now, under a doctor's care. If anything, happy news was just what everyone needed.

Will cleared his throat. "Me neither. I'll make it happen, Dad."

Peter jostled Will harder this time. "That's my boy!"

Will flushed, pleased, all while eyeing Tessa nervously. "I'll need some time. I want to do it right, for Tess."

Peter lifted a hand. "Say no more. I'll have the press kit updated, and you let me know as soon as we can run with it. The *Globe* is running a feature in a couple of weeks, lots of pictures from tonight. We can list her as your fiancée in the captions.

"A couple of weeks?"

"Don't overcomplicate it, now. All you have to do is get down on one knee."

Will buried his face in his wine glass, not wanting Peter of all people to glean from his expression that in fact, four excruciatingly long months ago, his interminably perfect son had already done exactly that, and he still had nothing to show for it.

Cathedral Bells (Cup-and-Saucer Vine) / *Cobaea Scandens*

Knots.

———◀◉▶———

ELEANOR

ALL THESE YEARS LATER, why was she still shocked when her husband failed to play within boundaries he only *pretended* to let her set?

Seating Tessa at the head table was concession enough. The gala was Eleanor's signature event, one she'd spent the past six months coordinating to the last painstaking detail. But Thornton was AG now; keeping the pompous ass happy was crucial to tonight's success—and Peter's. Ties to provincial government were key in mayoral elections, something no other candidate in the race had. Quite usefully, Tessa had kept him sucked into her orbit all through dinner. Calling her into the family shot at the podium, however, without so much as a discussion or heads up, was too far.

Eleanor's cheeks twitched; clearly, Peter intended to push up the engagement after all. Sure, she'd been warming to the idea herself, but that was beside the point. He'd promised that play was off the table. How easily he forgot she was equal partner in all of this. How he'd be nowhere without her. She threw back her chocolate martini and scanned the gaming tables. Predictably, Peter was losing to Thornton by the thousands at Texas Hold'em. Will was at the roulette table, compulsively stacking chips onto number eleven? *Right. Tessa's birthday.* Eleanor rolled her eyes out loud.

She'd nearly convinced herself Tessa had the mettle to stand beside Will when it came time to hand all this over. Peter had worked tirelessly to get where he was, but Eleanor had sacrificed every bit as much and overlooked a great deal more. Tessa would fold like a cheap card chair under that kind of weight, leaving Will in a freefall. Eleanor wanted the mayor's office—deserved it—but her firstborn would not be collateral damage. King Westlake was long overdue to remember who wore the real crown.

As the band slid into a slow number, the perfect chance presented itself. Bradley Thornton cut in on Will and Tessa on the dance floor. Will, patience wearing visibly thin, stepped aside. Peter swooped in after Olivia. Portia Taylor all but trampled what remained of Hunter's balls trying to get to Will, but Eleanor got there first.

"Hello, handsome." They glided across the floor. "Are you enjoying yourself?"

Will was distracted, his gaze heavy on Thornton and Tessa, but his reply was perfectly cordial. "You did a wonderful job as always, Mom."

Eleanor beamed. She really had raised the loveliest boy imaginable. It would be dreadful, this next part, but does a mother let a wound fester in her baby because cleaning it out is painful? Her job, above all else, was to protect him. "You and Tessa look so happy tonight. I just know those rumors will be long dead by tomorrow."

Will stopped swaying. "What?"

"Sweetie, you don't need to save face with me! I didn't believe a word of it myself. It's just, once these things get going, the momentum gets hard to contain. I want to help."

Will grew panicked. "How did you . . . did Dad say something?"

It was not the reply Eleanor expected, but it proved what she'd been saying for weeks; life with Tessa was far from idyllic.

"It's no big deal," he continued. "We just need time to figure everything out. *Privately*. How many people know?"

Eleanor elbowed her curiosity aside; she had to stay focused. "Gosh, there's really no telling. Practically everyone has a landscaper nowadays. I'm sure I'm not the only client who keeps her windows open."

Will exhaled, then a wave of contempt curled over him and tore straight towards her. "This is about where she *works?* I should've known you and the wife-bots would have fun with that one. And you know what? I'm so done defending you to her! She could've taken a handout from me, but she's been killing herself at that place to pay her own way. You need to give it up already. At least she has a job."

Well, that certainly makes things easier. Eleanor revved for the finish line. "Yes, and I hear it comes with quite the benefits package."

Darkness crept across Will's face like the leading wall of a monsoon. "What?"

"Even if there was the tiniest seed of truth to it, seeing as these things rarely do start out of nowhere, I'm sure it's all out of her system now. You two really seem stronger than ever."

Will's voice hugged the curve of hysteria, his hand on her ribcage tremoring. "Tell me exactly what you heard."

Eleanor threw her head back and laughed, lest any bystanders notice the tension, then cuddled close to her son. "The landscapers were at the house a couple of days ago, and well, you know how men talk when they think women can't hear." In fact, Eleanor had no idea what they'd said because the crew spoke only in Spanish, but Will would have no way of knowing this. The point was, the intel was credible; no need to reveal her real source.

"Mom. What did they *say?*"

"Oh, I couldn't repeat such language. Suffice it to say, it had to do with the new girl at the Blue Iris who helped load their trucks."

Eleanor's side tingled where Will's grip relaxed. "That's the hot gossip? A bunch of nobodies checking out a girl in shorts? Come on, Mom. You're better than this."

"I wasn't finished." This next part required unwavering precision. Eleanor had to apply enough heat for the idea to stick, without leaving a charred mess. "It seems she and a coworker have gotten . . . close." Eleanor winced. "I'm sorry, darling, but it sounds like he's bragging about seeing her naked."

"Mom, guys make stuff like that up all the time! Tessa would never—"

"Of course not. Only, the details were quite specific. I don't suppose she has any unusual markings? Something resembling a thumbs-up sign?"

Will pulled back, looking her dead in the face as the song finished. He excused himself, Eleanor staring after him, a discordant mix of pride and fear and victory in her chest. *My son is going to be the best litigator this city has ever seen.*

Will barely flinched, but right before he turned away, his mother watched a single droplet of doubt fall into his eyes like India ink into a clear green lagoon, and Eleanor knew the other morning had been well worth the risk.

Yes, one last time with Tony had paid off in more ways than one.

Thuja / *Arborvitae*

"We are unchanged."

———◄◦►———

LUKE

H E LEANED AGAINST his pickup in an unlit corner of the hotel's valet lot, trying to understand how he ended up here. One minute he was headed out for a pack of smokes, the next he was camped outside the Royal York like some kind of stalker.

The cherry of his cigarette flared in the darkness. He recognized the shape of her movements instantly, though all the rest was different. They were hightailing it out of the lobby, strappy heels swinging from her fingers like stolen jewels. She was long and lean in a shimmering gown, the perfect compliment to whatshisname's well-cut tuxedo.

It suited her, the dress and the makeup, the shock of tumbling locks. Just as well as sneakers and a ponytail did.

Earlier today, after Tessa had breezed out of the shop, Luke went against his better judgment and his therapist's every talking point by hanging back.

"You're Ainsley, right?"

"Yeah."

"You've known him a long time. Tessa's boyfriend?"

"Sure, as long as she has. Why?"

Tessa would hear all about this later, no doubt about it. But in that second, Luke needed to *know*. He'd caught himself racing down a treacherous road, and he needed something heavy to bring it all to a quick, certain stop. "Is he really all that? I mean, I get the looks and the money and the car and everything. But is he a *good guy?*"

Charlie let the bouquet in her hands drop to the counter and looked at him.

"What?" Luke asked her. "You don't think it all sounds a bit too good to be true?"

They both looked at Ainsley.

"Yeah," Ainsley said finally. "He is. It's hard to believe, but those two really are as good as it gets."

"Glad to hear it." Luke rounded the building to the yard, Charlie's X-ray stare tracking him through her window.

And he *was* glad.

Really.

So why was he standing out here in the dark?

His stomach clenched as Tessa murmured in Mr. Prettyboy's ear, laughter consuming them both, those rich pink nails from earlier now concealing an exclusive joy. Her chin tilted to the marquee lights as she giggled, her glimmering lips like a shooting star, oblivious to the bystanders staring as they clamored into the limo.

It was true; they were good together. So good, Luke decided he'd just seen what it looks like when two people are meant to be.

Good for you, Tess.

By now, Luke understood she deserved the very best kind of man.

One who could give her everything, love her without reservation. Seeing firsthand she'd found him brought a swell of . . . well . . . relief more than anything. Tessa was as happy as everyone said, and that made her truly off limits. Officially unattainable. Should his subconscious decide to go rogue again, it was comforting knowing the matter was out of his hands.

Consciously, Luke would never make a play for Tessa. He knew how it felt to go all in, then get tossed like a used napkin. He wouldn't wish hurt like that on any guy, much less a decent one. Sure, he enjoyed hanging out with her—no expectations, no pressure. She was the only one on the crew besides Flash who didn't look at him like the box cutters might need locking up. But what a coincidence the first woman to get in his head, after all this time, was in love with someone else.

Like Dr. Lutchman explained, old patterns would pop up again just to test him. Half the battle was recognizing it, then loving himself enough to break the cycle. It didn't matter if Tessa crossed this parking lot right now and swore she was done with whatshisname forever. That she wanted nothing more than a broken, broke-ass sap like himself. She'd change her mind.

In the end, they always did.

The kind of love in that limo didn't *let* you walk away. Luke didn't care that her laugh was the cool side of the pillow in August; he'd already learned this lesson once, and he wasn't going to be ravaged twice.

Snapdragon (Lion's Mouth) / *Antirrhinum Majus*

Used as a spell breaker.

━━◀O▶━━

TESSA

ESSA ROLLED OVER and forced a damper on her breathing, pretending to fall asleep. Next to her, Will's fingers drummed his chest, the vibrations tracking along his damp sheets and up through her pillow.

Nothing was the same after Thornton cut in on the dance floor. Was Tessa wrong to agree to the dance? It was one song; surely he didn't want her snubbing the *attorney general?*

When the music ended, Will swept her straight from the ballroom without a word, without even saying goodbye to his parents. Tessa fled with him like an inmate granted early parole. Back in the limo, he kissed her voraciously. Her back hit the seat with a commanding *slap* as he tore at her heavy underskirt. Tessa tasted a brand-new flavor of arousal that left her re-energized, and open to all possibilities.

The downtown streets made for a turbulent ride on the low, narrow bench; her head kept jamming against the armrest. Will's condo was two minutes away. More than once, she suggested they wait until they got upstairs. But Will was so insistent, his hunger so rabid, he didn't seem to hear. In the end, she'd practically thrown him off her.

"Will, STOP!"

Remembering it now left her queasy; the haunted pitch of her own voice, the pull of her jaw as he backed away, eyes a spilled bag of beads, fly unzipped and black tie dangling. His gaze darted, disoriented. Like she'd shaken him from a terrible nightmare. Over and over, he pulled his hands through his hair, sputtering breathless apologies.

It must have been Thornton who unhinged him.

By the time they spilled into the penthouse, he was trembling. He started kissing her again, begging her to say she loved him. Imploring her to prove it. Never had her Winning Westlake been in such broken need of reassurance. Tessa, certain by now it was she who set him on this course months ago by putting his diamond back in the box, shushed him gently. Promised all was forgiven. Led him like a lost, whimpering child to the bedroom and tried to put back whatever piece of him had snapped loose.

It was nothing like last time, before Nano's dinner, or any other time. Will was rougher, more forceful. His body closed around hers like a blood pressure cuff, twelve o-clock shadow chafing like Velcro. He didn't hurt her, not exactly; Tessa could have overpowered him anytime she wanted. Rather, it was like he wasn't there in the bed with her at all.

At dawn, Tessa left Will snoring fitfully and slipped into the Uber downstairs. For the first time, it was a relief not to look at him. She didn't know how to step out from last night's bizarre shadow into the present.

Luke and Darryl were pulling away snow fencing panels. Flash and Tony leisurely unpacked the aisles. As July approached, landscapers slept later, waning the pace from all-out sprint to distance run. Rowan rounded the corner with coffee, six chutes of steam in the early light. Wordlessly, he handed one to Tessa, who smiled in silent appreciation. It was an unspoken rule; in the mornings, the day laid out like clean linens before them, nobody talked until they absolutely had to.

Today especially, Tessa's soul softened in the peace like wildflower seeds after a drought. She cranked open the checkout umbrella, pausing to peer up the middle; Tony's re-enactment of a bat flying out of it and hitting him in the face had everyone weeping with laughter in the beer garden, but she'd been on high alert since. The crew drifted over. Rowan plugged in the till. Darryl rationed newspaper sections. Still, nobody spoke.

Tessa arranged pints of strawberries along the counter, smiling proudly. The fruit she'd selected at the terminal was at the perfect stage of maturity—plump and shiny, bright stems, no white flesh at either tip. One broke loose and rolled across the newspapers. In a practiced motion, never looking up from his page, Luke popped it in his mouth, ejecting the stem into his fist.

Tessa's eyes nearly popped out of her head. *You didn't wash that!*

Luke rolled his back at her. *Right, I forgot. Everything from the terminal is covered in hork and piss.*

Her expression shot back the reply. *It IS, you JACKASS!*

Luke hunched his shoulders and puffed his cheeks, silently pretending to hurl.

Tessa pressed her lips together, one hand flying to her mouth, silencing the jolt of laughter without a second to spare.

LUKE

Across the weather-beaten counter, the newspaper headlines dissolved to grey before Luke's eyes.

It was the flash of those pink fingernails flying to her mouth that did it, the laugh he couldn't hear against her naked lips. They rocketed him backwards in time to mere hours earlier, when he was absolutely sure the only guy who could ever be in on the joke with the woman in front of him was William Whatshisname Westlake.

Luke gripped the counter with both hands, wishing like hell he could talk to Sam for just five minutes.

And then, the phone inside the shop began to ring.

Love Lies Bleeding / *Amaranthus Caudatus*

Desertion.

———◀○▶———

CHARLIE

NOT ONE SICK day in her life; certainly not in late June, with proms and graduations in full swing.

The later start was a major perk of working the inside counter. Charlie was dead asleep in her bed when the Parry Sound coroner's office called the shop at six forty-five. But by six forty-seven, a silverback gorilla was thumping her front door off its hinges.

Darryl's face pinched. "You sleep in *that?*"

Charlie looked down and cringed, wishing she'd thrown on her robe before answering. Her sleepshirt was migraine red, a spastic bird splashed across the chest, the words *Crooked Crow* in chicken scratches. A triple extra-large, it hung around her like a Christmas tree bag.

Not that she cared how Darryl saw her. She simply preferred not to invite conversation about why she was sleeping in Sam's clothes.

Luke had found the shirt in an old box of Sam's at the Lodge. They went through it together, rooting around for the smallest flicker of the man they deeply missed, laughing through tears trying to guess how he'd come upon such a godawful, tremendously too-big garment. To know Sam was to be sure there was one hell of a good story behind it. Charlie brought the shirt home; it was all she had of him. Harper would sooner burn the rest than let her have one shred.

"G-string's in the wash. What do you want?"

Darryl hesitated, like maybe it wasn't worth mentioning after all.

"Spit it out, Brick, before I punch your face."

"Coroner's office called."

Charlie's eyelashes dropped like a velvet curtain.

Fuck.

"Body washed up on Waubuno Beach."

She swung the door the rest of the way open. "I'll be ready in five minutes."

False Strawberry / *Potentilla Indica*

Deceitful appearances.

———◄⟨○⟩►———

TESSA

THE SHOP WAS PACKED. Rowan was on the landline, the phone held away from his ear as a woman's voice screamed inside it. "Find Luke," he said. "Tell him 217 Strathallan, stat."

Tessa rolled her eyes. If there was such thing as a *landscaping emergency*, presumably the caller had a *landscaper* she could call, instead of bullying Rowan into sending one of his crew while short-staffed. The whole neighborhood knew he was incapable of saying no.

Luke was offloading soil from a flatbed blocking half of Cresthaven, seemingly oblivious to the line of honking SUVs. He palmed the forklift's heavy wheel, his bicep a softball, maneuvering the machine on a dime in roars and beeps. He'd been withdrawn since the call from the coroner's office.

Tessa would deal with the so-called emergency herself. She was headed to cover Darryl's deliveries anyhow, and the last thing Luke needed was to be screamed at. Besides, she owed him for covering when she left early yesterday for the gala.

At 217 Strathallan, Tessa followed the flagstone around the stucco mansion to the backyard, where she stared in stupefaction. Textured greens flowed between colorful bursts. A boxwood hedge curved like human ligament. Birds of paradise. Heliconia like low-hanging fruit. A cobalt infinity pool beckoned, surrounded by King Sago palms and dipladenia the color of wild flamingoes. Tessa knew without counting there were twelve of each. She'd hand-selected this order herself at the terminal, on Rowan's request, at a market price that left Darryl choking on his Mountain Dew.

A figure strode from the cabana trimmed in rose gold. Sun hat, celebrity-width. Messy-perfect fishtail braid. Tony would have abandoned the lame sports analogies and declared an outright *smoke show.*

The woman's shimmying sarong fell silent. "Who are you?"

Tessa stammered, unsure where to place her gaze. The customer's bikini was so suggestive of kinky lingerie, it seemed an invasion of privacy just to be near it. Inside the open cabana doors, by the daybed, a sleek bottle sat on ice next to a fluted bowl of strawberries. Tessa frowned, confused. Why would the customer want Luke servicing her flawless garden with a poolside rendezvous imminent?

Her insides did a backflip. That first night in the beer garden, Luke said rich women around here loved a man in work boots. Tessa looked back at the bowl of berries, heat crawling up her chest.

This was meant to be a midday booty call.

With Luke.

Hadn't he popped a ripe, filthy strawberry straight into his mouth just this morning? The man *obviously* liked strawberries . . . but so what? Tony did this sort of thing all the time. Why did it sting to discover Luke was no different?

The woman looked vaguely familiar; she was probably a model, or a local TV personality. She lifted her sunglasses in thinly veiled horror. *"Tessa?"*

The air squeezed from Tessa's lungs, her brain tripping over the implications.

It was Olivia Thornton.

Last night, Olivia had appeared so demure, her conservative gown ten million light years from the come-fuck-me getup she wore now. *For Luke.* Tessa fumbled an explanation. They were short-staffed, Luke couldn't make it. "It sounded, ah, *urgent,* so I came instead."

Olivia gave a forced smile. "Oh, I only called to thank Luke for pulling together such quality product, and let Rowan know how pleased we are." She waved the matter away, wrist jingling. "Someone got their wires crossed."

Tessa flicked her gaze towards the cabana. "Sorry to have disturbed you, then."

Olivia laughed lightly, gesturing to the daybed. Those perfect strawberries. "Bradley's due any second."

Right. Tessa, still stunned, could only nod. "Have a nice day, Mrs. Thornton."

"Please, call me Olivia." Then, in case Tessa decided to go blabbing to Will, "It was great meeting you last night. I'm sure we'll be seeing a lot more of each other on the gala circuit." She smiled. "Lucky us."

"Yeah," Tessa said, making a break for the gate. "Lucky us."

Black Mulberry / *Morus Nigra*

"I will not survive you."

—◄○►—

CHARLIE

KILLARNEY TO PARRY SOUND was a disquieting distance for a body to drift, to say nothing of what ice damming would have done in the weeks leading up to the thaw. Charlie tapped the maps app closed and made herself as small as possible in the passenger seat. Outside, sections of guardrail shifted past like flipbook animation.

"I don't want to think of him going out like that, either," Darryl was saying. "But Waubono is—"

"I know." Waubono Beach was downwind from the cabin, along the same current where the snowmobile had washed up a few weeks back.

Charlie stared into the distance. She'd never stayed anyplace longer than a few months, rooted evenly by her love of the shop and the insatiable urge to fix all she could beyond it. But in pursuing a life that was decidedly both, she'd ended up with one that was neither.

There had been other men. Good, decent men who varied in creed and color but all had in common a finite amount of patience for a woman who refused to stay put. A woman who could be flung open like a trap door by a 2 a.m. text from another man.

Men who all wanted kids.

Which left Sam, whose most reliable quality was pouring her every emotion into a cocktail shaker and agitating to a cloudy swirl. He'd be right there in her bed, present and cogent and surging with life, until suddenly, he was a staircase spiralling to dark all over again. He'd be lying next to her, vowing to her popcorn ceiling he couldn't breathe anyplace else, then show up to work married. Barking about a missing pail of waxflower.

Six years ago, while running deliveries in Forest Hill, Sam stumbled upon Harper sunbathing topless by her parents' pool, fresh off her divorce from the housepainter. By then, he was gun-shy of marriage and told Harper as much right off the bat. On the surface, Harper was cool about it. Assured Sam she was only looking to have fun, piss off her stuffed-shirt father. But with the others, she was clear as a flawless diamond; only a ring would do.

"Hold one hand out and one over your ass, see which fills up first," Darryl told her as she stalked the sidewalk, waiting for closing.

"He'll never go for it," Rowan agreed. His divorce had cost a fortune, and Sam realized how easily he'd gotten off with the first two.

Harper's bronzed shoulder gave a little wave inside her halter top as she aimed her smirk straight at Charlie's window. "He'll change his mind."

Two months later, Sam propped himself up on one elbow next to Charlie's pillow, traced her collarbone with his knuckle, and told her Harper was pregnant.

With twins.

Charlie scrambled from the bed, sheets flailing like Sam was a saw-scaled Indian viper, hurling insults along with his clothes. At a certain time of day, you could still see the pucker his steel-toed boot left in the drywall.

Whatever they had, screwed-up as it was, it had been working. Sort of. But now there were babies involved. Two innocent heartbeats. Just like that, Charlie was done. Full stop. The same part of her Sam had ruined beyond repair, barring her from properly moving forward, became the reason she couldn't go back.

Charlie made a toast at the reception. Wrapped toilet paper around Harper's exploding belly. Watched them share everything she had come to want so badly.

Sam never could get it through his thick skull there was no crossing the counter. People either shopped at the Blue Iris, or worked there. Same neighborhood, worlds apart. Between his generous salary and the dividends from his parents' shares, he made a lot of money, but his new bride spent it in ways he never knew existed—weekly microdermabrasion, in-home masseuse, a personal chef specializing in prenatal nutrition. The Lodge, cozy and adorable at first, was pronounced entirely unsuitable. Harper insisted on a semi in Davisville they couldn't afford and filled it with furnishings from stores with names Sam couldn't pronounce.

All the while, Sam still lingered at the counter after unloading the cube, dishing his marital dirt while helping her wipe the already-spotless shelves. Having relocated Sam off property, it seemed Harper was set on extricating him from the shop entirely. How was she expected to raise two babies by herself, she demanded to know, while he was off working eighteen-hour days for four months straight? To which Sam had countered, how were they going to manage the growing stack of bills if he didn't?

Eventually, Sam started showing up to Charlie's bedside again like she was some twenty-four-hour confessional. She kept her covers sealed. Rolled her eyes. Claimed not to give *two shits* about his self-inflicted problems while hanging on every word. Wondering if she could have done everything differently.

"I can't stop picturing it," she whispered across the front seat. She felt seasick.

"Don't bother." Darryl twisted to look at her. "You're waiting in the car. I swear to God, Spider, if you—"

"I'll wait in the car."

SAM

He turned up whisky-hazed at her bedside for the
same reason as always:
she was the only place that had ever felt like home.

And she'd come back.
To him, the shop.
Every time.
Still it was the leaving he never could push past.
The barren months in her sweaty freedom zip-cord,
the blacked-out holes of need and regret between plantings.

Always on him to *talk about it,*
always on about the people who *did* want her help.
Trudging her slippery steps, he still believed her the martyr,
suffering him at will.
The barbed wire in her tears proved her his prisoner,
shackled by tragedy bigger than both of them.
For all her fair-weather fleeing,
she *couldn't* walk away.

Not until he cleared her a path.

Spindle Tree / *Euonymus*

Likeness.

CHARLIE

THEY WERE WAITING on her to crank out the usual sarcasm, lob a few shots at Darryl or Tony. Let them know they didn't have to worry about her. Instead, Charlie stared into the blue bulb a few feet above Tessa, the one that would have kept his expression unreadable until the second beer, when he sat all the way back. Tonight, she couldn't bring herself to reassure them. She was worried, too, by her own reaction when Darryl returned to the car and said the body wasn't Sam's, and by Darryl himself, acting as though he'd been identifying mutilated corpses all his life.

In a way, she supposed he had.

Like his brother, Darryl never spoke about that night. Charlie knew only what Rowan did; he was seventeen when Iris was taken away by

179

ambulance, Henry by cop car. Two funerals in under a week. Darryl had lived in that same house, alone, ever since. Hadn't so much as swapped out the mangled honeysuckle wallpaper. At seventeen, Charlie's most pressing concerns were which T-shirt made her boobs look biggest, and whether Sam noticed. Darryl was a prick from day one, but after today, it didn't seem hard to understand why. Did she have to be such a bitch in return?

When Darryl pulled away from the morgue, Charlie felt a patent sock of disappointment, as if she'd been hoping the body *was* Sam's. She was still weighing what kind of a monster that made her. Truthfully, she'd mourned him a million times while he was alive. Now, she almost craved a gravesite to lay flowers on, beat her fists against.

God knows she'd tried to walk away. But Charlie was incapable of loving any man as wholly as she did that horribly tortured one. Never could bring herself to change the lock on the bungalow, turn off the damn phone. And yet, she'd hated him throughout. In the space of a single moment, Charlie could ache for Sam while genuinely never wanting to see him again. Every fall, when she boarded that plane, she felt light as dandelion fluff to be freed from his bullshit—save for the crippling phantom limb without him beside her.

Here again, he'd left her dangling. A wee insect lashing by a thread. Waiting under these sagging rainbow lights to be swallowed whole, or set free. Or both.

Charlie hadn't set foot on the Blue Iris property during winter since she was nineteen. This past New Year's, she could have spent her layover in a hotel by the airport, and the crew would have been none the wiser. Instead, adamant there was nothing worse than paying a premium rate to spend New Year's Eve listening to people barf in the hallway, she gave the driver her bungalow address and left her porch light on. And when Sam appeared by her bed in the middle of the night, as she knew all along he would, she uncorked a twenty-seven-years-aged bottle of rage and poured it all over a not-so-recovered addict, on the eve of a trauma anniversary he couldn't put words to.

What was wrong with her?

The guys tucked their empties into the case by the fridge. Tessa screwed the lid onto her water bottle. "You want us to stick around?" Luke asked.

Charlie surveyed the rumpled, sweat-stained group. "Go. Get some sleep. Heat's really socking in tomorrow." He looked at her, unmoving. "Lukey-boy, I'm *fine.*"

Luke stood with a sad smile. Sam made fast friends everywhere, but he had cheesy nicknames for only the handful he cherished most.

They bent to hug her in turn; even Darryl squeezed a shoulder on his way past. Tessa, sunken and small in Sam's old chair, made no attempt to move.

"What's happening over there, girlie?

"Tired, I guess."

"I could use the distraction."

Tessa gnawed at her lip. "I'm okay."

Bullshit, but no use dragging it from her. "How was the gala?"

Her cheeks puffed in exhale. "I smiled, made small talk. Tried to be there for Will."

"Tried?"

Tessa shrugged. "Supposedly, I shine at those networking things. Will says I make inroads in ten minutes he can't manage in six months. I don't see how."

Charlie smiled. "Your energy really is something."

"My energy?"

"Vibes, aura, whatever you want to call it. Yours pulls at people like a magnet because it's gorgeous, but also because it makes them feel seen."

Tessa thought about this. "Last night, I felt like a rag doll. Ripping at the seams trying to make small talk. Twice, I worried I might literally fall over. If it were up to me, I'd spend all my time with just Will. Or my grandparents, or Ainsley. Or here. I'm such a weirdo."

"Fake conversations, negatively charged environments, even going too long without food can leave some empaths totally depleted."

"Depleted. Exactly. How do you know all this?"

"There was this Reiki master in Phang Nga for a while. Anyway, the point is, you have to protect that high vibration of yours, throw a shield up once in a while."

Charlie moved over one place to Darryl's chair, taking Tessa's hands in hers. "You're not a weirdo. It's a gift, and as far as I can tell, you got it from your mama."

Tessa's eyes rounded into blue quarters, the rest of her falling slack. "You knew my mother?"

Charlie took the girl's face in her hands, grazing those smooth cheeks with her thumbs in a startlingly mom-like gesture. When Tessa first stopped into the shop this spring, grown and capable, mere months younger than Charlie's own child should have been, Charlie remembered her instantly. Swelled with illogical pride. Too many times since, in the haze between sleep and waking, she'd allowed herself to fantasize that her unborn baby was a girl, that she'd lived, and grown up to be Tessa Lewis.

"She came in once," Charlie said. "You were with her, but you were probably too young to remember."

Tessa shot upright. "No, I do. Do you remember what she wanted?"

Despite serving countless customers since, Charlie did. "American bittersweet—a shitload of it. But it wasn't in season. I offered to get Sam from the back, see if he could ask around at the terminal, maybe bring some in on a special order."

Tessa leaned so far forward, she practically folded in half.

Charlie chuckled. "Back then, calling him up to see to a woman like that would have set my teeth grinding. But she was so genuinely . . . *nice*, I really wanted to help. He was drunk off his ass from the night before, though, hadn't shown up for work yet. I went on sort of a rant about it, actually. She must've thought I was a real piece of work."

Charlie explained how the pair hung around awhile, shoppers

gathering around Beth like children drawn to the chimes of an ice cream truck, plunking their life stories like linty pocket change, Tessa growing weary of having her head patted. Charlie rang through a few purchases, and when she next looked up, the two of them had vanished. She never saw them around the neighborhood again.

A few years later, Charlie had stared at Beth Lewis's photo in the paper for a long time, thinking of that sweet little daughter robbed of her mother too soon, and how horribly cruel a world it could be.

Twinflower / *Linnea Borealis*

Conflicted.

—◄○►—

TESSA

WELVE DAYS of heat alerts had turned the city into a bulging
water balloon. Tessa, armed with Charlie's details about her mother's
flower request, had voluntarily worked all of them, even her days off,
hoping to jog her memory. Summer was short; she was running out of
time.

As for American bittersweet, the internet was highly conflicted.
Some considered the plant a treasured cure-all, others a poisonous pest.
Symbolically, it was said to represent bad luck, fidelity, and a call to war.
Why did Beth want so much of it, and when it wasn't in season? They were
living in the tiny apartment on Morrow at the time, it didn't even have a
balcony. Shortly afterwards, they'd moved into the coach house, but there
wasn't a stick of bittersweet anywhere on Nano and Pop's property.

Tessa's stomach gurgled. She recalled her lunch, untouched in the cooler. It was too hot outside to eat. There was too much to think about.

Back-to-back shifts had also prevented Tessa from seeing Will since the night of the gala. Their conversations had taken on a detached edge, but neither had so much as hinted at what transpired after they left the Royal York. Tessa preferred never to relive it, and presumably, Will was too ashamed. Instead, he inquired exhaustively after every detail of her day, as though concerted interest in her job was his least awkward path forward.

Yesterday, with one day's notice, he invited her to spend the Canada Day holiday on Lake Muskoka with his friends. Rowan would have given Tessa the time off, but Will's never-ending questions and the tension crackling through their phones was wearing on her. After Charlie's talk in the beer garden about energy and shields, Tessa recognized that a whole weekend of it, plus Hunter and company thrown in, would be too depleting right now.

Will, however, desperately needed a reprieve; he was under so much pressure at work, and it was obviously wearing on him. Tessa encouraged him to go have fun. Hopefully, it would act as a circuit breaker of sorts, a much-needed reset between them. Still, Will was miffed she'd declined to go along, and Tessa had felt off since the conversation. This morning, she drove to work in a daze, inadvertently running a stop sign.

Thankfully, the shop was quiet; the heat was keeping people away. The air hung like a wet blanket in her lungs. She peered at the clock, thinking she'd call Will right now, clear the air. But he'd be in a car full of people already, on his way to Muskoka.

A convertible rolled up to the curb. The driver, dressed all in white with a yellow sweater over his shoulders, fanned a wad of hundreds at Tessa like paint chips. "I need fifteen bags of soil delivered an hour ago."

Tessa rolled her eyes; that much dirt cost around sixty bucks. "Truck's out for today. Might be able to set it up for tomorrow?"

He reacted like she'd asked him for a kidney. The landscapers were at the house *now,* he was having a Canada Day party, he needed the dirt *immediately.* While he carried on, Tessa recognized him as a Sunday regular at Peter and Eleanor's country club, along with his surly wife and three bread-tossing children.

After she'd convinced him his only option was to take the soil with him, he sat there, engine idling, air conditioning blasting from the open roof. Tessa fetched his change, moved his tennis gear, lined his trunk with plastic. Each bag she lifted grew heavier. Twice, she lifted her ball cap to wipe the sweat dripping into her eyes. She glanced around, hoping to snag help, but the guys were tied up, including Luke, "on delivery" for the fourth time this week.

Exactly how many times did it take to apologize to Olivia Thornton?

Tessa steadied herself against the skid as a wave of dizziness hit. One bag left to go. The driver, on the phone now, glared impatiently in the rearview mirror. An idea crept in, sparkling with guilty pleasure. Tessa hesitated. This guy definitely knew the Westlakes. But he'd never make the connection; Phil Taylor and Olivia Thornton hadn't recognized Tessa here. He tapped his horn, hurrying her along, and that settled it.

"Trunk's full," she called, and before he could clue in, she flung the last bag into the car's ivory interior, where it belly-flopped with the satisfying *pop* of a weakened seam. One that would blow the second he lifted it.

The car squealed off. Tony rounded the fence and saw Tessa propping herself against it. He hopped on a skid and lit a cigarette. "Everything okay, Tee? You don't look so good."

"A bit gassed, I guess." She held out her hand for a drag. She still wouldn't call herself a smoker, but the occasional hit of nicotine definitely took the edge off. "Loaded fifteen bags of top while that jerk sat and watched."

"Who, the M-6?" Tony knew every customer by the car they drove, which he could identify just by hearing the engine. "That guy's a piece of shit. I should totally fuck his wife."

Tessa laughed weakly. "Maybe while he's crying the stains off that ivory interior."

Tony looked puzzled, then it clicked. "No . . ."

Tessa grinned.

"NO. A brown bomb? *Inside* the car?" He reeled backwards, laughing, then high-fived her like a dad on graduation day. "But fifteen bags, that's a shitload in this heat, Tee. You should've tagged me in."

"Better you finished watering before Darryl lost it."

Tony stretched himself taller and puffed his chest. "HEYCH-two-OH, kids, or we might as well go into the SHELF business."

Tessa chuckled; his impressions were dead-on.

"I'm about to start on the back," he said. "Unless you'd rather do it? Leave the front lines to me and Flashy for a while."

Tessa pressed her palm to her forehead, a dull headache emanating. "Perfect. Holler if you get swamped."

In the yard, heat wriggled from the asphalt. Every leaf and bloom held still. Tessa dragged the hose to the shady corner way in back, working through the rows, her thoughts jumping to Will, and how much she wished things between them were back to normal again. To her grandparents, likely exhausted from all the upkeep on a house they'd have sold years ago if not for her. Finally, stubborn images arose of Luke's thick, tanned arms pinning Olivia Thornton's body to that daybed in her cabana. Olivia feeding him strawberries with her manicured fingers.

Tessa's arm cramped up. The rubber hose in her hand turned to brick. Desperately thirsty all of a sudden, she twisted the nozzle and leaned over to drink. Next thing she knew, she was spread flat as a picnic blanket on the blistering asphalt, looking up through candied swirls of Summer Fantasy phlox into the vast lemonade sky.

That's when everything went dark.

Tessa could hear their voices somewhere in the yard, but her own was stuck.

"How long ago?" Rowan asked.

"I don't know, an hour?" Tony said. "She looked like shit, too."

"So you sent her back here. Alone."

"Take it down a notch, okay? I took over the heavy lifting as soon as I noticed. You're the one letting her work two weeks straight in a heatwave."

"She insisted!"

"You're the *boss,* Rowan. Start acting like it anytime."

Tessa shuddered, cold water from the hose gushing beneath her.

Rowan's voice cracked like lightning. "TESSA!"

Luke now. "What's up?"

"We can't find Tess."

"What do you mean, you can't *find* her?"

"She came back to water an hour ago. Nobody's seen her since."

Tessa mustered a small gurgle. A shuffle of sneakers, then the cart she lay behind swung away to reveal her lying there, ponytail afloat in soupy soil, water darkening her clothes like bloodstains. Rowan screeched.

Luke pushed in front of him, dropping to his knees with a splash. "Tess. You okay?" He propped her to sitting. Tony shut off the hose. Rowan stared, paralyzed, as Luke pulled away her sunglasses. "Tess." He snapped his fingers, the breeze of it grazing her nose. *"Tessa."*

The world slid back into focus. She cleared her throat. "Yeah. Fine."

The men exhaled in a single waft.

"What happened?"

"I was watering, and my legs gave out."

Darryl waddled up behind them, a pepperette hanging from his mouth.

"Oh. I'm up there going where the fuck did every . . . *whoa,* what happened to you, Princess?"

"She passed out," Tony said.

"I did not!"

"You weren't answering us," Luke said.

Darryl tore off a bite of sausage, jaw smacking. "Heat prostitution."

Four sets of eyes squinted at him.

"You know," he jiggled his hands in clarification, *"heat prostitution."*

Tony sighed. "What are you talking about, man?"

Darryl finished gnawing. "As in, Princess here has been fucked by heat."

Tessa's head sank against her forearms, her body shaking weakly with laughter.

Rowan's voice fell a few octaves. "Heat *prostration.*"

Darryl shrugged. "You want to keep jerking each other off, or get her some water?" Tony dashed out of the yard. Darryl stooped over Tessa. "When's the last time you ate?"

"It was too hot. I will, after I'm finished back here."

"No chance," Rowan said, turning to Luke. "Get her to the Lodge, keep an eye on her. Give her lots to drink, and make sure she eats."

"You got it, boss."

"Tessa, you're off the next three days."

"What? But I'm fine!"

Rowan's palm signaled an end to the discussion. Tony reappeared with water, and Tessa emptied the bottle in seconds.

Luke helped her to her feet. "All right, Lady of the Heatwave, you heard him."

"Honestly, I'm good. I'll just go home."

"No way you're driving right now." He steered her up the Lodge's back steps and through a sleepy screened-in porch. The cool air inside the house pricked her skin. She took in the tidy laminate countertops, the dish cloth folded over the tap. Much cleaner than the bachelor's lair she'd been picturing. "Washroom's there," he said, pointing. "I'll run to the cooler and grab your extra clothes."

Shit. Tessa sighed at the ceiling. "I was so out of it last night, I forgot to reload my bag."

Luke fetched a clean towel. "It's okay. I'll find you something."

After smelling each manly bottle in the shower, Tessa scrubbed until the water ran clean. By the time she'd slipped into the T-shirt and sweats Luke left by the door, she felt almost normal.

In the kitchen, he handed her a smoothie and pointed to the living room. "Go sit down."

"Mmm, this is great. What's in it?"

"Coconut water, mint, celery and banana. Very hydrating." Luke ushered her along.

"I'm totally making this. Was it a whole banana, or—"

"Sit!"

She looked at him. "You don't have to be pissy."

"And you don't have to be a pain in the ass."

Tessa traveled a few steps, then succumbed. Luke led her by the elbow as she gazed drunkenly around the living room; Maple Leaf blue paint. Bench weights. Two worn recliners and back issues of *Men's Health* and *Maxim*. A giant flat screen. All stark and tidy as an art gallery. She sank into one of the recliners, already half asleep. "Not even a stripper pole."

She awoke in the dark, a blanket tucked around her. Rain streaked the windows. Tessa followed her nose to the kitchen, where Luke stood plating food in fresh clothes. His black hair was wet, and wildly unkempt without its ball cap, but in a perfect, underwear-model sort of way.

He looked up. "You really will do anything to get out of closing."

Tessa scrunched her face at him, then shivered in the air conditioning.

"The heatwave broke, we can eat on the porch if you want."

Outside, the wet storage yard exhaled relief. Conversation was easy, the silence as natural as talking. Luke had become one of her closest friends. It bothered her that he was having an affair with a married woman and still didn't trust her enough to tell her about it.

Tessa waved her fork at the penne sautéed in garlic, oil and chopped tomatoes. "How are you such a good cook?"

"I have to be. Tony would have us living on Corona and pizza pockets."

Tessa looked up. "Where is he, anyway?"

Luke shrugged. "He's been rushing out every night. Usually, I'd get the full rundown, but—"

"Weird." Usually, they'd *all* get the rundown.

They looked at each other. *Ainsley.*

Tessa would use some of her time off to catch up with her friend, find out once and for all if Tony was a legend in his own right, or just in his own mind.

"Thanks for everything," she said, finishing her last bite. She stood. "I'll help you clean up, then get home."

Luke's face filled with alarm.

"What?" Tessa asked.

"Your bag. I meant to grab it when I went to help close up. But we were racing to beat the storm, and Rowan was rushing me back to check on you . . . mine's still in there, too."

Tessa frowned. Her phone, wallet and keys were inside the cooler. "Do you have a key?"

"To the shop, but not the cooler. Only Rowan has that, and—"

"He sleeps with his phone off." Rowan was vocal about the effects of cell phone radiation.

Tessa chewed her lip. She could use the landline in the shop, but Will was still in Muskoka. She couldn't put Nano or Pop on the road this late.

"Sorry, Tess. My spare truck keys are here, I'll drive you."

Luke had work in the morning. She'd put him out enough already. "It's fine. I'll crash here, get my stuff first thing and head out, if that's okay?"

"Why do you think they call it the Lodge?"

Tessa smiled.

Luke forked his pasta. "You can have my room."

She raised her eyebrows.

He lowered his. "You wish, Princess. I meant I'd take the recliner."

"Sure, you did. Jackass."

Luke grinned.

Tessa sat back, blissfully full. The temperature was perfect, the couch wide and worn. The green flock before her emitted a near-audible sigh, lulling her into a calm Tessa hadn't felt in months. "Would it be weird if I slept right here?"

Luke chuckled. "Sam never slept anywhere else. Swore he could hear the flowers growing, and it was better than Ambien."

Tessa glanced around the outdoor room. The more she learned about Sam, this troubled stranger she'd never met, the more she found herself really starting to miss him.

Viburnum / *Tinus Lucidus*

"I die if neglected."

———◀◦▶———

WILL

THE BOAT'S DECK was slick with coconut sunscreen and spilled Jäger. The lake sparkled. The bikini bottoms and bass gyrated as one. Will rapped on the bar top, prodding Hunter to keep pouring, his stomach pitching like walleye caught on a lure.

For as long as he could remember, envy hovered close. Guys strived in secret to be him, their girls vying in the open to be his. Like white noise, he never much questioned it. Tessa's attention, her heart, was the first to invoke any real sense of need, and to this day, he'd do anything for it.

He just never, in a million years, anticipated having to beg.

The longer she held him off the more affronted Will became, her clinging to threadbare excuses like Pop's care (Will could look after that with one phone call) or her job (temporary, of no consequence whatsoever), unwilling to spend even the occasional night at the penthouse.

He hadn't helped matters by taking his mother's bait at the gala. Will knew Tessa hadn't done whatever Eleanor suggested, it was just that, by that point, it felt like he didn't know her at all. The Tessa he adored was all pause-and-check, slow to warm up, attuned to his every twinge, and here she was neck deep in a whim of a job, light years from her comfort zone and skill set, bending over backwards for a bunch of strangers at precisely the time he needed her more than ever. Everything was subject to question.

And then, that one detail Eleanor mentioned cut him to the quick. The cheeky thumbs-up on Tessa's left breast, in bold defiance of the shy modesty layered above it, was something of an intimate running joke. The sight of it evoked a tender sense of privilege, even now. It was unthinkable that some losers in his parents' backyard were laughing about it. Laughing at *him*.

Jealousy catapulted Will outside himself. He had no words to explain what happened when the song finished that night; he wasn't even sure he trusted his own recollection of it. All he knew was the long-muffled fear that he wasn't enough—for Tessa, and without Tessa—dragged itself kicking to the forefront of his mind, and he'd been unable to quiet it since.

He should just tell Tessa what Eleanor overheard. Together, they'd applaud the creativity of the rumor, then dismiss it out of turn. But Will couldn't lend breath to the words; acknowledging the possibility of being cheated on out loud was more than his pride could handle.

Instead, he set about some due diligence. Probed gently but thoroughly as she recounted each day, grid-searching for guilt fibers. Hunting for inconsistencies. As expected, he found none. Still, she could be here on this boat right now if she wanted. How could they put that awful gala behind them, when she consistently refused to meet him halfway?

Ashore, at the chalet, nightfall clung heavy to Will's eyelids. Music and laughter blinked like a migraine aura. He clung to the back of a chair, scanning the room for Hunter. Will spotted his friend face down, red cup dribbling in his hand, a ping-pong ball knuckling his shoulder. Will muttered to himself, stumbling onto the deck, the square bottle still launched in his hand. He squinted at the yacht, glittering in its slip. *Is something moving down there?* The alcohol made it hard to be sure.

It's then that he spots her, deep in the shadowy cavity of the boat. Rolling and fumbling with a formidable stranger. Her bedroom giggle skips across the water and Will's pulse spikes with the same vengeance it did at the gala. In a telescope-turned-backwards sort of way, he understands his mind is playing tricks on him. Tessa isn't actually there, making a mockery of him in front of all his friends. But like waking disoriented and panting from a nightmare, the physiology of it lingers, and for a moment, he loathes her anyway.

He knows then he has to go directly to his room, wait for the exploding inside his chest to peter out, then *call her.* Pull her from lavender sleep and let her pillow voice drown the one crying with pleasure down at the water. Let her assure him, *there's no better man.*

His steps are slow but deliberate down the hallway, some faceless, nameless other stalking after him. Still taunted by Nightmare Tessa's transgressions, his mouth a cracked sheet of cotton from thirsting after the real one, the *swish-swish* of long hair behind him becomes an affirmation.

You're William Fucking Westlake.

You're William Fucking Westlake.

He flops onto the bed, sloppily ordering the ceiling to right itself. It hits him with agony that he isn't so different from Teddy after all. Will, too, is hooked on being in first place, on being at the front of every pack, the same way his brother itches after coke.

The door closes behind him, Portia's bony fingers winking over the lock like the cool leather of a Town Car. The room spinning, his ego the only driving notion, he lets himself be shuttled home. Back to where he started, and where he belongs.

Back on top.

Southern Magnolia / *Magnolia Grandiflora*

Ensures faithfulness when
placed under the bed.

———◀◦▶———

TESSA

L UKE SWIRLED the dishcloth across the cutting board. "Are we going to talk about it?"

Tessa stopped mid-scrub, a hot lump rising in her throat. "Huh?"

"Why you're so afraid to take a day off lately."

Oh. That. Tessa placed the saucepan on the drying rack, considering. The job consumed her waking hours, the outdoors and hard labor exhausting her in uncomplicated measure. At night, her body surrendered to sleep before her mind could object. She nodded towards the back window. "It's those plants. Somehow, they quiet all the noise."

Luke laughed. "I think that's why we all stay. But all those fancy

degrees, a soul mate who's rolling in cash. Don't mind me saying, but your life doesn't seem noisy."

"It's not that simple."

Luke hung the cloth over the tap and leaned against the counter, arms folded. "Break it down for me, then."

Tessa hesitated. Hadn't he done enough tonight, without listening to her whine about her problems?

"Come on, Tess. Talk to me."

Before she knew it, all her uncertainties went plunking into the suds. What if she didn't find her *big,* a career that would hold up next to Will's? What if she *did,* and hated it? How much longer could she dither selfishly, grandparents strained by a property they could no longer handle, Will sleeping alone, all because she couldn't bring herself to pack up the apartment she'd shared with her dead mother and act like a grown up?

Luke nodded, prodding her to continue.

Tessa described how, after losing her mom at age eleven, change of any sort became dismantling. Simple decisions felt heavier than they should, because what if she didn't get a do-over? She'd tunneled deep into academia, answerable questions becoming her solace, each course syllabus a tidy inkjet map.

But now, at twenty-six, thirty loomed large. Like a speech running too long, it was time to wrap up the student thing, roll next segment. Only, for all the depth and breadth of her transcripts, Tessa didn't know how to do that part. No textbook unearthed any inkling towards one path over another. Choosing one, without any clear sense of where she might end up, felt impossible. "It's like hurtling yourself out of a plane and just hoping for the best!"

Luke cocked an eyebrow. "People do that. It's called skydiving."

Tessa smiled. "Thanks, jackass. I'm just saying, people get this big thrill out of surrendering to what might go wrong, but for me, everything already *did* go wrong, and now it's like I need to know every ending before I can begin. And that's not going to work anymore."

Luke's eyes lifted, but his stubbled chin stayed aimed towards the floor. It was completely gone now, the boarded-up façade that revealed him only in pried-off slats. In his troubled gaze, Tessa saw all the way to his concrete footings.

She tilted her head. "Everything okay?

"What you said, about needing to know the ending first. I've been living that for a long time. And you're right, it doesn't work."

The kitchen fell silent.

Luke's smile glowed off her skin. "For what it's worth, just the word skydiving makes my gut flip."

The emotions swelling inside her popped in a spurt of laughter. "I know, right? Who voluntarily signs up for that?"

More laughter. More silence.

"Tess. You know you've got this. Apply, interview, decide as you go. If you end up in a job you don't like, you can always find another one."

True. Except every co-op placement and internship further amplified Tessa's fear that no workplace would feel right, in which case, how could she rise to the top of any one of them? Cubicles were padded cages. Meetings rendered her zombie-like. Her computer constantly malfunctioned in ways tech support couldn't troubleshoot. The communal microwave smell, the constantly brewing inter-office politics, all of it eroded her senses like water torture. Managers praised her results, but the work itself never sparked to life. Failing to reach *big* was worrisome, but the thought of eking her way there, inert and dispassionate, was paralyzing.

"Moving into the penthouse makes sense," she said over the *swoosh* of the drain. "Will's salary would cover us, and the jobs I'd be applying to are all downtown, anyway. Nano and Pop could cash out, live worry free. Afford care down the road."

Luke speared cutlery into the drawer. "Then what's the issue? You're marrying him anyway, right?"

Tessa could trust Luke with the rest of it. She wanted to. But she respected Will too much to have the conversation with anyone, until she'd finished having it with him. "Right. But if I don't get my own life figured out first, I'm afraid I never will."

Life married to Will would be so comfortable. Easy to the extreme. With nothing forcing her into the unknown, the years would tiptoe past like footsteps after curfew. She'd slip into the supporting role of Mrs. Westlake, every win filtered through her husband, just like Eleanor, and Tessa would have her *big*, but really, it would be Will's.

Luke's voice pulled her back. "I thought you said you lived downtown before?"

"I stayed at the penthouse a lot through grad school, but I always had my own apartment behind my grandparents' place. I'd stay there forever if I could, but Will's life is downtown now. His dad's running for mayor, he's being groomed to take over the firm. He barely sleeps as it is without adding in a commute."

"You lit up just now, talking about your grandparents' property. This amazing guy you talk about would do anything to help you hold onto that."

Luke was right; Will's empty trust fund was proof. Yet still, Tessa couldn't make the leap. "He needs me to meet him halfway on this one. I think—" It socked her to say it aloud, never having dreamed such words could be true. But Tessa was the one who had pushed Will to take over the firm. She'd promised to help, stick by his side, whatever it took.

"I think it might be a deal breaker."

Luke's eyebrows drew together. "He told you that?"

Tessa traced the pattern on the dishcloth. "Not exactly."

"Come on, give the guy some credit. It's not ideal, but it's not impossible, especially not with his means. Talk to him. He'll make it work . . . you'll see."

"What makes you so sure? You don't even know him."

"I know you. And you're worth it. No chance he can't see that."

"I thought I was a pain in the ass," she teased.

Luke grinned. "You're definitely that. But he's lucky to have you."

Back on the porch, the anxieties that had bubbled up in the kitchen skated from view across the platinum blooms. Tessa sank into the couch. "If you ask me, you're the lucky one."

Luke settled into the armchair, curious. "Why's that?"

Tessa sipped her water. "Because I've seen Olivia Thornton in a bikini, and it practically gave *me* a hard-on. Sorry I ruined your plans, by the way. I didn't mean—the whole call from the coroner's office thing. I thought I was helping you out by going."

"You lost me."

"Relax. I'm not about to blow your little arrangement with Olivia."

Luke remained perfectly—annoyingly—*chill.* "It's not exactly a secret."

A flare of indignance shot up. She'd guess that Tony knew, but *everyone?* "I just spilled my guts to you in there, and you still don't trust me? What are you worried about? Tony talks about his sexcapades all the time, it's not like I go around—"

Luke's burly hand objected. "Wait. You think I'm sleeping with Olivia Thornton?"

Tessa's cheeks burned. She shouldn't have gotten so worked up. Now, she'd turned the Luke-Olivia thing into a *thing.* No wonder he didn't tell her things! She swallowed. "Um, yeah."

"You know she's married, right?"

"I'm not judging, I swear, I—"

"You seriously think I'd be down with that?"

"She summoned you in the middle of a weekday, dressed like a porn star! Clicquot and strawberries by the daybed! What was I supposed to think?"

Laughter simmered in Luke's chest. His head tipped to the sky, the rich sound boomeranging. He laughed harder, teeth glowing in the darkness, eyes melting to black gold.

"What's so funny?" she asked.

"I'm picturing your face!" Luke puckered his lips, wiggling as he howled, performing his best uptight-Tessa expression.

She lobbed a cushion at him. "Okay, fine, if you're not fucking her, then what?"

When his hysterics abated, he explained that he'd landscaped her backyard. "Technically, I ended up subbing out the labor, but the designs were mine."

Tessa looked at him, stunned. "That job was *yours?*"

"I've been getting my landscape architecture degree in the off seasons. When the Thorntons moved here in February, local landscapers were already booked. Olivia came around asking Rowan for a referral. He brokered the whole thing."

"Luke, that backyard was spectacular. Does this mean you're starting a landscaping business?"

Luke nodded. "One co-op credit left. I was supposed to apprentice with Frank this summer, but with Sam gone, I decided to stick around one more season."

"Well, I'm glad you stayed." When Tessa first started at the shop, Luke was the load-bearing wall down the center of her day; how would she have managed without him? "Not as glad as Olivia, obviously."

Luke rolled his eyes. "Olivia Thornton is spoiled and lonely. She kept dragging out the job. When I started saying I was too busy, she'd yell at Rowan for recommending me. He'd cave and send me there during work hours to shut us both up. And yeah, it started to seem like she had more in mind, but then she transferred the final installment a few days ago, and not a word since."

"My visit spooked her. I met her and her schmoozy husband at the gala the night before."

Luke pretend scowled. "Thanks, Tess. Now I'll never get to see that bikini."

Tessa stuck out her tongue. "So those deliveries were just . . . deliveries?"

"If you actually thought otherwise, you don't know me at all."

Tessa felt a smug little flutter, because it was just the opposite. She curled one leg under her. "All right. My turn to ask a question."

"Fair enough."

"What's the deal with your ex?"

Luke's chin drew inward. "Who told you about my ex?"

"Olivia-on-a-mission would be tough for any single guy to resist. I watch women hit on you every day, I can tell you're stuck on somebody."

Luke's gaze found the floor. "You could say that."

"You fell pretty hard."

"You know something? I'm not sure I ever loved her."

Tessa frowned. "Then how come you miss her so much?"

"I don't. Not at all."

Tessa's hands shot up with impatience. "Okay, *Darryl,* who do you miss, then?"

Luke let out a long, shaky breath. "My son. I *really* miss my son."

Red Bay / *Persea Borbonia*

"Love's memory."

———◄◉►———

LUKE

H E PULLED TWO lowballs and the Jameson from the cupboard, then gripped the edge of the counter. He'd tried backing off the subject, but Tessa sang his own words from earlier straight back at him. *"Come on, Luke. Talk to me!"* Now, pain in the ass that she was, she was refusing like a five-year-old to go to sleep until she heard the whole story, and he needed something stronger than beer to tell it.

He carried the drinks to the porch and sank resentfully into the couch. Beside him, Tessa spun on a dime, already sipping at her whisky. He looked at her sideways, this same person who wrinkled her nose at beer out back night after night, now taking her Jameson straight. Luke took a generous sip from his own glass, remembering what Dr. Lutchman said. *Bottling things up only increases their power.* With a deep inhale, he began.

"We were together about a year when she got pregnant. I was just out of college. I met Tony through friends, found out he made more at the shop with overtime than any of the office jobs I was applying for. He put in a word with Rowan, I worked nonstop. By the end of that summer, I had a down payment. Painted the nursery, hung safari animals above the crib. I even did that class where you swaddle a teddy bear."

"*That* I would've paid to see," Tessa said.

Luke chuckled. "I was twenty-three. Everything about fatherhood scared the shit out of me."

"Same. No way I'm having kids."

Luke shook his head. "That's because you don't *know*. When I held Kyle for the first time . . . I can't explain it. Done. All in."

She smiled. "Lucky baby."

Luke looked away. "Brittney checked out on both of us, ran out every chance she got. Thankfully, Tony hooked me up with some plowing contracts for the winter. I got to be home with Kyle, and when snow hit, I brought him in the truck with me."

With a clamp tightening around his heart, Luke explained how he'd fallen profoundly in love with his boy. They were two dudes in the trenches, muddling through those first endless weeks. Luke paced the hall every night at sunset, swaying and shushing himself delirious with the baby cradled over his arm, inhaling the scent of Kyle's head like smelling salts. When Kyle got his first cold, Luke held him in the tub with the hot water running. He figured out *O Canada* was the only song to get him to sleep, and that he loved mashed banana at dinner but gagged on it at breakfast. Eventually, Luke forgot he'd been anyone but *da-da*. He no longer recalled how he used to fill his days, or what life without his son felt like.

Tessa held still, cradling her glass in her lap.

Luke lit a cigarette. He'd never divulged so many details before, not even to Charlie, who'd been remarkably supportive for someone without kids.

He took a slow drag and held it. Jutted his jaw as the smoke crawled free. "Then, one random Monday night when Kyle's ten months old, Brittney walks in and says he isn't mine."

In his periphery, Tessa's mouth stretched into a very large *O*.

"She was off and on with her ex the whole time." More whisky. "Kyle's his."

A long pause.

"Are you sure?"

Resentment shot from Luke's nostrils. The first time Kyle smiled for real, Luke's fingers flew to the dimple on his own chin, so proud he cried. As if a dimple was some unique genetic tag, like every third person on Morrow didn't have one. "I saw baby pics of her ex. There's no question. Rowan arranged for a DNA test anyway, and for once, she was telling the truth."

Tessa's mouth was still open. "Luke, I . . . that's *awful*. What did you do?"

Luke pressed a thumb to the corner of his eye. "I met with the guy a few times. He was all right. Brittney played both of us, but he wanted to try. For Kyle. Who am I to get in the way of that?"

"And the house?"

"I walked away. I didn't want to uproot the baby, and part of me liked knowing he'd grow up in that room, even if it left me broke as shit. I moved in here, worked from dawn until I dropped. Rowan left groceries on the counter. Sam taught me horticulture. Charlie checked in constantly, Tony kept me laughing. Believe it or not, Darryl convinced me I had a shot at this landscaping thing. And I'm good now, because of them." He cleared his throat. "But I still feel so stupid, you know? Kyle turned three a few weeks ago, and he has no idea I exist. It was all for nothing."

Tessa squeezed his elbow. "You can't look at it that way. You gave him a great start, loved him when his own dad couldn't. And hey, at least you found out when you did, right? Plus, now you know you want to be a dad someday. Think how prepared you'll be when the time comes."

Luke smiled, swirling the ice in his glass. "Now you sound like my mom."

"You should listen to her. She sounds awesome." Tessa grinned in her smartass way, but the pity behind it now made Luke's heart twist like a slipped tendon.

"That she is." Luke tipped the glass, dropping fire into his throat just in time to torch the words he very nearly blurted next. *She's going to love you.*

TONY

Shortly after 2 a.m., Tessa's car was still in the driveway. Two empty glasses and the old bottle of Jameson sat on the counter. Tony fist-pumped in the dark. *You getting this, Sam? Lukey-boy finally went for it!*

Staring into the black yard, he could almost hear Sam's reply from the porch, whip-sharp even as he dozed. *Fuckin' A, Suave!*

Tony looked down, and his grin dropped away as he noticed the spill of hair where Sam's gruff mop used to be. Tessa. Tucked inside the spare blanket from the closet.

He made a mental note to call Luke a pussy first thing in the morning.

Not that he was one to talk, returning to his bed tidy as a boy scout for the sixth time in a row. He thought he'd read Ainsley loud and clear at first. They met for what he assumed would be a simple hookup, and ended up hanging at the bar instead. She didn't turn all dramatic after two drinks, speaking instead about her art—drinking straws in multiple sizes, credit cards turned sideways. Peeling gold flakes and tinted epoxy. It was all pretty cool, actually.

He waited two days for the text assault to begin, to be voluntold to spend his next five Saturdays on double dates with her friends. Next time out, he found himself agreeing to a booth, where he purposely checked out the waitress, waiting for Ainsley to get bent. But the only heat he caught was from watching her eyelids flash and glimmer as she skimmed the wing menu.

Did he still want to hit it? Like MacGregor on fight night. But the talking was all right, too.

Golden Wattle / *Acacia Pycnantha*

"The answer is yes."

———◀◦▶———

TESSA

A T THE CREAK of the back door, Pop and Nano's heads stretched three inches above their recliners. Tessa bent to kiss them, the all-day news blaring at her backside.

"You've been busier than a two-headed cat in a creamery!"

"You must be exhausted. Have you eaten?"

Despite heat prostration and staying up half the night talking to Luke, Tessa felt great. Waking in full daylight was a forgotten decadence. When she opened her eyes, the storage yard was waiting for her, the rainbow flock swaying like birthday candles in the breeze. Her backpack sat by her feet along with her work outfit from yesterday, freshly laundered. Tessa's face burned at the idea of Luke folding her bra and panties, though relieved they were among her nicer ones. There was also an unopened toothbrush, a banana muffin, and coffee. Tessa didn't know anyone better suited to fatherhood than poor Luke.

Except Will.

Luke's account of being strapped to an unpredictable infant day and night underscored Tessa's desire never to have one. But the void Kyle left gave her new appreciation for the pain felt by someone who *did* want a child and was deprived of one. Had she been too eager to accept that Will, patient and intelligent, utterly gorgeous, heart as deep as the sky, was okay with never being a father?

A ripple tore through her stomach; it was a conversation they needed to revisit.

"Nonsense," Pop was saying, "hustle's in her blood. Look at her, the kid's never looked better!"

Nano stood, squeezing both of Tessa's hands, performing her usual workup. After eyeing her granddaughter carefully, she released her grip. "Pop's right. That place agrees with you. How about quiche? I have all the stuff. It won't take a minute."

Pop flicked off the television and creaked from the recliner. "I'm in. Nothing on the tube anyway but death and nutbars. Whole bloody world's gone to the dogs!"

Tessa chopped broccoli. Nano whisked the eggs while Pop set the table.

"Paper says Will's dad is the favorite for mayor," Nano said.

Pop snorted. "There's someone I want in charge of my tax dollars. A lawyer."

Nano shot him a look.

He waved it off. "She knows I don't mean Will."

"I know, Pop." Tessa flipped on the faucet to rinse her hands. A glint beyond the window made her lips part as the sweep of green lawn was swallowed by an exquisite haze, everything suddenly dipped in gold. A cedar-shingled gazebo appeared out of nowhere. Fluffy banks of Endless Summer hydrangeas in that impossible-to-maintain blueberry hue. Tessa's eyes pushed bigger as a swimming pool popped up next, then a gushing waterslide carved from tiers of armour stone. A hot tub. A sunken fire pit. The unmistakeable smell of wood-fired pizza.

Before, the idea of anything besides Pop's criss-cross mowing pattern beyond this window would have sent a fracture through her heart. But now, gold emanating from everywhere, music and laughter exploding like glitter bombs, Tessa fought off blinking in case the vision before her disappeared. Slowly, she pressed her fingers to the glass, her whole body now thrumming a single, solid word—*YES*.

For an atom of time, the golden haze set her reflection aglow in the glass. Her chest did a tuck-and-roll. It was her mother's face staring back. Tessa's hand flew to her own cheek.

After years spent clinging to her mother's memory, it all became suddenly clear. The illogical happenstances, the indecipherable sensations she could never quite put words to; every one of them had been Beth.

The vision collapsed back to green lawn. Despite the recent strain between them, Tessa's heart clamored for Will. For the life they'd been building all along.

Nano reached past her to shut off the tap; the sink was nearly overflowing. Tessa stammered an apology, voice garbled and foreign. Nano smiled. "Your mother used to disappear like that all the time." She scooped coffee into the filter. "How is Will managing, anyway? I haven't heard that engine coming down the driveway in a while."

Tessa sighed. "He's under so much pressure. I'm worried it's starting to get to him."

"If anybody can handle it," Pop said, "it's our boy."

At finding no message waiting when she got her phone back this morning, Tessa hoped he'd finally unplugged in Muskoka. Now, the backyard vision had injected her with new confidence; Will would return from cottage country refreshed. They would talk it out, and the strangeness hanging over them since the gala would be gone. Tessa would join him downtown in the fall, sure now it was only temporary, and start earning a salary. Nano and Pop would be fine. Tessa could feel it now, the rightness of what she'd glimpsed through that window, and she wanted it without reservation. Could no longer do without it.

At the table, Pop lifted his fork, and the thick layer of gauze around his finger stopped Tessa midchew. "Pop! What happened?"

Nano made a face. "He tried fixing the lawnmower again."

"What *try*? I fixed the damn thing, didn't I?"

"That thing is older than me," Tessa said. "I wish you'd let me buy you a new one."

"They don't make them like that anymore. Nothing but cheap garbage nowadays."

Tessa spotted her chance. "Wouldn't it be great not to have to worry about the lawn at all?"

"Here it comes, Nano. The nursing home speech."

"Nobody's talking about a nursing home. But in a lovely *retirement community*, you wouldn't have to deal with grass. Or snow." She looked at Nano. "Or cooking. And there's all kinds of fun activities."

"And old people in shitty diapers," Pop said. "And the Grim Reaper's rotten breath down my neck." He shook his head. "If it comes to that, take me out back and put me out of my misery."

Tessa looked at them, hoping they saw they didn't have to pretend anymore. She was ready.

After Beth passed and adolescent Tessa moved from the coach house into the main house, her grandparents' unspoken financial strain leached through the walls. The weight of everything left unresolved with their daughter pressed down harder on her own grief. Tessa stole back to the coach house at every chance. Once, they found her there while touring the property with a man she recognized from the flyers. A realtor. Tessa fled, sobbing. How could she leave the one place she still felt her mother around every corner?

In hindsight, Tessa understood Nano and Pop wanting to sell for the same reason; they couldn't heal in the same place they broke. Still, they never went through with listing it; clearly, they couldn't bear to uproot her. But now, it was time.

"Be honest," she said. "Isn't it too much, staying here?"

Nano sighed. "Getting old is too much. But nobody's dragging us out of here before we're good and ready."

"Or cold and stiff," Pop added.

"But what if Pop needs . . . help? Down the road, I mean."

"Nobody's caring for my husband but me. And I plan on doing it right here, for as long as the good Lord allows it."

Tessa searched their faces. "You're not staying on my account?"

Pop chuckled. "If this kid could turn worries into dollars—"

"We could never part with this place, honeybun."

Tessa chewed her lip. "But you met with that realtor. After Mom died."

Nano's eyes narrowed, backtracking along the trail of Tessa's anxieties. "Oh, sweetheart, he was doing an appraisal! We were updating our wills, taking out extra insurance. We had no intention of moving!"

Tessa's body expanded in her chair. "Not even now?"

"It might take three days to cut the lawn, kiddo, but where else do I need to be? You gotta use it or lose it."

"And we're not ready to lose it just yet."

Hyacinth, Pink / *Hyacinthus Orientalis*

"Let's play."

◄◦►

TESSA

JULY STREAKED by like the sweaty Snowbird pilots performing their annual air show. Will worked nonstop, barely able to squeeze in a quick goodnight call from his desk, while the pace at the shop slowed steadily. Landscapers appeared only when clients requested replacements for plants such as blue lobelia (much of which had turned to crispy fried noodles in the heatwave), and retail traffic was mainly on weekends again. Which meant that on a sweltering Monday like this one, the flora had full run of the place.

By 11 a.m., the buckets of cuts sat in fluffy, monochrome rows. Outside, all aisles were watered and dead-headed, every picked-over tray consolidated. Tessa walked out to the corner for a wide-angle view of the front display, grinning proudly.

With Rowan's blessing and Darryl's lack of protest, she'd reconfigured the shop's gateway into a lush garden scene. Four rusted shelving sections were replaced by a cedar pergola and wrought-iron benches from the supplier catalogue. Tony put a new valve on the hose bibb, Luke ran electrical, and a new fountain bubbled. Hooks were installed along the pergola, and Charlie demonstrated how to suspend potted wisterias, lending the appearance of one mature, fluffy vine. There were pink columns of dipladenia, gardenia for fragrance, spiked balls of cleome like pastel pufferfish. People stopped to take selfies. Children ate ice cream, their toes dangling from the bench while their parents browsed. Mrs. Bucket Hat had peered out from her pots of woolly thyme to declare it the prettiest corner on Morrow again.

The best part? Tessa's creation was constantly on-peak. Whenever the plants went off-bloom, she simply swapped in their fullest, brightest inventory. As soon as Will came up for air at work, and they'd finally set things right again, she would bring him to see it.

She was still standing there, marveling at the living picture postcard display, when something propelled her shoulder forward with a *thunk.* She glanced down the boulevard and saw Darryl and Luke doubled over in laughter. At her feet, the football they'd been tossing teetered.

"Whoops," Darryl yelled. "Sorry, Princess!"

Tessa's glare vowed revenge. They *oooooh-ed* like third graders as she stalked to the counter, plucking a fresh peach from the display. Bruised, unfit for sale. She tossed it gently, turning it over in her hands, examining. Then she hurled it straight at Darryl's face.

The fruit bounced off his skin with a pulpy *splat,* and it was war. All three skidded through the aisles, hurling peaches like snowballs. Pots were overturned, branches flailed. Luke grabbed a handful of elastic bands, laughing devilishly as he fired them between the shelves. *Snap. Snap. Snap.*

Darryl clapped himself on the neck. "OW. You prick!" He lunged.

Luke dipped past him and around the corner, where Tessa was already charging. He ducked. She jumped. But it was too late. Tessa vaulted over his shoulder, face barreling towards the concrete at heart-stopping speed.

His arm caught her thighs at the last second, and she sprung back like a bungee cord, lungs whooshing at the near-miss, and the alien sensation of skin across her bottom half that wasn't Will's. Darryl closed in. Tessa's legs flailed by Luke's cheek as she twisted to see around his thigh. Luke seized the hose.

"Do it!" she yelled.

The thick blast hit Darryl square in the chin.

He gasped. *"GODDAMN* that's cold!"

Luke took off, Tessa still over his shoulder. Darryl aimed the hose like a firearm, herding them into the shop with an apocalyptic grin. With a tad of remorse, Tessa assumed the game would end now that they'd reached indoors.

But Darryl pressed on. "Say your prayers, motherfuckers." With a jungle sound, he opened fire, sweeping the nozzle back and forth in merciless assault. Tessa and Luke screamed as frigid water soaked their clothes and ricocheted off the counter, the register, their faces, drumming along the windows and the display cooler. Cellophane sleeves rattled. Pots were picked off the shelves, soil and foliage erupting like shrapnel. It was . . . *too far.*

Ponytail in her eyes, view largely obstructed by Luke's leg, it was difficult to tell if Darryl was still messing around, or if he'd completely decoupled with reality. Either way, there was no escape. Luke flung open the cooler, hauling her inside. He plunked Tessa down and swung the door shut to block the onslaught as Tessa, breathless and claustrophobic in her wet tank and shorts, began to violently shiver.

Cactus / *Cactaceae*

"I burn."

DARRYL

W HAT HAPPENED to his mother in their kitchen had quietly numbed him, like a subtle prick of lidocaine while he was fixated on the sky, waiting for some massive boulder to drop. All these years later, the arc of that old football through the sunny belt of July finally prompted a thawing of sorts. The tingling sensation of feeling returning. Then, chasing through the aisles, juvenile and reckless, turned him into some deranged confetti canon, too much life exploding inside of him at once, and all he could think to do was go aim it at the shop.

Darryl had long decided keeping everything the same would help. But *who* had it helped? His dead parents? Sam, also dead? Himself, walking around these wasteland years, deader than all three? Every overturned plant, every sweep of the hose revealed *more* of Iris, not less, exposing all that would have been under her luminous reign. Then, it was his father slamming out of him, the elfish version long scrubbed from memory, whose grin used to set their footed pajamas squealing, his wife protesting from the sink, "*No wrestling before bed!*"

Darryl leaned against the cooler door to keep Luke from pushing it open, rummaging through the clutter by the phone. *Bingo.* A classic blue Bic. He chortled as he slid the pen snugly into the padlock hole, then flicked the light switch, plunging the fridge into bone-shuddering darkness before turning to leave.

"You kids have fun in there."

TESSA

Every cell in her body glitched. She waved a hand in front of her face; it no longer existed. It was so dark, she couldn't detect if she was blinking. Nearby, Luke was panting. "Enough," Tessa told him. "Open the door."

The *click* of the metal handle. A thud as he heaved his weight. "I can't."

"I'm serious, Luke. Let me out."

"I *can't*. He's jammed it."

Panic swept to the ends of her. It was the stuff of horror movies, trapped in an oversized coffin, being frozen alive. None of which seemed too far a stretch for Darryl at the moment. "*DARRYL!*" she screamed. "It's not funny anymore! Open the door!" But the hum of the compressor, the insulated walls left her voice nowhere to go. "Luke, I can't stay in here. I'm freaking out."

Luke thumped his fist against the door. "Come on, man. You win. We're tapping out. Open up." Nothing. "At least put the light on, asshole!"

Tessa's voice broke. Fleeting warmth around her eyes signaled she was crying. Her breathing thinned, her jaw convulsing. "He's really leaving us in here."

"He's not. He's just messing with us."

"You saw him, he's gone completely psycho!" Tessa stammered. "He traps us in here like slabs of meat, soaking wet, then *turns off the light?* Who *does* that?" She was full on crying now. "He's not okay, Luke. And now we're stuck in here and it's just him out there and who knows how long until—"

"Tess." Luke's hands landed on her shoulders, his words at her forehead like the flickering of a lighter. "Tessa. Breathe with me, okay? Close your eyes. Imagine the light is on, and the door is wide open. *Breathe.* Come on, let's hear it."

Tessa did as she was told. She pictured the cooler as she'd last seen it—a windowless room the size of a walk-in closet, flowering buckets all around. She felt the curved plastic of a Clock pail, followed it up to the cellophane sleeves, fingered the velvety contents. *Snapdragons.* Her memory filled in the rest—purple shafts of liatris beside the snaps, then bushy tiki fern. Million Star along the back, Ecuadorian roses, the half-empty flat of peaches. The mound of backpacks shoved in the corner.

She gasped. "Our bags!"

Luke's hands disappeared. The light from his phone was the blinding beam of a rescue chopper. He left messages for Rowan and Charlie while Tessa jogged in place, rubbing her arms.

"Being wet makes it so much worse," she said.

"We do have dry clothes."

"I can't change in here."

"You do all the time."

"Not like this."

"You'd rather stay like that?"

Tessa considered, teeth clattering. "We'll have to go one at a time. There's no room."

"Fine, whatever." In the phone's halo, Luke's heavy eyebrow ticked up. The frigid air took on weight. "You first."

Tessa hung her spare tank and shorts off a pack of Leonidas roses. Luke turned his screen off, sinking them into unnerving blackness again. She drew a breath; it was counterintuitive, removing clothes when she was this cold, even if they were sopping wet. Stranger still doing it with Luke a fog of breath away, acting totally casual, as if he wasn't the second man in the world she'd completely undressed beside. As though, in a different kind of darkness, it would still mean nothing. "Keep it off until I tell you, okay?"

"Got it."

"And don't move. Stay exactly where you are."

"Okay."

"Luke, I mean it."

"May I breathe?"

"I'm serious!"

Luke sighed. "Jeez, can you wrap up the riot act? I'm freezing my balls off."

No sooner had Tessa lifted her shirt did the screen light up. *"Luke!"*

Luke laughed, waving his empty hands innocently. "It's a text. My niece. Okay, see, now that's impressive." He held the phone to her face. "No-handed cartwheel!"

She scowled, ignoring the video. "Maybe flip it over this time, jackass."

"Sure thing, Princess."

They fell back into darkness. Tessa wrestled with her wet clothes, the cold biting her skin. "Please just don't with the princess thing right now, okay?"

"It does kind of suit you."

"I am the furthest thing! Why does everyone assume I'm some kind of—"

"Would you lighten up? It's ironic, that's the point. At least until you're crowned Mrs. . . . what's his name again?"

Tessa bristled. "Westlake." It was incomprehensible that *Mrs. Westlake* could refer to anyone but Eleanor. She'd half-joked once about remaining Lewis, and Will laughed, but the hurt in his eyes made her own start to water. Tessa vowed right then to safeguard *all* the pieces of him, surname included.

Luke's turn. He relit the screen, retrieved his clothes, then shut it off again. "Same deal. No peeking."

Tessa snorted. "I think I can restrain myself."

The silence lasted a beat too long. "Can you, though?"

His tone was light, joking, but Tessa felt a reverberation inside, like the plucking of a guitar string. He pulled off his shirt, and she tiptoed into the scent of him, a musky blend of sweat, the body wash she'd scrubbed herself with the night she stayed at the Lodge, and the detergent he'd used to wash her clothes the next morning. Memory flashes collided in a disjointed heap; the walls of Luke's shower. His forearm across her thighs. Her bare chest, slippery with soap.

Tessa's mouth went dry. Involuntarily, she stepped forward, deeper into his scent. Panic surged as her body plunged further forward still, her limbs seemingly beyond her own control. Frantically, she tried reeling herself back, but from what she didn't even know. What exactly was she planning to do here, now, in the freezing darkness? *With Luke?*

A clicking sound. This time, the shaft of light landed like the headlights of a cop car. Caught, not saved.

"What the—?" Rowan flicked on the light. "I thought that message was a prank." He swung the door open as Tessa, awash in self-reproach, stole a glance at the hard moguls trailing Luke's abdomen before he'd finished pulling on his clean shirt.

What was wrong with her?

They spilled into the muggy staff room. The shop had weathered a tropical monsoon. Water beaded along the walls, the windows, the till and card readers. Droplets slipped from plants, bouquets, the ceiling. Tessa and Luke looked at Rowan. Would he be furious? Was he even capable of yelling?

But he just floated out the door, distracted, pausing only to mumble over his shoulder.

"I'll bring back chicken wings."

Pincushion Flower / *Scabiosa Atropurpurea*

"I have lost all."

———◀◯▶———

ROWAN

THE SHOP WAS RUINED, and he didn't care. It wasn't the worst thing to happen today—or the weirdest.

In the pub two blocks along Morrow, he turned the envelope in his hand; a notice from the city's bylaw office. Apparently, Trucks—a commercial entity, situated on residential property—was operating without a permit, which meant Rowan owed nearly thirty years' worth of fines.

Simon would never have invested in the Trucks expansion without the proper permits. Nonetheless, Rowan had ten days to produce a copy, or pay the fines and apply for a new one, which he'd never get. Half of city council was backed by the same developers who had been trying to buy the Blue Iris site since he was a kid.

Rowan had already been home where he tore his dad's study apart and found nothing. His mother had been nagging him to sell the Tudor-style mansion for years (*No point in passing it onto you, it's not like you need room for a family*), but after she'd migrated to Arizona, he found the place wasn't so bad. Closer to work than his condo in the Annex, and with the Lodge getting full, he'd quietly moved in four years ago. If his mother were a different sort of mother, he could speak to her about transferring it to his name, or refinancing it, so that Rowan might access some leverage. But Rebecca had never been that sort of mother.

Even with the recently improved buying margins and the expansion into big-ticket items like pergolas and fountains, it was still the wholesale division keeping the Blue Iris afloat. Without Trucks, Rowan would have little choice but to close the shop, sell off the land. Put his crew out of work *and* their homes.

With Sam gone, Darryl's joints buckling, and Luke on his last run, the place was coasting on fumes regardless, but still, it would be Rowan who tanked it. One by one, their glances would cut him to the quick. *How could you let this happen?*

It was bloody lonely, being the boss.

Rowan tossed the envelope onto the bar, pulling another from his pocket—the latest offer from EnvidaCorp. The terms couldn't be better if they'd let Rowan craft the deal himself. A five-year leaseback would give the crew plenty of time to resettle, find new jobs. The three condos thrown in, free and clear, would give them places to live. The time to cash out was now, before the developers figured out Sam wasn't coming back, and Rowan was financially desperate without him.

Just contemplating it was giving him an ulcer; the Blue Iris was everything good he'd ever known. The alternative? Go bankrupt and leave the people he cared for most in the street.

Unless there was still a third option. One look at the inside of the shop, dripping water from skylights to cement mere days after Tessa got away with making a new front display, suggested Darryl was finally snapping out of it. He could hardly protest a new, modernized checkout after waterlogging the existing one. With a few more updates, maybe Rowan could make a go of it without Trucks, return the Blue Iris to its original footprint. He could raise the rent on the houses, cut back on the freebies and food. Demand actual *money* from his so-called friends when they swung by to fill their trunks. Hang up the bottomless pocket shtick and be a boss for once.

Rowan flipped the offer back and forth between his hands, weighing whether to sign it, or light it on fire.

Crowsfoot / *Erodium Crinitum*

"Let's begin again."

———◄○►———

CHARLIE

SHE FOUND HIM pissing by a pile of empty skids like an overgrown bulldog and shoved the back of his shoulder. "What is your problem?"

Darryl cursed, fumbling with his fly. "Can't stay gone one goddamn day."

"I had three missed calls from Luke. How very *Darryl* of you to go postal, then mosey back here with your dick in your hand, store unattended, staff hypothermic and asphyxiating."

"Please. You and I were in there a shitload longer than that."

Charlie made a sound, half laughter, half repugnance. Indeed, way back, on a day they'd behaved particularly viciously, Sam had locked them in that same fridge. Told them to *work their shit out.* Apparently, their father did the same when the brothers refused to stop fighting. Said they'd learn to get along or kill each other, but either way he wouldn't have to hear it anymore.

And this was the reason Charlie had come charging through the yard on her day off, in her sports bra, all her fresh-flowing *savasana* up in smoke. All these years later, locking people in a *refrigerator* with a *blue pen* remained the gold standard for conflict resolution in that family, and she no longer accepted it.

At her sides, her hands curled into fists. "You know what really pisses me off? *You* had shit to work out. My only problem was, I was sick of it . . . *and I still am!*" She drew a breath. "What happened to your parents was horrible, Darryl. But you need to move *on*. Let everybody else move on! Fucking *evolve!*"

He half-turned, staring over his shoulder at her.

"They weren't even arguing, Brick. They said you started it with the football!"

Darryl flung a blush-colored Grandiflora onto a metal cart. "Yeah, and they wasted no time going full contact. Ask me, plenty needs working out there."

Charlie let out a chopped laugh. "They're *friends*. It's what happens when two people spend tons of time together, and one of them isn't a sociopath."

"You're too busy zoning out behind that counter, Spider. The kids are not all right."

Charlie put a pin in her anger, temporarily shifting to mama bear mode. Losing a baby she'd never even met still broke her to this day; Luke saying goodbye to Kyle was unfathomable. He'd fought *so hard* to come back. Charlie was incredibly proud of Luke's progress, and acutely aware of its fragility. But surely a little workplace banter wasn't the end of the world? It was such a relief to see that smile returning.

Then again, Luke wasn't Tony; he was incapable of skating along the surface. Developing feelings for Tessa, who was deeply involved with Will, threatened his chances of ever properly trusting again. It might very well suck him under completely.

Charlie added it to her worry list for later, returning her attention to Darryl. "Well, I'm sure they're much better off now that you tried to kill them. Worked wonders for our relationship."

"You know, half my problem was, I *wanted* to want you back then. But once we got in there? Nothing but tundra, clear as a goddamn bell."

"Great. Now it's my fault you're gay, too."

Darryl snorted. "When you're trapped in an ice casket and can't find your own eyelids, bullshit's first to tap. Maybe Sam had me figured out before I did. Maybe he was hoping we'd take a roll through the birds of paradise." He snapped a dead bloom off a New Guinea, tossing it aside. "All I know is, being in there, with you, I *knew*. Messed me up more for a while, but at least I knew."

They looked at each other.

"Then I'm glad he did it." Charlie was startled by the sincerity behind her words. "But Brick, what good is knowing what you want if you're never going to act on it?"

Darryl squinted into the distance. "I acted today. Trashed the whole tired place."

Charlie studied him. Yes, something inside that pitted barrel psyche had definitely shifted. Moreover, he might be onto something. "Maybe it's good you took it all down. Maybe that's the only way you get to start again."

The next morning, the shop was put back as it had been, and differently. Quieter. Darryl mumbled something resembling an apology, then watched quietly as Rowan ordered state-of-the-art checkout systems to be installed on both counters. Charlie would have expected the boss to be ecstatic at such a leap, but he, too, was unusually somber. Meanwhile, Luke and Tessa's interactions were noticeably distanced. Overtly cordial. The crew looped to and from the cube, unloading the buys of the day.

"If Charlie's not going, I'm not going," Tessa was saying.

"She's coming this time," Tony told her. "Right, Charlie?"

Every year, on the August long weekend, Rowan took the crew for a night on the town to thank them for sticking it out through the busy season. A tradition Simon started. Charlie had attended during her first two summers at the shop. Then, never again. Watching Sam in action at those bars, effusively oblivious to the wreckage he'd caused her, was too much. But this year, Tessa was insistent.

Charlie shook her head. "I don't do staff night."

"Come on, just this once. Please?"

"It's not as great as they make it sound. They never agree on where to go, so they end up wasted in the back of some rancid peeler bar that pays off the health inspectors."

Rowan made a face. "Last year, I had to throw out my shoes. Couldn't get the sticky off."

"Darryl got the calamari two years ago," Tony said. "I tried *one* piece?" He made a fist and slammed it into his other palm. "Puked three days straight."

Luke groaned. "The Lodge smelled like a sewage plant."

Darryl shrugged. "I was totally fine."

Charlie folded her arms. "See what I mean?"

Tessa laughed. "Well, now that *we're* going, we'll come up with something better. I'll talk to Ainsley. She lives to organize stuff like this."

Rowan sighed relief. "Great. Invite her if you want."

"Yeah," Tony said into the freesia he was carrying. "I mean, whatever."

Luke, balancing potted orchids like cocktail trays, stopped to catch

Charlie's eye. "He'd want us all together. He'd want us to have fun."

Charlie didn't deserve fun. Not after letting Sam walk out the door that night, of all nights, in the state he was in. But after all that preaching to Darryl about evolving, tearing down old to make way for new, it didn't appear she had a choice.

SAM

The Chevy was a toaster swung by its cord on the cabin road,
a forty-ounce touchstone between his knees,
out of never at last.

He wasn't scared,
just lulled by the promise of it being over.
Of never again having to outrun this day,
another New Year that brought no fresh beginning.
The humble kitchen in shambles.
Splintered table overturned,
cupboards like backhands.
Iris's violet irises
expanding like blown glass.
Henry's earth-stained fists a bottleneck at her throat.

He'd tried every way he could think of to quiet the squeal
of his mother's star-dusted soul
skidding on black ice,
his father's clattering after it like newlywed tin cans.

Every cowardly-assed way but one.

Moonflower / *Ipomoea Alba*

Variety of morning glory
that blooms at night.

———◀◯▶———

CHARLIE

TWO HOURS seemed a painfully long time to primp. But here they were, Tessa and Ainsley, coming up her driveway in a whirl of duffels and leggings and brown liquor store paper. Oddly, Ainsley was also wheeling an aluminum tower that looked stolen from a mechanic's garage.

Charlie turned from the window. Staying out past nine, in clothes that in no way qualified as pajamas, would be the breakthrough; she had zero expectations of enjoying it. Time seemed to have lasered her ability to style her own hair, or pick a proper outfit by herself, but she refused to get stuck like Darryl. Staff night was as fitting a time as any to start moving again.

In this very room, she'd pried Sam's fingers from the edge, knowing full-well the ravenous wolves waiting for him below. But he'd lived his whole life on that same edge, purposely seeking it out time and again. Was she expected to be his safety net forever? Wasn't she entitled to a breaking point of her own?

The girls turned her quiet bungalow into a Cyndi Lauper video. A tiny cube on the counter emitted impossibly big sound as avocados were mashed for guacamole, the cupboards scoured for a pitcher to hold sangria. They trash-talked customers, dished on which landscapers were sleeping together, and twenty minutes in, Charlie was near tears with gratitude they'd come.

In her bedroom, the mysterious aluminum tower flew open, blow dryers, curling irons and flat irons spilling like popcorn kernels. A drugstore's worth of compacts and brushes exploded onto the dresser. Tessa gravitated to the corner, her gaze fixated on the red sleepshirt draped over a chair, her head tipped as though the shirt had come alive and started talking. She reached for it, and Charlie bristled; irrationally, she did not want anyone else touching the shirt. Tessa pulled back, like the fabric was flame, her voice barely audible over the music.

"Where did you get this?"

Charlie affected nonchalance. "Oh, it was Sam's, or at least we think so. It's way too big. There was a bar called The Crooked Crow up on Morrow. Must've been a giveaway or something."

Tessa cradled the shirt. Charlie crossed the room and eased it from her, smiling nervously, and tucked it away in a drawer. Tessa's eyes lingered after it, her features pulling together. "I think I've been there."

"Oh, it closed ages ago. Probably before you pups were born."

"But the logo . . . it's *so* familiar."

Across the room, Ainsley applied eyelash glue. "You're thinking of the Black Raven on Richmond. The one Jax played at? God, he turned out to be another winner. Sometimes I think it's sex with me that ruins them."

Tessa snapped back to the moment, eyes twinkling. "Well, from what I hear, sex with Tony fixes *everything*. You'll see new colors, hear musical notes you've never heard. I'm pretty sure it cures the common cold."

Laughter spurted from Charlie. "Sooner or later, we will need someone to confirm whether he lives up to his own hype."

Ainsley shrugged. "I went in expecting a hookup. Now, I have no idea what's happening."

"I've never seen him like this over a woman," Charlie said. Then, choosing her moment, added, "He's almost as bad as Luke."

In the mirror, Ainsley's eyes jumped to Tessa's, a fuchsia line halting mid-lip. "I knew it!"

Tessa fiddled with a tube of concealer. "Please. I help him scope out girls, beautiful, made-up girls who don't smell like sheep shit."

Ainsley whirled around. "If Will saw the look on your face—"

"What look?" Tessa looked from Ainsley to Charlie. One hand lifted to her hip. "There's no look."

"Whatever you say, girlie. Do me a favor, anyway?

"Anything."

"Be extra careful with our Lukey-boy."

Tessa's nod confirmed she knew about Kyle. Charlie couldn't decide if she was relieved Luke had told her, or even more concerned.

"Will, too," Ainsley added.

Tessa had both hands on her hips. "I've had guy friends."

Ainsley scoffed. "Yeah. Notice how fast they fell off? Even the dumb ones knew to steer clear of Westlake's girl."

The women stared at each other. Ainsley returned to her makeup. "Don't get me wrong, I love him to death. I just always felt like he had a jealous streak."

"*Will Westlake* is jealous of no one, and why would I give him reason to be? He's my whole life!"

The party bus squealed to a stop out front, and the tension evaporated. Ainsley swept highlighter over Tessa's every contour, then pronounced her look finished. Charlie stole a glance in the mirror and felt a girlish tingle.

Her mouth was a nude filigree, her hair like smoked glass. The crepe romper, borrowed from Tessa, cinched and billowed to optimal effect. The glittery plum around her eyes was ridiculously overboard, yet exactly enough.

In the hallway, Ainsley twirled. Charlie and Tessa *oohed* at the sandal-boots criss-crossing her calves, the flat slice of bare midriff. Her hair, platinum blonde and ultra-thick thanks to extensions from the magic tower, hung in a long ponytail that gradually morphed into the same shade of fuchsia as her lips.

"Ainsley Murphy," Tessa said as they left, "if you don't close the deal soon, I think Tony might implode."

Charlie stared after them. With Ainsley's help, Tessa's natural iridescence had intensified threefold. If anyone was going to implode tonight, she could only hope it would be Tony.

Angel's Trumpet / *Brugmansia Candida*

"This must end."

───◄◇►───

DARRYL

THE LIGHTS INSIDE the bus changed in time with the music, a hyper color Milky Way of blues and greens bleeding to purple and red. Sam would've shit a brick.

The brothers might have opted to stay in here all night, cold beers in hand, cracking off through the window while the others went about their pub-hop or club-crawl or whatever young people's agenda the girls had cooked up. Darryl squinted sideways at his house through the tinted glass. Suddenly, he couldn't fathom how he'd stayed.

Sure, there had been pillow forts and living room campouts, chocolate pancakes and balloons tied to the chair on birthdays. But poking like weeds between those memories were all the rest. Quiet mornings that began with his mother pouring rainbow cereal, ending with shards of the bowl embedded in his father's forehead. Somewhere along the line, it got so that the alarms sounding between his parents faded to white noise—until that night.

Funny how one night could change all that followed.

Darryl had been playing freeze football at the field. He heard screaming from the driveway, but it hardly fazed him. In the off-season, without the shop to tether their focus, Henry and Iris were either pawing each other like newlyweds or pulling each other's hair out. Only days prior, he'd found them slow dancing in the kitchen, cuddly as kittens, a split in his mother's lip and bloodied gauges down his father's cheek. Their dysfunction could be switched on and off, easy as a welder's torch.

Until the switch broke.

Henry was shitfaced, Darryl could tell by the snarl. Undaunted by Henry's temper while he was sober, Iris got off on it when he was drunk. Still, Darryl's mother's voice was different somehow. The calm, calculated madness of raw steak being pulled from a tiger's mouth. And what did Darryl do? Stood eavesdropping in the hall like the limp dick he was.

"Fine, Henry. We'll all keep pretending the rest of our lives. For you."

"Don't act like you give two shits about me! *You* made this mess! Treating him like an overgrown pansy since he was born. You think it's gonna be easy for him? For any of us?"

"It's not a *choice!* It's not picking out a pair of fucking pants! He's our *son.* You think that comes second to your macho bullshit?"

Darryl's mouth turned dry. Panic seared. His mother knew. And now, so did his father.

Henry scoffed. "*My* macho bullshit! You're a real piece of work, you know that? You've been gunning for me since I got in the goddamn door! How long you been saving this one up, eh?"

Darryl hardly had time to wonder. He jumped at the roar of the kitchen table flipping. One by one, chairs smashed off the walls, wood clattering like bowling pins. More screaming. The usual threats (*get out of my face, or I swear to GOD . . .*) twisting darkly into dares (*what are you waiting for? DO IT!).* The thud of flesh against drywall. And then, another noise he couldn't place. One he'd never stopped hearing.

Sam, living next door at the Lodge by then, must have heard it from there. He flew in, hissed at his brother to *get out! GO! Run to the shop, call 911!*

Darryl snapped from his stupor, leaving Sam to storm the kitchen alone because in that moment, he was sure Henry would have killed him instead.

Afterwards, Darryl came to wish it went down like that. His cowardice cost them their mother, and then, in a jail cell two days later when Henry processed what he'd done, their father.

Darryl spent the rest of his life trying to atone, to keep his brother together. But the freight train in Sam's veins only picked up speed. Nobody could stop it—not Darryl, the three wives, not even his achingly perfect twin daughters. The sponsors, probation officers and court-mandated therapists never got far, either.

Only one person could reach back through time and pluck snippets of the Sam who existed before. Indeed, though his actions, and his dick, pointed everywhere else, there was only one true north on his brother's perpetually trembling compass. Only one name he ever cried in the dark.

Charlie.

Boarding the bus now, Darryl half expected her to sprout wings and flutter up the steps like a black-eyed faerie. He tipped his beer, gulping the knot in his throat. He'd been so damn unfair. She showed up that first summer he and Sam were running things by themselves, oblivious to the steaming pile of shit she'd stepped in. The brothers never talked about it to anyone, not the government-appointed social worker, not Wannabe-Dad Simon or his screechy four-eyed kid. Not even to each other. Still, Charlie stuck it out all this time. And how did he thank her? By letting her blame herself for tripping Sam's wire, when it was Darryl who planted the bomb.

He shoved over, inviting her to ride beside him. Slowly, like it might be a trap, Charlie obliged. Before he could talk himself out of it, he collected her hand and squeezed.

Her black eyes jumped to his.

"It wasn't your fault, Spider. Believe me. It wasn't."

Her shoulders fell, mouth hinting worriedly at a smile.

What Darryl wouldn't give to be loved the way this woman had loved Sam. How his big brother squandered it, summer after summer, he'd never understand.

Good old Sammy, God rest his soul, was a fucking idiot.

Tulip, Wild / *Tulipa Gesneriana*

"I want you."

◄○►

LUKE

I T HAD BEEN, by all accounts, the most legendary of staff nights.

The lounge, so low-key they practically needed a password to get in, lent an illicit kick to the cocktails themselves. The steakhouse that followed had heated toilet seats, and you barely needed a knife to cut the meat. Then, a rooftop bar with sweeping twilight views, a bioluminescent nightclub where even Darryl's movements passed for dancing, and finally, a traditional pub complete with jukebox, billiards and darts, where the fellowship was still underway.

And all the miserable while, he hadn't been able to stop looking at her.

He'd maintained a respectable distance, shored up between Rowan and Darryl. He danced with some girls at the club, flirted with a few more at the bar as he tried to appear generally unruffled by the fact that every other guy in the room was checking her out. Even next to Ainsley, it was impossible not to.

The trouble was, she was so . . . *sparkly.* Tessa's turquoise top set her blue eyes flicking like mirrors. Everything from the dangly earrings down to her chunky metallic heels behaved as though charged by the moonlight. Her hair, loose and full and free of its ball cap, thrashed wildly at the shores of her, a deep swoop to one side which Luke had longed all night to tuck behind her ear with two fingers. And how was it her every sunbaked surface was reflective, as if her skin was permanently wet?

She looked like a friggin' mermaid, is what she looked like.

Once, at the club, she caught him in a dead stare. Luke was immobilized; should he stay the course? Look away, act like it never happened? But Tess made it easy, smiling guilelessly and giving a little wave. Why did it always have to be so *easy* with her? It was becoming a real problem.

Now, she was dancing with Charlie and Ainsley again, the kind girls break into spontaneously wherever they happen to be standing, because the song, in this case, Shania's *Man! I Feel Like a Woman!*, seemed to command it. Luke stifled a groan. Back at the club, chest-thumping glimpses were dangled then retracted in a fit of strobes, but here at the pub, he had full view of the straps of her top plunging to a *V*, her back a flexing arrow of flesh pointing to her hips, her distressed jeans swiveling in a way her cotton work shorts did not. Resignedly, he lay another piece into the puzzle that had been stubbornly building in his mind all summer—Tessa's naked body, one peachy section at a time.

He stepped out for a smoke.

When he returned, Tessa and Ainsley were facing off against Darryl and Charlie in a game of eight ball. Rowan tallied the score while Tony maintained a casual-on-purpose perimeter. The girls won, then challenged Darryl and Rowan to another. Again, the girls took the early lead. Meanwhile, a man in Bermuda shorts circled over and handed Charlie a drink. Luke shot her a look that said, *Whoa! How long have I been outside?*

Charlie threw back, *HELP!*

Luke prodded her with his chin, smiling encouragingly.

Tony appeared at his elbow. "Ainsley's dad had a table in his basement. You believe those two went undefeated all through high school?"

It was harder to believe Tony had retained this much biographical information about a woman. Luke threw his arm around his friend's neck, sighing as Ainsley and Tessa bumped hips. "Face it, buddy. This one's got you locked up."

Tony laughed. "You know something? It doesn't suck."

They clinked bottles. Drank. "Glad to hear it," Luke said. And he was. His eyes flicked back to the pool table. Tessa chalked her cue, some zero who couldn't take a hint steady up behind her, schooling her on technique even though any idiot could see she didn't need help.

"What are you going to do?" Tony asked.

Luke took another swig. "About what?"

Tony's expression flattened Luke's façade like a soda can.

Luke shrugged, eyes still on the table. "She's in love with whatshisname." He knew the guy's name. He just couldn't say it out loud. "He's good for her. They're happy."

The lilt in her tone when she spoke of him, the softening around her eyes that left no doubt who the text was from, confirmed this to be true. Despite himself, Luke was glad; he wanted her to be happy. Almost as much as he wanted the same for himself—with literally anybody else. Luke's persistent lack of self-preservation when it came to Tessa, the glaring temptation to cross that same line he intimately detested, was deeply troubling. It had gotten so his imagination was picking up ghost signals.

Tony studied him. "Ainsley said the same, and yet, Tee's been tracking *you* all night."

Luke scoffed.

"Dude, you think I don't have radar for this shit?" Tony said.

Luke recalled being locked in the cooler. At first, his primary focus was keeping Tessa from going into cardiac arrest. But after they found the phone, he'd sensed a shift. Then, the look she wiped from her face when Rowan opened the door; Luke knew that look when he saw it. Didn't he? He'd been out of the game so long, maybe not. Freezing, pitch-black terror was hardly conducive to foreplay.

"I don't know, man. We're friends."

Tony looked at him.

"Okay, *good* friends. Working there, who wouldn't be?"

Tony set down his drink. "Fine. I'll prove it." He scanned the bar, then sidled up to a curvy brunette gulping a glorified Slurpee, reverting to lady-killer mode with astonishing ease. One overplucked eyebrow arched as she followed his finger to Luke. Heels wobbling, she trailed Tony back through the crowd.

"Hi, Luuuke," she sang too slowly, the top of her straw chewed flat. Her furry eyelashes flapped. "I'm Brianna."

Luke shot Tony a look as Brianna settled well inside his personal space, firing questions then answering them herself. Luke's eyes strayed over her shoulder to where, wouldn't you know, Tessa monitored the exchange with covert interest. He turned his head sideways to sip his beer, mostly to avoid hitting Brianna in the face with the bottle, leaving his eyes on the billiard area. He pressed the glass to his lips and held it there as everything else slid from focus.

Tessa took her time choosing her ball, then planted herself at the foot of the table, facing Luke. He scanned the arrangement on the table; she'd picked one hell of an ambitious shot. His stomach tightened as she folded at the waist, hand splayed across the felt, index finger curled over the cue tip. Her other hand pulled back along the shaft and she held a wink, like she was peering down a rifle scope. She glided the stick back and forth, lining up her shot. Somewhere in the background, Darryl heckled her to get on with it. Their section grew quiet, save for Brianna's droning and Bon Jovi's blooming crescendo in the background. As if Luke needed any reminder that he was halfway there, but living on a prayer.

All eyes were trained on the white cue ball. Tessa focused with laser precision, striking it neatly. It banked off the long rail and across the center string, prompting a *whoosh* of collective inhale as it narrowly avoided two stripes and potted a solid. From there, the ball cut left, sinking the last solid into the corner before softly tapping the eight ball.

Click.

The room was on pause. The black ball crawled towards the corner, lingering on the lip of the pocket. Gravity arm-wrestled. The ball tipped in, and the girls won again. Whooping and wild applause erupted, but Tessa remained exactly as before, locked on target, back arched over the table, brow set in hungry determination.

From his vantage point, only Luke could see she hadn't looked at that white ball once since she'd hit it. Rather, her sight line had skimmed the table altogether, lifting towards the bar and over Brianna's shoulder. Directly—unmistakeably—at him.

Japanese Cherry / *Prunus Serrulata*

"Return to me."

CHARLIE

SHE DRANK just enough wine to stop worrying if her outfit was age-appropriate, laughed so hard she snorted—and she danced. Somewhere, Sam yelled, *Look out! There she is.*

The bus slowed to a halt in the 2 a.m. taxi crunch on Spadina. Charlie stared through the flashing neon sign of a second-storey tattoo parlour. *Sam, Sam, Sam.*

There was no reason to feel guilty, yet she did. The infuriating witchery of Sam made you love him, but only between wanting to kill him. He'd own all his shortcomings, taking all the blame you could throw, but in this resigned, pitiful way, like he was genuinely baffled by his own capacity for wrongdoing. It made it impossible to hold him accountable, robbing you of the rage you were fully entitled to.

Charlie startled at the warm press of her own hand on her belly, a familiar gesture, briefly, until the life inside was gone. Also gone now was the encroaching fear, the all-consuming paralysis that came with monitoring a reckless pilot from the ground, loving someone who lacked the internal coding to love back. A strange void, but one she could get used to.

She could no longer deny the allure of a clear, attentive male gaze that didn't come with a soul-crushing guarantee. Tomorrow, she would call Adam, the man from the pub. Let him buy her a cappuccino, maybe an almond croissant.

But first, she needed off this bus.

Charlie yelled to the driver to open the doors, vaguely aware of Tessa clamoring after her up the narrow, pulsing staircase and into the red faux leather beside her. The women held hands as Charlie quietly lay Sam and their unborn baby to rest the only way she knew how—along the slender curve of her breast, right above her heart, in the shape of one dark and nimble little spider.

TESSA

Charlie's stalled engine had sputtered to life. Darryl was considerably less terrifying when he smiled, and they'd successfully coached a tequila-lubed Rowan through buying a pretty divorcée a drink. Tessa seemed to hover above the ground at all this momentum, each peal of laughter buoying her higher.

Drawn to the Blue Iris by a frail memory of Beth, working there on a carousel wish that the market held some lost piece of her, it was finally clear; the ease radiating from inside Tessa now like sun through stained glass *was* her mother. Almost as if Beth had been riding around in this tricked-out bus all along, waiting for her daughter to figure that out.

Tessa's pocket shimmied with a text from Will. Over a month had passed since the gala, and Tessa was still ducking him, never acknowledging the reason he tipped so off-kilter in the first place. She ached to lay her hands on his skin and let the glory of this moment soak through, tell him she'd seen it now, through her grandparents' window—his plan for their future could work. But he was at Peter and Eleanor's annual pool party and barbecue, catered, so the barbecue stayed covered. Everyone wore linen suits and dresses, so there was no swimming, either. At least Will was out of the office.

Across the aisle, Luke's ocean-bottom hair was a tidal wave. He nodded towards the back of the bus, where Ainsley giggled, the pink tips of her ponytail splayed across Tony's chest, his voice a bass line in her ear. Luke's brow lifted, flooding with light then shadow in time with the streetlights. *Looks like tonight's the night.*

Tessa flicked her eyes at the ceiling. *FINALLY!*

Luke's head tipped in silent laughter. Her insides scrambled after his full, easy grin like the bus had crossed train tracks and caught air. The choppy lighting, late hour and the buzz in her blood permitted her gaze to linger. She'd done a hundred double takes tonight, her gaze briefly snagged then her chest slammed yet again by the sober realization that it was Luke.

She did not slipstream his joy tonight as she had with the others. Watching that girl cozied up to him at the bar, uttering God-knows-what in his ear, set Tessa prickling with indignation. It made no sense; she held no claim to him. Did she expect him to be off limits to the rest of the world along with her? She was a horrible friend.

"Did it hurt?" he asked.

Tessa blinked; she'd been staring right through him. Luke gestured to her abdomen, where the hot throb shot back to consciousness. "Yeah. But it was quick."

Too quick. Tessa had never acted so impulsively. The mere suggestion of metal shoved clean through her navel should have made her cringe. But tonight, with Charlie in dire need of moral support, Tessa didn't think twice. Next thing, she was back on the bus, proudly flashing her bejeweled belly. Tony and Ainsley whooped. Darryl grunted. Rowan averted his eyes with a smile. Luke studied it intently, saying nothing.

And that was it; no derisory glances, no poking judgment. Over the past seven years, Tessa had gravitated to golf balls over billiards, to white tablecloths over back-clapping bars—to Will, despite all that surrounded him. But she'd never appreciated dancing in neon anonymity or shooting pool in a wood-panelled aisle so much as she had tonight.

"We could crash at Darryl's," Luke told Rowan, who was in no shape to drive home. "Give them the Lodge to themselves."

"Fine by me," Rowan said, still grinning into his phone.

But as the bus pulled away shortly after 3 a.m., Darryl proved less than accommodating to his would-be overnight guests. Ainsley, flustered now at finding her imminent hookup the subject of driveway debate, said she'd crash at Charlie's with Tessa as initially planned. Tony shot Luke a panicked look.

"It's fine," Luke said, steering Rowan towards Darryl's porch. "Darryl wanted us to come in for another beer, anyway. Right?"

Darryl, half-limping, stopped on his front steps. "Fuck's sake." He turned, squaring his hands up quarterback style. "Here's what's going to happen. Tweety, you've got my spare room. Luke, you're on Charlie's couch. Charlie and Tessa, as you were. Tony and Ashley, congratulations, the Lodge is yours. Don't forget to hydrate." With a half salute, he headed for the door.

"Wait!" Charlie said. "Your couch is bigger. Why wouldn't you take Luke?"

They looked at each other. It was plain to see Darryl was edging Luke towards the precipice they all knew was there, while Charlie was throwing herself in front of it. Finally, Darryl shrugged. "I'm off tomorrow. In two hours, I'll be wide awake and on that couch in my tighty-whities, eating pizza pockets and watching Breakfast Television. Luke wants to join me, he can have at it."

Luke made a face. "Ugh. I'm good with Charlie's."

Tessa exchanged the briefest of glances with Ainsley before they parted, her friend banking right towards the Lodge, Tessa veering left towards Charlie's, Luke trailing her inside.

Bone Flower / *Polianthes Tuberosa*

"This pleasure will inevitably cause pain."

LUKE

HE DID THE RIGHT THING.

But that didn't mean he was done sulking about it.

Luke had stared at Charlie's living room ceiling in the dark for who knows how long, trying to rein in his thoughts. Sometime before dawn, he pulled on his jeans and trod to the bathroom to take a leak. Afterwards, he swung the door open, ensuring it made no sound, then startled with such force he nearly tore the knob off.

"Jesus Christ!"

Tessa's reply hissed across the threshold. *"You scared the shit out of me!"*

"What are you *doing?*"

"What do you think? I have to pee!"

"You couldn't knock?"

"How was I supposed to know you were in here? You couldn't put the light on?"

"Why would I?"

"So you don't give somebody a heart attack, you *jackass!*"

Luke grinned. "Sorry, Princess."

Tessa jabbed his bare chest with her fingertips, teeth gritted. "I *told* you, stop *calling* me that."

Luke caught her wrists with his fingers, encircling them like handcuffs. She made no effort to free herself. Gently, he lowered her arms, inching her closer. Her smile faded, eyes wide. The fly of his jeans pulled so tight his temples pounded. For too long, they stood there, faces searching, her pulse galloping under his thumbs. With every breath, her thin camisole grazed his chest, siphoning the air from his lungs. Their eyes synced, four stoplights changing to green.

GO.

He will never understand how he stopped himself from covering her in lips and palms and carrying her straight to bed. Now, he'd spend the rest of his miserable life wondering what it would've been like if he had. But Luke hadn't forgotten the pain of betrayal. Crazy as it drove him, Tessa and whatshisname had something worth holding onto. Something her heart couldn't walk away from, no matter what promises her body made in the dark. In the end, Luke would get burned.

Maybe she had too much to drink, or the looming changes September would bring had her acting impulsive. In that moment, all he knew was if they did, Tessa would regret it, and by extension, so would he. Guilt would drive her away. She'd probably quit the shop, and the brightest spot in Luke's days would be gone. He'd much rather have Tessa's friendship over the long run than all of her once, mind-blowing as it would have been.

His voice was pinched. "Tess. We can't."

"I know." Her mouth spoke the words, but the rest didn't seem to hear. She bit her lower lip, which only implored him louder to kiss it.

"I'm serious. You can't throw your whole life away. I can't be that guy."

Tessa seemed to float off then, looking at him but *through* him. When she finally spoke, her voice belonged to a frightened child. "What if it's not even my life?"

Huh?

The trance crumpled. Tessa backed away, stammering. She clamped her eyes shut. "God, Luke. I'm *so* sorry. Did I just mess everything up?" Her words gathered steam. "Is it going to be all weird with us now? Please tell me it's not going to get weird, because I don't think I can—"

"*Shhhh.*" Luke put one finger to her lips; a consolation prize. "It's fine. Tess, look at me. We're *fine*. Nothing happened. Let's just forget it, okay? I won't get weird if you don't get weird."

"You swear?"

"Cross my heart."

Now, Luke was at work, trying not to be weird. Of all days, it was just the two of them on shift, but aside from one *Carlo's* delivery and a trickling of hostess gifts inside, Monday of the August long weekend promised to be the quietest of the summer. He'd arrived early and set up alone, then managed to keep a low profile out back.

Tessa poked her head into the yard. "You good to cover the front? I need to gas up the cube for tomorrow."

She didn't sound weird. Luke peered around a cart full of clematis. She didn't look weird. "Okay . . . sure. Unless you want me to go?"

"All good. See you in a few."

As far as Luke could tell, it was the same Tess, which was great. And also, a bit weird. He walked up front, found the aisles deserted. Doubled back to the laneway and hopped on a skid, work boots dangling, and lit a smoke, willing his brain to stop churning.

Because Tony was always shouting out car names based on the engine sounds, or perhaps because his conscience half expected a reckoning, Luke knew without looking up that the distinctive growl on the approach belonged to a Porsche 9-11. And when the matte custom-width rim rolled to a stop at his feet, he knew the driver was none other than Whatshisname Westlake.

Fucking great.

"You can't park here, man. You're blocking the laneway."

Will held up the coffee cup in his hand. "I'll just be a minute."

"It's a tow-away zone."

Will glanced around the empty storefront. "I'll take my chances."

Luke took a long pull on his cigarette, then deployed a swath of smoke rings across the car's open roof. "Suit yourself."

Will looked at Luke with disgust. "People still do that?" he scoffed. "Now that we all know how badly it ends, how hard can it be to walk away?"

Luke felt like telling him to go ask his girl about walking away, or how many smokes she bummed last night. He pinched the cigarette between thumb and forefinger. "This? Nah, I only smoke when I'm here." Not entirely true; lately, Luke had been smoking like a brush fire. He looked Mr. Prettyboy in the face and hauled another drag. "Helps drown out the entitlement."

Will's smile was straight off the side of a bus. "I'd have to drown out a lot to work here."

Ouch. Tessa made this guy out to be all princelike, but so far, all Luke saw was a condescending douchebag. He decided to have a bit of fun; he'd earned that much. "I don't know. There's a few perks."

Whatshisname played it cool, but Luke definitely hit a nerve. "Lucky you," Will said. "Anyway, I don't want to keep Tessa waiting." He pressed the key fob in his other hand. The car yelped in Luke's face.

Luke called after him. "Tessa? Yeah, she's not here."

Will stopped. Glanced at the hunk of metal around his wrist. "Did she leave early?"

"Nope."

An irritated sigh. "Then where is she?"

"Gassing up the cube truck."

The flawless collection of features twisted into a single, gold-plated question mark.

"For tomorrow morning?" Luke offered. "Tuesdays are—"

"Buying days, I know," Will snapped. "You sent her to get *gas?*"

"Nobody *sent* her anywhere. She offered."

Another scoff. "Tessa offered to drive a cube truck."

Luke ground the butt against the heel of his size twelve, easing slowly off the skid. His broad frame at full extension had a scaling effect; where Westlake was a plainclothes Batman only seconds ago, he'd now been downgraded to Robin. Luke shrugged. "She seems fine with the bigger rig."

The pale eyes, simmering now behind the Ray-Bans, snapped sharply to Luke, who stared back evenly.

"How long has she been gone?"

Luke frowned. "I'm supposed to keep tabs on her?"

Will sneered at the cup in his hand, as if blaming it for his agitation. "It's getting cold."

Luke looked away, up the street. "She'd rather have coconut water."

"Tessa loves coffee."

"Not when she has to wake up at four."

"I know exactly what Tessa wants, thanks."

Luke lifted his hands in mock surrender. "I'm just saying she should stay hydrated. That episode she had gave us all a good scare."

The half-bored *GQ* expression clouded, dark and fast.

Luke waited a beat. He should probably stop here, but like a bullet already out of the chamber, he kept going. "Don't worry. I took excellent care of your girl."

Will took a step forward, pulling off his sunglasses. Looked Luke dead in the eyes. *"Fiancée."*

Luke's smug air dropped away like a finger pulled from a drinking straw.

"She didn't tell you?" A short laugh. "But then, she can't go flashing a ring like that around here. Her face when I slid it on her finger, though? *Wow.* Blown away. Speechless, in fact. I went a little overboard at Tiffany's, but a girl like Tessa deserves the full package, don't you think?"

Luke had no idea what to think.

"Anyway, she did mention you helped her out. Between wedding plans and running my law firm, it slipped my mind. But thanks, uh . . . what's your name again?"

Luke cleared his throat to answer.

Will eyed him stiffly. "Right. Luke." He set the steaming cup on the fence post. "Tell Tess I'll catch her at home . . . Luke."

Luke blinked. The engine roared, and in a squeal of rubber and smoke, it was over.

Nightshade / *Solanaceae*

"You lie."

———◀◉▶———

WILL

ENGINE NOISE pinballed through the empty financial district as his foot hammered the gas.

Last night, he'd sat in his parents' backyard at the party, watching his mother discreetly dabbing her nose with tissue. Trying to crack why it mattered. Mid-briefing today, it hit him—*seasonal allergies.*

Eleanor suffered with them since Will was a kid, refusing to take antihistamines because they made her foggy. All these weeks, he'd fixated on how the *gardeners* had learned of Tessa's birthmark, overlooking the crucial hole in the testimony—Eleanor claiming to have overheard them. She never would've left the windows open while the lawn was being cut!

It was the kind of sloppy oversight Will would never have made before, and it changed everything. Eleanor knew where Tessa worked; generating the lie's framework would have been easy. That thumbs-up birthmark detail would have proven trickier, but his mother's resourcefulness was unparalleled, and she knew Will needed more than fuzzy conjecture. For all Will could guess, she'd been stockpiling the tidbit for years in case of emergency, and Tessa in the campaign stock photo surely qualified as such.

Half of him was in awe of the extent his mother was willing to go to protect him. The other half felt compelled to apologize to Tessa for not believing her about Eleanor's cruelty all along. Will couldn't wait another second to clear the air. He and Tessa had barely talked—properly *talked*—since the gala, and that was on him.

But then, from the second he'd pulled up to the Blue Iris, that jerk Luke was bent on provoking him. Mocking him. Acting like he knew Tessa after what, a few *weeks?* Will had never leaned so far towards violence in his life.

His phone pinged. Will ignored it. It pinged twice more. He kept driving; it was a holiday Monday, it could wait until he got to his desk.

Luke. The stranger of his nightmares, Will knew it on sight. Doubt tunneled like termites. He couldn't blink without Eleanor's words popping back up like clickbait. *"These things rarely start out of nowhere . . ."*

Will's gut wrenched. *Canada Day.* He was so relieved that she didn't call him out for missing their nightly call, after he was such a dick about instituting them in the first place, he forgot to question why his own call log was empty. If Tessa really did fall ill that night as Luke implied, not unlikely working those hours in that heat, then why had she never mentioned it?

It was this, all the not knowing between them now, that made the rest unbearable. Not knowing had quietly rooted for months, and shoots of doubt were sprouting faster than he could yank them. Making him question Tessa's loyalty. Her commitment. His own desirability. His worthiness. His ability to hold first place. Not knowing was turning him into a condemned building on the verge collapse. Desperately capable of anything to prop himself up.

Like bragging to Luke about there being a ring, even though Tessa was going to be furious.

Or worse.

He'd milked the work excuse for all he could, didn't balk when Tessa opted out of last night's pool party. But how much time had to pass before he could look her in the face without feeling woozy? What if next time Portia—his best friend's fiancée—aimed her pepper spray gaze in his direction, Tessa just *knew* in the eerie way she always seemed to know things? Could he properly explain that what happened in Muskoka had nothing to do with either of them?

Not that Will had cheated, not in any true sense. He was desolate that night, consumed by uncertainty, uncharacteristically tipsy. He could summon a yachtful of witnesses to attest to his compromised mental state! If anyone were to blame, it was Portia; that girl just didn't let up.

"SHUT UP!" he screamed at the dash. Fucking phone was relentless.

Besides, Portia wasn't a choice, she was a fallback. And that was different. Will's *choice* was Tessa. He'd chosen her over countless others, every time, in every way. But what did she expect? She'd neglected him for weeks, then practically shoved him up the 400 to those libidinous shores, Eleanor's wicked seeds germinating. At the time, it felt like Tessa was begging him to even the score.

The only thing to do now was move forward. The future they'd envisioned all along had to start today. *Now.* Obviously, he hadn't planned on revealing their news so inelegantly, but Will couldn't let Luke's cocky expression rest. Many a guy had worn it before, each claiming to be her *friend.* Until they saw up close who William Westlake was and backed the fuck up.

Will balled up his suspicions as he drove, stuffing them and their spiral of consequences into a mental trash bag, which he flung out the open roof. He pictured them landing with a clang at the corner of Morrow Avenue and Cresthaven. *The Blue Iris.* Had his head been properly in the game, Will would have kicked that file into high gear weeks ago.

At first, it was just a bunch of lot numbers on a country club napkin, of no consequence to Will one way or another so long as it got him where he needed to be. Now, although business remained strictly business, the pleasure Will would take at seeing the whole place bulldozed to dust, carved four levels deep and backfilled with steel and cement, would be highly personal.

"WHAT?" His screen, now a bubbling whiteout, forced him to pull over. Will slammed his palm into the gearshift. "You've got to be kidding."

The *Globe* was running their piece on Peter Westlake tomorrow, and the campaign team wanted approval to reference Will and Tessa's engagement in the media packet.

Will knew their wedding would be bittersweet for Tessa; no mother welling up in the bridal suite, no dad to walk her down the aisle. He could see how the onset of Pop's Parkinson's might have stirred up all sorts of painful feelings, and he'd resigned himself to patience and compassion, prepared to keep their news secret for as long as she needed. But Tessa was notoriously indecisive; even basic forward steps required a small nudge. The longer this limbo kept up, the more things kept spinning out of control. Will had no choice but to take back the wheel before one of them did something they couldn't recover from.

Forgiveness, not permission.

Surely, he could make Tessa see why now was the perfect time to remind everybody in this city, from his meddling mother to the grubs at the Blue Iris, that they were an unbreakable force. Worst case scenario, he'd blame the campaign team.

Will tapped open the thread and replied to his father.

RUN WITH IT.

Lobelia / *Lobelia Inflata*

Ill-will. Storms.

◄○►

TESSA

IT WAS, AS POP would call it, a blue-skies-and-green-lights kind of day. Everything was clicking into place, though it had seemed impossible only yesterday, after the hallway encounter at Charlie's. Thankfully, Luke had the clarity to call time when he did, mercifully *chill* about the whole thing. Compromising their friendship would have been almost as unbearable as ruining her relationship with Will.

On this cloudless August day, she saw the close call with Luke as the turning of a corner. Now that she'd faced head on the real possibility of losing Will, she'd never risk it again. Forcing this distance between them, skirting her *big* and allowing her childish indecision free rein had led her grossly astray.

Poor Will was so swamped at work, they hadn't been able to connect before she fell asleep last night. But at four this morning, a voicemail was waiting.

"Hey, you. I know it's late." Will's voice was naked. "I just wanted to say sorry, for . . . *everything*. I love you, Tessa, more than I know how to deal with sometimes." He cleared his throat. "Come after work, spend the night with me. No more questions, I promise. I just need to feel you in my arms again. I swear it's like I'm going crazy without you."

A fresh band of guilt cropped up. Will needed her now more than ever, and she hadn't made him, *them*, a priority. Tessa loved the shop more than logic dictated, but wow, she missed him. The old him, before the corner office and corporate functions, the incessant jockeying for position. She missed the couple who boarded that plane in February and had yet to return home. But the voicemail was proof they were of one mind again. They'd found their way back. She tossed some makeup and a slinky sundress into her bag, firing off the text as she headed out the door:

I'm sorry, too. I'll come straight after work.
I love you, William Westlake. Forever and ever.
XXX

She skidded to a stop on the porch, then hurried back in to unearth the turquoise box from her drawer. Her jaw still fell a little whenever she flipped it open; four-and-a-half carats in the shape of a heart, shimmering like a bottomless bag of pixie dust. She tucked it in her backpack. Tonight, she and Will were going to sit down and set their plans in stone. Together.

Tessa's high continued all morning. She and Darryl, now a noteworthy buying team, scooped prime inventory at the terminal, then set bidding price on nearly every lot at auction. Back at the shop, she sold every spectacular Eugenia topiary straight from the bumper, landscapers whooping their approval. Afterwards, eager to boast about how she'd edged out three competitors on those topiaries while Darryl was in the burger line, she set off in search of Luke. Yesterday, when she'd returned from getting gas, he was tied up out back and then on a last-minute delivery that went past closing. But thankfully, they'd spoken enough beforehand to satisfy her things definitely hadn't gotten weird.

The yard fell silent when she walked in. Luke turned and began watering the tuberous begonias. Tony stubbed out his smoke and slid past, eyebrows raised.

"I'll cover the front," Tony told her.

Tessa looked at him, puzzled. "Okay." To Luke, she said, "I did those yesterday."

Luke lifted the hose one shelf higher, waving it over the alliums instead.

"They're good too. I did that whole section."

"Great." Luke snapped the nozzle shut, wrangling the hose over his elbow like a rattlesnake. "Then I'm all done back here."

"Is everything all right?" Tessa fished for eye contact, but his gaze was nailed to the ground. "What'd I miss?"

"Nothing. I'm good."

"Did I do something?"

"Nope."

"You're clearly pissed off."

Luke huffed. "So? Do we have to tell each other everything?"

"We spend fourteen hours a day together. I talk more to you than my own boyfriend."

Luke dumped the coil to the pavement with a rubbery slap and glared at her. "Fiancé."

Adrenaline shot down Tessa's legs. *"What?"*

"That's what he is, right? Your fiancé? This whole time, all of . . . *this,*" his sun-stained hand swept fierce circles between them, "and you didn't think to mention you're *engaged?* Whatever fucked-up game you're playing, Tess, I'm out."

"I'm not, I swear! How did you—?"

"Right. We're *friends.* And I keep telling myself that, I do. But dammit,

Tessa, we came pretty close to the line, don't you think? And now I find out the whole time—"

"No! I meant . . . I'm not *engaged!*" His anger passed through her skin like a rhino through a straw fence. "Would you slow down and let me—"

"Really? Whatshisname thinks you are. Told me all about it when he was over here pissing on my leg yesterday. So yeah, Tess, please. Tell me how him sliding some gigantic rock on your finger has us both so fucking confused."

"I . . . it's . . ." Tessa's mind clamored to catch up. *Will was here? He told Luke?*

"You know what? Forget it." His dark eyes blazed. The break in his voice struck her like an uppercut to the stomach. "You almost turned me into the *one* thing I hate."

Tessa raced after him as he stormed through the yard, frantically sputtering the explanation as best as she could. Technically, when Will sank to one knee in the floury Caymanian sand back in February and asked her to marry him, she *did not* say yes.

But then, she didn't exactly say no, either.

Woodbine / *Lonicera Periclymenum*

Peace of mind.

TESSA

Last February

H E SHOWED UP the night before winter break and asked her to do two things—throw her bikini in a bag, and trust him.

The private villa was deep on a narrow peninsula, the Caribbean tide a hypnotic embrace through the panoramic windows. For three days, they did nothing other than flounce in the waves and make love under a four-poster canopy in the sand. On the fourth day, Tessa woke to a Catamaran docked out front. Will flashed his sleepy smile and suggested she eat a big breakfast.

They spent the day courting stingrays, skimming psychedelic reefs, and feeling the gentle suck of starfish against their palms. Not since Will first tilted her chin to his at age seventeen had Tessa known such bliss. On the way back, they lay entwined on the rear deck, cheeks pink with wind and lips like saltlicks, watching the blood orange sun sink into their wake.

On the beach, a crackling bonfire waited. A driftwood arch wrapped in breezy linens. A blanket strewn with pillows, red petals and candles piled all around. Tessa took it all in, heart somersaulting. Will, on bended knee. An orange blaze reflected in his hand.

His lips mouthed the question, though she couldn't actually hear it for the rolling tide. Tessa clung to him, the surf slamming and fizzing, her tears clotting in the sand. Every cell wanted to marry him. Always had. Still, as he slid the ring onto her finger, she said nothing.

Back indoors, the roar of wind sealed out and the villa aglow against the black sea, a living fairy tale took shape; a small, elegant ceremony in their favorite chapel at twilight. A string quartet, then a live band at the outdoor reception. A constellation of white string lights. Throw blankets for guests in case it got cool.

And how many nights before this one had they spent musing over cake flavors, what to name the dogs? Yet, as they talked, made love across the California King, the diamond on Tessa's finger grew heavier, the new angle of her wrist exposing a facet of herself she'd long kept hidden—she was defective. The parts of her capable of real commitment, of making a choice and sticking to it, had been pieced together wrong by a mother who departed without goodbye and a father who didn't hang around long enough to learn she existed.

Will was kissing the length of her arm, asking if she'd like to redecorate the penthouse, when two words lodged unspoken in her throat. *I can't.*

Being downtown with him, freeing Nano and Pop to downsize and enjoy retirement, made the most sense. Still, Tessa wasn't ready to say goodbye to the coach house she shared with her mother, the property that held so much of her past and herself.

Will smeared a runaway teardrop from her jaw, smiling, as though reading her thoughts. He opened the nightstand, handing her a fold of papers. The letters *Purchase Agreement* swam in front of her. Enough zeroes to stop her heart. Then, a bank draft made out to her grandparents.

Week by week, Will had cleaned out his trust fund to buy Tessa's dream home—Nano and Pop's. The plan was perfect. It would be an investment at first, with Tessa's grandparents remaining in the main house as long as they wanted, rent free, while the coach house was rented out. Alternatively, Nano and Pop could use the proceeds from the sale to move anyplace they wished, in which case both dwellings would be rented, generating a tidy income. Either way, her grandparents would live out their years worry free, and Tessa could join Will at the penthouse during this crucial time in their careers knowing their forever home, her one true home, would be waiting.

The answer was obvious. Still, she couldn't manage to say it as she tearfully wrapped her arms around him, then her legs once more, the diamond reflecting off the ceiling in an iridescent spray.

Back in Toronto, word of Pop's tumble in the washroom waited upon landing. They raced straight there, Tessa choking back a new pair of words now—*people disappear.* She slipped the ring back into its satin-lined box. They agreed to tell no one it existed, not until Tessa was sure Pop was going to be okay.

The next morning, she barely registered Will's expression when she unpacked her suitcase at the coach house instead of the penthouse. In the end, everyone was one unforeseen incident from starting over. The best laid plans could vanish under a car bumper. Tessa couldn't be too reliant on anyone—not even Will, no matter that her soul belonged to his. She had to figure out her own plan, be self-sufficient and solidly on her way to *big*, before she put that kaleidoscope ring back on. Otherwise, she might get too caught up in its glow.

Days went by. Weeks. There was her degree to finish, and Will's schedule got busier. The campaign forged ahead. Tessa took the job at the shop, where the plants didn't keep time and no one was waiting on menu selections or venue deposits, and it proved surprisingly easy to pretend Will's proposal had never even happened.

Field Poppy / *Papaver Rhoeas*

Revelations.

TESSA

HER FACE BURNED in the beer garden as Luke described an encounter by the skids with an alpha egomaniac she'd never met. Will's blanket apology on her voicemail this morning, after dodging her calls last night, took on new meaning. His lack of self-control, once again, was unsettling.

She apologized to Luke; she hadn't acted like somebody else's fiancée and they both knew it. But now, she was glad he knew the truth. He was the one person who wouldn't make her feel crazy for holding Will off, and he could be trusted to keep it a secret.

Luke shifted uneasily.

Tessa's eyes widened. "Who have you told?"

"Just Tony, but—"

"Ainsley knows, then. She'll be pissed for a minute, but—"

"Tess. You need to go look at today's paper."

Rowan spread the newspaper across a skid of soil. The crew circled in around Tessa. The headline: **WESTLAKE ROLLS DICE ON MAYOR SEAT**.

The feature tracked Peter's evolution from eagle-eyed lawyer to business tycoon. The elite client roster, famed courtroom charisma and loud philanthropy. His longstanding ties to Attorney General Bradley Thornton, which gave him an edge in the race. Photos from the gala were sprinkled throughout, with the infamous family shot front and center. Beside it, a candid of Will and Tessa, locked in the passionate kiss they'd shared upon entering the ballroom. The caption below it read:

Westlake's lawyer son William, successor to the Westlake empire, with bride-to-be Tessa Lewis. The high school sweethearts' wedding plans remain under wraps, but sources say it promises to be the social highlight of the year.

The world fell away. Tessa stared in disbelief. With a gasp, she dropped the newspaper and raced inside; Nano and Pop would be halfway through it by now.

TONY

"Help me out," Darryl said. "Is she marrying the guy, or what?"

"That's the million-dollar question," Luke said.

"Literally," Charlie said.

Tony pulled off his sunglasses, taking a closer look at the spread. Tee was a ten in that getup, but also a bit like a bunny in a snake pit? And was that—

No way.

"Uh, guys?" Tony said.

They paid him no attention. "But he did propose?" Rowan was saying.

Luke nodded. "Tess never actually said yes, though."

"She turned him down?"

"She wanted more time."

Darryl let out a low whistle. "Guess her time was up."

"I don't understand," Charlie said. "Why would Will let this get out if she wasn't ready?"

Darryl nodded. "Ask Princess, the guy walks on broken grass for her."

Tony's hand was in the air, like he was seeking permission to use the bathroom. "Guys—"

Luke scowled so hard at the lip-lock photo Tony feared the page might go up in smoke. "I'm telling you, the dude who showed up here yesterday *wasn't* that guy. I almost bashed his face in. No way Tess falls for someone like that. And then he goes and does *this?*"

Poor Luke had it bad, even before Westlake rubbed his nose in the shit. And now, Tony was starting to formulate a loose understanding of why the kid came gunning for Luke to begin with. He tapped two fingers against the newspaper. "*Guys.* Check the blonde."

Rowan peeked over Luke's shoulder. "Eleanor Westlake?"

Tony grinned. Rowan's eyes bulged.

Yeah, she'd fed him a fake name, and she was kinda-sorta Tessa's future mother-in-law, which was messed up in ways Tony was still bending his mind around, but he couldn't help peacocking a little. He and Toronto's future first lady were *tight.*

That first summer, he was the newest Flash, jotting down details for her mandevilla delivery. By noon, he was taking payment handcuffed to a padded headboard in Hogg's Hollow. It wasn't her first midday rodeo. In many ways, Tina—Eleanor—shaped Tony into the Olympian he was, always sending him from her garden gate with something new in his repertoire.

Sometimes, he hung around afterwards. Eleanor was always on him to make her laugh, do his impressions. She'd cackled that day when he, balls-naked in her ivory-on-cream bedroom bigger than his front yard, re-enacted the moment Luke inadvertently found himself staring straight down the new girl's shirt, Tessa's unique birth mark offering the first "thumbs-up" his friend had seen in a long while.

"New girl, huh?" she'd said, super casual. "You think you have a shot?"

"With Tessa?" Tony liked to think he had a shot with any woman, but like he told Eleanor, it wasn't that way with Tess. Besides, some hotshot lawyer had her locked down, and if that ever changed, his boy Luke definitely had dibs.

Come to think of it, Eleanor had been acting sketchy that whole last round. Asked twice if Tony remembered to skirt the security cameras. Said their meetings had to stop—*"for real this time."*

"She's gorgeous," Charlie said. "I see where Will gets it."

"Don't you recognize her?" Rowan asked. "She used to shop here. The last few years, though, she's been strictly—"

"Deliveries," Darryl said, catching on.

Charlie's jaw dropped. "Blonde Tina from Hogg's Hollow is Eleanor *Westlake?*"

Tony frowned. "She told me her last name was Turner."

Darryl tremored. Coffee sprayed from Rowan's nose.

"You thought her name was Tina Turner," Charlie said.

A knuckle formed between Luke's eyebrows. "That's his *mother?*"

"I mean, she never, like, introduced herself. Like, *oh hey, what's up, I'm Tina Turner.*"

"You're literally fucking his mother," Luke said, his face blank.

Tony aimed a finger at Luke. "*Was.* I'm a one-woman show now, so let's be sure to play that up for Ainsley, shall we?" He slapped Luke's shoulder. "Sorry you didn't get to beat his face in, bro. Ask me, I did you one better."

Luke guffawed, still staring hard at that newsprint.

Behind them, a Prius bearing the government logo pulled up. The driver flashed a laminated badge and dropped yet another paper-based bomb—a stop-work order, due to unsafe working conditions.

The Blue Iris Flower Market was ordered closed, effective immediately.

Scotch Thistle / *Onopordum Acanthium*

Willpower.

—◄○►—

ROWAN

THE LABOR INSPECTOR was a mall cop on Red Bull. He ordered Rowan to wait outside, grilling the entire staff, even Tessa, found in the bathroom with tear spots all over her grey T-shirt, the phone cord wrapped around her like butcher twine.

A complaint had been filed alleging unsafe working conditions at the shop. Combined with the outstanding bullshit fines for Trucks, which Rowan would have paid by now if he could have, it was enough to shut him down pending a full investigation.

Rowan wasn't some arms-length investor raking dividends from behind a desk. He knew firsthand the long hours through weather alerts, the gruelling physical demands. The geo-concentration of privileged, whiny customers. That's why he paid the highest wages on Morrow, handed out bonuses like cinnamon hearts post-Valentine's Day. Gave breaks and time off on demand. Ate the overages on their homes. He'd be nothing without his crew, which is exactly why he never pushed them to do any more than they wanted to. They just always seemed to *want* to.

After the inspector left, Rowan dismissed the group to call his lawyer. But instead of going home, they followed him like worried ducklings into the shop. He made the call on speaker phone; he couldn't summon the energy to continue the lies, and there was little point anyhow.

Attorney Bobby Benedetto assured them the inspector's claims were mostly smoke in mirrors. "If no health and safety violations were found onsite, and the staff corroborated you're following heat stress and overtime protocols, I should be able to get the stop-work order squashed in no time."

A collective sigh. Indeed, Rowan had been firm about staff taking regular breaks and days off ever since . . . Tessa's fainting spell in the yard.

The thought seemed to rise to everyone's mind at once.

Tessa looked up. "You guys think it was me."

"Stop it, girlie."

"I wouldn't blame you. I pass out, and suddenly we're being interrogated about heat stress?"

"After a spotless record all these years," Bobby said, "it does seem strange. First bylaw comes after you about the yard, and now the labor department a few weeks later? Word must be out about Sam."

Darryl's eyes bore into Rowan. "What's that about the yard?"

Voice shaking, Rowan brought them up to speed. Trucks was on residential property; without permission from the city, it wasn't allowed to operate. And without Trucks, he was out of ways to keep the shop afloat.

"So, we need a permit or something?" Charlie asked.

"More than that," Bobby explained. "We need a zoning variance, converting the property to commercial usage."

"Which my father *got*," Rowan said. "Why wouldn't he? But the city is insisting he didn't."

"I bought us some time on account of the original owners being deceased, but unless we can produce a copy—"

Rowan looked at Darryl, then Charlie, and shook his head. After the reading of his father's will, his mother had lit a crackling fire in the open brick fireplace of Simon's study and burned every paper in the file cabinet.

Apprehension rolled through the room like tumbleweed.

"So, we apply for a new one," Charlie said.

Bobby sighed. "Developers are dying to get their hands on that block, and we all know the pull they have at city council. If you filed now, it would get denied in the hopes you'd be forced to sell."

Charlie's cheeks puffed in weary exhale. Rowan nearly threw up. She was his dearest, most loyal friend. This place was her sole constant. Her *home*. The last piece of Sam any of them had left.

"What if I ignored it?" Rowan asked. "Keep paying fines or something?" He contemplated how far he was willing to go. Would they make him do jail time? If he hacked white-collar prison, customers would definitely stop pushing him around.

"The penalties would be astronomical," Bobby said. "At best, you shut down the wholesale division, sell off the houses and yard, float the storefront as long as you can. But taxes for small businesses are only going up."

Clearly, there was no lawyering out of this. Rowan couldn't see much choice but to sign that offer. Get as much money as possible for the one place in the world that was everything he couldn't buy.

Summer Rhododendron / *Rhododendron Maximum*

"Who is against me?"

———◄○►———

TESSA

HE ELEVATOR ROCKETED to the penthouse, the evening she'd envisioned hours ago sinking further from reach with every floor.

The hurt in Nano's voice had torn Tessa's heart like wet tissue. *No, Tessa* explained, sniffling into the phone, she hadn't left them to *read about her engagement in the paper like everyone else.* Yes, it was *right there in black and white*, but—well, yes, there *was* a ring—but the paper got the facts wrong! Nothing was official!

The caption listing Tessa as Will's fiancée could have been an unchecked assumption by the reporter, or a tip from someone at Tiffany's. A ring like that, a man like Will, would have stood out. Hell, Tessa was ready to blame autocorrect, so long as it didn't happen on Will's go-ahead. But hadn't he callously dropped the word *fiancée* to Luke just yesterday?

And why was he the only person she hadn't heard from this morning? *No.* He was too mired in figuring out how this mess happened, too busy tagging heads to be rolled. Tessa, at the penthouse early due to the work stoppage, would sit on his leather sectional and wait, thoughts firmly in check, until he walked in with the perfectly logical explanation.

When Tessa stepped off the elevator, candles were flickering. Wine breathed in the crystal decanter, and the scent of filet mignon filled the air. Will stood at the counter, plating food from cartons belonging to the French bistro a few blocks away, the one that didn't offer takeout. He brightened when he saw her, so much, that for a half-beat, Tessa wondered if he was in court all day and word of the news article hadn't yet reached him.

He strode over. Kissed her. "You're just in time."

Nothing had changed. Yet, his demeanour felt altered from head-to-toe. Robotic, almost. A Will Westlake hologram. Tessa stalked to the windows—not the airy set overlooking the amber-streaked harbour. The other ones. She searched the hard gridlines of the financial district for what to say, how to feel. Nothing made any sense anymore.

His fingers grazed her hip, and Tessa recoiled. The glass of red wine he'd brought her tumbled across the carpet. They stared at the burgundy river creeping along the hand-knotted fibers, neither making any attempt to stop it.

"I don't even like red wine," she murmured.

It was true. Will simply began pouring it one day, assuring her it was an acquired taste, but all she'd ever acquired was a headache and the stifled urge to dump it down the drain.

He sidestepped the mess, moving towards her the way he would an injured animal. "You saw the article."

The words were a lit match in freefall. Tessa's ears a slick of gasoline. "Of course I saw it! Did you think I wouldn't *see* it? The whole fucking COUNTRY saw it! Nano and Pop think we *lied* to them! I have a thousand messages, everyone I know thinks we're engaged!"

"We are." He spoke with infuriating calm, like she was some irate caller on a customer service line. "I'm sorry word got out earlier than you wanted, but don't you think we've kept it secret long enough?"

She squeezed her eyes shut, trying to teleport him to reality. "I never said *yes*."

Will tilted his head, patiently standing by while she finished being irrational. "Tess, you let me put the ring on your finger."

"I'm NOT ready, Will. You knew that."

He sighed, haughty impatience beginning to swirl. "It's jewelry! Our plans are still the same, we're still the same, the only difference from yesterday is optics. Do you really care all that much if—"

"YES! I do! And what is that picture of us kissing even doing in the spread? It's supposed to be about Peter's campai—"

Tessa stopped, face freezing mid-wince as she recalled Peter beckoning her across the stage at the gala. Will prodding her along, Eleanor fuming. Was she imagining it now, the way Will angled himself, hiding her empty left hand from view? How that incredible kiss only moments before just happened to be artfully framed by the arched double doorway?

She had no clue how this fit into the campaign, but she'd overheard enough by now to know that Will's father left nothing to chance. In his business and his politics, there were no coincidences; Peter Westlake was *always* running a play.

And now, Will was part of the huddle.

Her pulse clipped, hot acid pumping. "Tell me this wasn't you."

His voice was pleading. "I know what change does to you. I was trying to make this one easier."

"Using the *media?* Do you even understand how fucked up that is? What were you hoping to do, strongarm me into *marrying* you?"

Will caught her charge, igniting. "I can't believe I have to! I've done everything. *Everything!* You don't want kids? Fine. Done. Pop's medical bills? Poof! They'll be taken care of. You want their house? BOOM! Wish granted!" He paced the room, eyes narrow. "I emptied my *trust fund*. I'm working my ass off twenty-four-seven to be the man you want! Give you the perfect life, make you happy!"

Tessa stepped in front of him, forcing him to a stop. "Except it's always about you, though. *You* parade me around at your corporate bullshit, plotting what I wear and where I sit. *You* told the world we're engaged, *without even checking with me!* All your life, you've gotten exactly what you want, exactly when you wanted it. Don't you stand there and pretend it's all for me."

"Really? You're insulting me now? *You* wanted me to run the firm, remember?" His voice barreled off the high ceiling. "WHAT DO YOU THINK THIS IS?" He pinched the bridge of his nose. "You don't want to help anymore, fine. Take another eight years to pick a job, go back to school, *do whatever the hell you like!* I'll be right here, making sure you have everything you could possibly want."

"I don't *want* any of it! Not if I can't trust you!"

Will's voice was ice and flame all at once. "You're one to talk about trust."

Tessa fell silent. This bizarre shift she was witnessing was supposed to have been a shuddering, short-lived anomaly, gone forever after the night of the gala.

"I heard about your sleepover. Makes sense now, why you never called on Canada Day."

"The night you got wasted in Muskoka?"

"I was not *wasted* in Muskoka!"

"Please. Portia tagged me. I'm invisible in person, but on social media we're besties, remember?"

At this, the perpetually unflappable Will teetered. "What's your point?"

Tessa's gut curled. The clip of Will throwing back shots on the rented yacht, a lubed-up Portia in the foreground with one devilish eyebrow cocked, should have sparked at least a flicker of propriety. But Tessa had scrolled on. *Not Will,* she thought. *Not ever.* Looking at him now, she wasn't so sure. She wasn't sure about anything. "I could tell in two seconds you were trashed, on some fancy yacht with the same woman who's been at your dick since *Mommy-and-Me*, and *I'm* being grilled about fucking sleepovers?"

Will's face twisted. "Honestly. Is the filthy language absolutely necessary?"

"It is, actually. Care to explain why I didn't have a missed call from you?"

"I was honest from the beginning about where I was! Who I was with! I *begged* you to come, but *no, you couldn't possibly*. Then you spend the night at some strange guy's place and don't tell me?"

She stared at him. "Oh, my God. You're jealous."

Will barked. "If you actually believe I'd be jealous, of an idiot loser like that, we have a much bigger problem."

"That's why you told Luke. That's why you put it in the paper!"

"All I'm saying is, why not just tell me about it afterwards?" Will rolled the next words around in his mouth like vile chewing gum before spitting them at her left chest. "Unless you threw him a thumbs-up."

Tessa's eyes popped. "Do you hear yourself? I had *heat prostration*, which I slept off . . . on the porch. I didn't tell you because talking to you is like facing a firing squad! Luke isn't some *strange guy*. And if you must know, it's not his house, it's Rowan's. Any of us can stay there."

Will snorted. "For now."

If he'd ever worn such a smug expression, if his tone had sounded so high-and-mighty before, Tessa, for all her freakish intuition, had failed to notice. She stopped cold. It was three in the afternoon; she wasn't even supposed to be here. If the Blue Iris hadn't been shut down due to a complaint the group could easily have pinned on her, she'd be on shift another three hours. So why was Will already plating their food when she stepped off the elevator?

Rowan had mentioned an earlier problem, too. Something about missing permits.

And city council.

Tessa whimpered. Knees buckling, she fell into a squat, as if bullets threatened the windows. As if she might dodge the realization that, like his father, there was no such thing as out-of-bounds for Will Westlake anymore.

"Today. The shop. That was you, too."

She hugged her knees, rocking as it pelted her; the reach he would have exercised, the layers of premeditation. The inside information *she'd* fed him about Rowan's unmanageable debt, and the shop's vulnerability due to Sam's death. She looked up at him, face on fire. *"Why?"*

"You could have been seriously harmed because of their negligence! Someone has to hold these people accountable!"

Tessa shot to her feet, her finger springing. "*These people* are my friends, and you're destroying them. Why, Will? For *what?* Because you had to prep a few cases with your pants on?" She grabbed the bridal magazines from the coffee table, whipping them like frisbees. "Because I didn't look at these fast enough? What *is* this? Is this you having a tantrum?"

"It's business, Tessa. You should probably get used to it."

She glared at him. "It didn't work, you know. Rowan's lawyer will have us back open by tomorrow. You Westlakes aren't the only sharks in town."

Will's eyes curved into a bone-shuddering smirk. "Rowan Miller is a law school dropout and a Bay Street washout, whose days were numbered regardless. It was pure luck the inspector didn't find more violations today, but that place can't survive without a permit—and I guarantee you, the city will not be approving one."

The sun slunk behind a skyscraper, recasting them in shadow. In another version of this day, she was pulling him close, the two of them whole again in the glow of all these candles. Instead, she stared dazedly, memories flashing like fireworks under a new moon.

Will crossing Ainsley's backyard to clear the busted screen door like a dragon slayer with dimples.

The flip of her diaphragm when he pulled his cashmere jacket around her shoulders, sealing out the autumn chill and the world.

His voice in her hair the first time he entered her, restraint unspooling to ecstasy.

The orange of the Caymanian sunset in his eyes, right before everything changed forever.

Will's image was stitched deep into every layer of herself. Yet, in looking at his face now, Tessa could find nothing familiar about it. "This isn't who you are," she whispered.

Will's eyes lolled like a watery dynamite fuse, his voice cracking. "That's what I keep trying to tell you. Lately, when it comes to you? I don't know who I am."

Purple Lettuce / *Prenanthes Purpurea*

Snake deterrent.

━━◄○►━━

TESSA

THIS WAS MEANT to be her day off, a day spent wearing Will's diamond and his softest baby-blue tee. Instead, Tessa's throat was sob-stripped, and her brain felt swollen from crying.

They'd fought in venomous upsurges and teary downdrafts all night as the even-handed man Tessa adored dissolved in front of her like a ghost. Patronizing, impervious, impossible to reason with. In the black truth of three in the morning, it was unthinkable that forever had ever seemed possible.

And then, it was time to go back to work. Tessa's body cried for sleep as she drove, but her mind was still outrunning these last surreal hours. The lines Will had crossed to further the Westlake endgame.

It wasn't a buying day, but Darryl was making a special trip to the terminal to pick up yesterday's product delivery, which the inspector had turned away. Tessa, determined to get Rowan out of the mess she'd unknowingly helped Will create by confiding about the shop, intended to tag along. She would speak to Carlo; he was well-connected in the industry, and Iris and Henry had been dear friends. Maybe he could help.

Tessa parked at the Lodge and made her way by the full moon's light through the beer garden into the storage yard. She wandered up the middle aisle, weeping softly to the sky, fingers trailing through the tufts on either side.

Before leaving the penthouse, she'd pried the truth from Will in grudging scraps. Peter's biggest campaign sponsor, EnvidaCorp, was a company set on redeveloping the Blue Iris site, and counting on Peter, as the next mayor, to steer the project through council's red tape. But there was one problem; unrelenting Rowan Miller refused to sell the land.

Tessa grew nauseous as Will admitted he'd been using the inside information she'd shared with him these past weeks. After botching that Hewson trial, Will needed to reassure his father he could handle running things, and scoring the Blue Iris site would be a huge win.

It was Will who had ensured EnvidaCorp's offer struck all the right chords for Rowan, while working Peter's connections to level sanctions at the shop until Rowan conceded. Tessa was only working there one summer, Will reasoned, and Rowan would have folded before long, anyway. Will would gain Peter's confidence and show his father he could separate personal from professional.

Tessa reached the laneway, where the cube truck sat unlocked. She climbed inside to wait for Darryl, staring numbly through the windshield, replaying the previous night's battle. For one, she'd called Will a *Westlake* like it was the filthiest insult possible. Rage mounting, he'd picked up the phone, right there at two in the morning, and instructed his banker, who actually picked up, to set a clock on the offer to buy Nano and Pop's. If the bank draft wasn't cashed by midnight on Labor Day, it was to be cancelled, and Will's trust money reinvested in EnvidaCorp holdings.

His exquisite plan, the one that would see her grandparents taken care of through their final years, while securing the house she cherished—the backyard she'd recently glimpsed their future unfolding in—reduced to a ruthless ultimatum with one phone call, just to show her he could.

"Why Labor Day?" she'd asked. It was as big a question as she could muster.

Will's voice was hollow. "You wanted the summer, take it. Finish—whatever this is you've started. But come fall, I need to *know*. You need to choose, Tessa. In or out. I'm William Fucking Westlake. I'm done begging."

Seething, Tessa had gathered her things, announcing she was going back to work, where *nobody exploited her for political gain*. Will fired accusations at her back. There she went again, putting strangers before him, prioritizing a stupid, dead-end temp job. *No wonder she couldn't get her shit together.*

As the elevator door slid shut, she fired the turquoise ring box at him. It bounced off his chest like a cardboard arrow and clattered to the floor.

Tessa checked her phone now—*4:06 a.m.* Darryl was still twenty minutes out. She closed her eyes and began counting her breaths, grounding herself by thinking about her feet the way Charlie had taught her. The phone rumbled in her lap. *Will.* With a bitter jab, she declined the call. Seconds later, he lit the screen again. Tessa powered off the phone and shoved it to the bottom of her bag.

Her eyes were sandpaper; she'd been awake since roughly this time yesterday. She needed caffeine. Tessa tucked a five into her sweatshirt and hurried to the twenty-four-hour diner up the block. On her way back, coffee in hand, a lone set of headlights on Morrow made her squint.

Tessa groaned as the driver made a U-turn, pulling up behind her.

Keep driving, asshole.

The driver called out. "Need a lift?"

She fixed her gaze ahead. The rumbling engine kept pace at her shoulder.

"Aww, come on. Not even a hello?"

Tessa picked up speed; the shop was in view. Darryl would be there any minute.

"What's the rush?" the driver badgered, rounding the corner onto Cresthaven with her.

Tessa patted her pockets. Panic stung; her phone was in the cube. She reached the laneway and hesitated. If she made it to the gate at the end of it fast enough, she could easily lose this creep in the yard. If she didn't, she will have literally led him down a dark alley.

"Tessa, right?"

She stopped, looking directly at the car for the first time. It was pumpkin-colored. The arm out the window wore a rolled-up dress sleeve and a garish metal watch.

The Rolex.

Tessa exhaled, fear falling away like a silk slip. "Mr. Thornton?"

"Are you alright? What are you doing out here?"

As he offered again to give her a ride, Tessa registered the pull of booze coming from inside the car. At last, she understood why, from the second she'd met him at the gala, this man set every cell in her body on edge. He was the sort of man who drove drunk.

"I'm meeting someone," she told him.

"Ahh, yes. Baby Westlake." A wet chuckle slithered into the night. "Here, call him from my phone. He'll love that."

"A coworker, actually. He'll be here any second."

"I see." The way he said it suggested he didn't believe her. "May I wait with you?"

Tessa paused, then nodded. She wanted far away from him, but how could she let him drive off in this condition? He half-pulled into the laneway, and as he stumbled from the car, Tessa instinctively took a step backwards. He noticed.

"I don't bite, you know."

She stammered, tried sipping casually at her coffee; it was still too hot. He smiled, letting her know all was forgiven. As he did, the alcohol proof oozing from his otherwise handsome face lent the appearance of a fat, ugly toad. As he reached to loosen his collar, the Rolex came alive again, taunting like it did at the gala. Gripping her body in irrational fear.

She had to keep him talking until Darryl got here. Together, they'd figure out how to get him into a cab. "What are you doing up so early?" she asked.

"So *late*." He croaked a laugh, impressed with himself. He nodded towards Morrow. "Poker game. Under the sewing shop. *Shhh!* Don't tell Olivia." He screwed his face into a hoity-toity pucker. "It's *illegal!*"

"Did you win?"

His expression hardened. "Always do."

Tessa's gut bubbled. She looked away, squashing the urge to squirm.

He cleared his throat. "I'd better go."

"No! Wait."

He paused, door ajar, gaging her hand before playing his own. "You'd rather I stay?"

Tessa didn't answer. *Darryl, where are you?*

Thornton nodded and started into the car.

"Stop!" She lunged, yanking him by the elbow.

He frowned at her hand, still on his arm. Tessa swallowed. Thornton's good favor was crucial for Will's career, not to mention the stupid campaign. But something terrible would happen if he got behind that wheel. She was sure of it. "You're drunk."

Thornton laughed. It was an airy sort of laugh, part *I-don't-give-a-shit,* part *isn't-she-cute,* and it landed in Tessa's privilege-weary ears like a pink rose on a poplar coffin.

Next thing she knew, she was charging him, a Spanish bull from its blacked-out box, as if it was Thornton himself who had stolen Beth away, left Tessa's beautiful mother busted open and bloodless on an empty street not so different from this one.

Her limbs exploded furious, pounding grief as the paper coffee cup, still in her other hand, flattened. Thornton roared as the steaming liquid spilled down his back. They grappled. Finally, he slammed her against the rear door of the car.

"You crazy bitch!" Thornton's breath on her face was flammable, the set of his jaw a seething warning to stay where he'd put her. The whites of his eyes grappled to make sense of her, to decide if she was punishable to the fullest extent or should be pardoned by way of insanity. Tessa thrashed, trying to free herself, but his fingers bit into her arms, unyielding.

Cold terror spread to her feet. In such a short time, power and resources had already eroded Will's conscience to a shocking degree; who could guess what Thornton was capable of?

Suddenly, she was back in Pop's garage in those weeks after Beth died, running nonstop boxing drills. Quick as a backfist, Tessa bit down with all her strength on Thornton's trapezius. His grip loosening, she buried her knee into his groin. He backed away with a guttural moan, and his hand took to the air, that horrid watch twinkling like a gold grenade.

The world was on fast forward and slow motion all at once. Tessa flailed, her feet fumbling with the curb as she tried to regain her bearings. She was making a break for the laneway when, like the inside of a flashbulb, everything turned suddenly, blindingly white.

Strangely, it was the sound of the metal she noticed, much more than its feel, as the watchband connected with her skull in a crackling, pulpy snap.

Goldilocks Aster / *Chrysocoma Linosyris*

"You're late."

———◀◉▶———

DARRYL

SIX LOUSY MINUTES.

His internal clock was conditioned to go off at the hair of four o'clock, buying day or not. But today, Darryl allowed his creaking joints to linger in bed awhile longer.

Six minutes longer, to be exact. But he was only making a quick trip to the terminal to pick up yesterday's inventory.

For the first time, there was no one to meet at the cube. Darryl had graduated to Sam's spot in the passenger seat on the same day Sam slid behind the wheel into Henry's. With Sam gone, Rowan climbed in, then Tessa. But today, this body, stiff-sore and sagging into the mattress, was it.

Darryl stared at the patina light fixture above the bed. *When was the last time anyone dusted that thing?* When had he last done anything besides cryopreserve the haunt of this place?

Those fines were hammering the last nail into Trucks' coffin, and it was just as well. Darryl was the last one standing, the end of the line. Sam's twin daughters sure as shit wouldn't pick up the family torch, even if they did move back from Europe; Harper barely let them near their own father, let alone scary Uncle Darryl. The whole beautiful, bloodied era would end with him.

He creaked his way into the cube truck, where Tessa's bag sat waiting. Darryl did a mental check. *Definitely Wednesday.* Her day off. Had she forgotten it yesterday? That dickweed inspector threw them all for a loop, and she was more tossed than a yard sale because of that article. But she couldn't have gotten far without her phone. Young people today were chained to those things like ankle monitors.

He fished through the glove box for the cell Rowan had given him. Sure enough, a text from Tessa:

I'm coming with you. See you @ the cube 4:30

Fuck's sake. It was 4:36, and the kid was nowhere. Darryl heaved a sigh, weighing whether to take off without her. As dawn peeled back a layer of darkness, Newspaper Norm seeped into view, arms flailing like windsocks. Darryl flicked on the ignition, spotlighting the laneway—and the human heap at Norm's feet.

The black tinge to her clothes turned his stomach to lead.

Darryl wanted to ride with her in the ambulance, goddammit. But Tessa, face bloodied and breath jagged, had insisted he go to the terminal as planned. Convince Carlo to help Trucks.

"You'll do fine, just don't be an asshole. And don't let Rowan sign anything!"

She was conscious, her clothes intact, and still a stubborn smartass. Everything he could've hoped for, under the circumstances. A relief really. Yet after that ambulance pulled away, Darryl, who had been piling back tears with the efficiency of a bulldozer all his life, couldn't stop them from spilling into his father's grey steering wheel at last.

SAM

He snorted the last of the eight-ball in the glove box.
Fell face-first into the storm cellar.
Not set on a plan, so much as the outcome.

Probably, he'd hit Manitoulin. Work his way south,
rack up enough heroin and Everclear to guarantee an implosion.
Tuck in deep someplace and ride to the end of the rainbow.

He looked back at the cabin one last time;
he'd always meant to bring her here.
Hopped on the snowmobile. Pinned it.

Grainy winds sliced like ten thousand circular saws across
the frozen water,
but he kept going.

So long as he could feel it, he still had work to do.

Eyebright / *Euphrasia Officinalis*

"I can see you."

———◇———

TONY

"RUN ME THROUGH the timeline again."

It was Luke's third time asking in under an hour. Tony kept the bumbleberry asters coming, hand-bombing them two at a time, the most inefficient way possible to offload the early fall crops.

All night, the cold section of mattress had nagged him awake. Ainsley was at her place, riding out *"the most epic creative surge of her life,"* juices kickstarted by Tony, no doubt. He was happy to leave her to it, then oddly bothered by her absence. Then, more bothered still by how bothered he was. They'd been together every night since staff night—three days and one lifetime ago. How did an empty bed go from sanctuary to exile so fast? Was it going to stay like this? Was he *okay* with that?

These were the thoughts grinding like teens at a rave when he heard the arresting shudder of a six-litre W12 beyond the open window.

Bentley.

He knew it right away, even nodded proudly at the ceiling. There wasn't a luxury engine in this neighborhood he couldn't pick out of a lineup blindfolded.

"Last I looked," he told Luke, again, "the clock read four-eleven. It was sometime after that."

"And you're sure it was Thornton's Bentley."

Tony never should've opened his fat mouth. "Well, no. I didn't see it, obviously."

"She met him at that stupid gala. Sounded like he laid it on her pretty thick."

Tony winced. "That's a big leap, bro."

"How many Bentleys have you seen in this neighborhood?"

Just the one. Orange, first popped up a few months ago. But no way he was telling Luke that. "That car could've peeled out anywhere in a two-block radius, man. Until we know more, all we can do is fall back."

Luke's chest surged, like he'd been hit with one of those heart paddle things. For a second, Tony feared his friend might pop him. "Fall back? *Fall back?*" Luke's thumb jerked towards the spot they all kept turning their faces from. "She was *right there.* You tell me how I'm supposed to fall the fuck back!"

Tony shook his head. He, too, was unable to stop picturing Darryl's account—Tessa curled in the road, steps from the skids he'd walked past a billion times, blood stretching in rust-colored ribbons from her face to her hands.

Yeah, it was a Bentley. Tony knew it, and Luke knew he knew it. But right now, his best friend was a grizzly bear on a choke chain. What good could come from saying aloud that every make and model of engine—

especially the high-end ones—produced its own acoustic fingerprint? It didn't prove a thing.

Nor would it be in Luke's best interest to learn Thornton's twin-turbo wasn't the only luxury engine growling in the vicinity this morning. Mind you, it wasn't as rare as a Bentley, making the exact model trickier to pinpoint by ear alone. But if Tony had to lay bets?

Porsche 9-11, hands down.

Prairie Rose / *Rosa Arkansana*

New growth.

———◀◯▶———

CHARLIE

CHARLIE TWISTED her pen in time with the reception area music, retracting the silver tip from its grenadilla barrel on beat. Rowan gave her this pen, the day she signed the papers establishing her not-for-profit foundation. She was so nervous this morning, she'd forgotten it, until the cup full of red ones by the bank's entrance reminded her. On the sprint home, she passed right by Martha Lavery's place.

Every spring for over a decade, dear Martha placed two crisp hundreds on the counter and left with sixteen special order Sarah Bernhardt peonies, eager as a baby goat to spend her summer staring at a wide stretch of dirt. Her vision for the space? A fragrant mess of blooms in full view of the kitchen, where the playscape should have been. But time and again, the plants refused to take. Charlie stopped by once to confirm the conditions—ideal sun exposure, richly tended soil, no scales of disease. No explanation. Just a pile of barren leaves shrugging spindly apologies in the breeze.

Charlie, too, was deliberate about her planting location—*elsewhere*. Fourteen shoeboxes full of pebbles, snow globes, broken shells, scraps of colored yarn. Every priceless token pressed into her palm by small, smiling fingers testified to her rootedness in a bounty of places, all of them far more oxygenated than a spider's glass cage. Translating charitable donations into on-the-ground realities let Charlie help people who wanted her help. Sowing pieces of herself across the globe was a privilege, one that fertilized her soul and flooded it with color. But what if, after all this time, it was still really all about the fact she could never help Sam?

Like the peonies, Charlie also refused to winter. The mosaic joy of watching her brainchild grow was supposed to be enough. Wrapping her arms around children in every time zone like a needy aunt was supposed to cancel out the loss of the one she never met.

From the bank's window, it was impossible to miss the shop's new front display; bright chroma splayed across concrete, each plant working together to achieve a desired visual effect, not one of them actually attached to anything.

Touching down here in peak season, her next flight out already booked, afforded Charlie a life that skipped straight to the good parts. Sunshine year-round, nothing tying her down. What did it matter if Sam was one frost away from turning into driftwood, or two barstools down from his next marriage? She wasn't sticking around, anyway.

Some lies root so deep, they start to bloom true.

Martha eventually threw in the towel, then came streaking in years later waving a single peony bloom. Blush in color, flecked with white, a vibrant swirl like raspberry coulis. Charlie had never sold, never *seen* one like it. Martha found the bud growing on the opposite side of the house, alone. Sam confirmed peonies could, rarely in this wintry zone, thrive from seed, and when they did, the cultivar was entirely unique. Nothing like the mother plant.

"So much for blooming where you're planted," Charlie said.

"That's a load of man-made bullshit, Spider. Plants bloom wherever they damn well want. Anybody who actually believes we're in charge is an idiot."

The bespoke peonies cropped up like quahogs at high tide, forming a spectacular sweep along the length of the Lavery house—on the one side that couldn't be viewed from anywhere in it.

In the end, Martha cut in a new window.

Charlie scrawled her name beside each sticky flag in the stack of loan papers, initialling every corner. For twenty-seven years, she'd kept to the shallow dirt, expecting fulfilment to flourish. Touching countless lives, never claiming her own. Like it or not, her peonies had taken root in *this* city. On *this* block. Right across the street, in a steady stream of stressed-out hostesses and shell-shocked new dads, rueful husbands with faulty calendar reminders, cemetery-visiting widows. Sooner would have been better, but it wasn't too late to go all in. Claim something permanent for herself.

Outside the bank, a warm gust lapped her shoulders. Charlie tipped her cheeks to the sky and smiled. Finally, she'd cut herself a window.

Bark of Barks Tree / *Cinchona*

Used as a fever breaker.

◄○►

WILL

L YING TO THE POLICE about his whereabouts was easier than expected. He sank into his chair, wriggled his tie loose and knuckled crust from the corner of his eye. It didn't hurt that the officer was cute, a blond, pale sheet of freckles. Young, too, probably still a rookie. Nothing to do but be himself.

Will was in the clear, and now he had to stay there, which he would, because he hadn't *done* anything. But if he admitted to being anywhere near that corner this morning, after that fight with Tessa last night, he'd be declared a suspect. Surely she didn't want that.

Will's fingers drummed the desktop as he waited for his inbox to chime. In nearly eight years, he and Tessa never truly fought. She flipped her lid when Will ended up on the wrong side of a case or if he pointed out the merits of scrapping bike lanes on Bayview, but her temper, quick to rear in flashes of heat and hands, was no more than a small kitchen fire with him. Will's adoring expression always contained it, and his arms around her porcelain waist were enough to snuff it out entirely.

But last night's blaze was a candle tipped into the spilled Merlot, out of control before he'd even realized it was happening. Rage snaked along the hardwood, crawled up the heavy drapes and licked the coffered ceiling black, the smoke so thick and wobbly they could no longer find each other.

Then, an hour ago, the frantic text from Ainsley knocked him sideways like an air-filled punching clown. Tessa had been taken to the hospital, and no one was sure what happened. When the witch at the hospital admitting desk refused to give out her room number (Tessa had been very clear: no visitors, no exceptions) and his calls went unanswered, he pulled some of Peter's strings to get a copy of the police report. Which his father would have received twenty minutes ago.

Sweat prickled as the document hit his inbox. *About fucking time.* Will scanned the pages, unblinking. He gasped relief at finding Tessa's statement coherent, but panic encroached nonetheless. She'd been involved in altercation with *Bradley Thornton,* of all people, recording it in the chain-link font of a police report. Without even talking to him first.

The facts were muddy at best, the blowback zone extending in untold directions. Will set about clicking and tapping, gaze vacant, running on full autopilot now. *Mitigate damages, restrict liability.* He vaguely recalled racing past that ugly car this morning, crooked at the curb of the Blue Iris. He didn't dream of stopping, or even slowing down. Whatever Thornton had gotten up to at that hour, no Westlake could be seen near. Given what Will *thought* he knew about Tessa's whereabouts in that moment, it never occurred to him she could be involved.

He checked his phone again. Dialed Tessa again. Voicemail, *again.* He whipped the phone across the room. How could she be ignoring him even now? Will yanked open his desk drawer and shook out a handful of chocolate mints. What, exactly, did Tessa want him to do, call up that blond cop, admit he drove to the Blue Iris this morning, moments after his fiancée threw his ring in his face and stormed from the building? Better yet, was he to call up good old Bradley, admit he saw his Bentley parked right where she was found injured only moments later?

Every legal mind in this province would agree that even if Will placed him at the scene, Tessa's allegations that Thornton was driving drunk, that he'd knocked her unconscious, would survive about as long as a worm caught out after the rain. Even if there was solid proof, which there wasn't, Thornton would make it disappear, like Teddy's drug charges had, and then, he'd make Will disappear. If pressed, Bradley would ruin Will's future, Peter's campaign, and the entire Westlake legacy before he was finished playing nine holes. Somehow, Will would make the asshole pay for what he did, but he was going to need his professional reputation intact and his father in the mayor's chair to do so.

Will rose to close the door, swishing water around his mouth to rinse away the chocolate. He picked up a photo on his shelf, tracing Tessa's cheek with his thumb until her colors puddled together. Imagining her scared and in pain was shoving his soul through a meat grinder. He wanted to go flip that hospital upside down until he got to her. He wanted to kiss every cut and bruise and never let anyone hurt her again.

But then, maybe it was just as well she was shutting him out. He wasn't sure he could look her in the eye just yet.

This whole mess never should have happened. Tessa, lightning rod to every lurking particle capable of carrying a charge, wandering the streets alone at four in the morning? And by her own statement, *she* got violent with Bradley first. Did she stop to consider what it might mean for Will? His family? Her own future? That shithole market was contaminating her judgment like an infected mosquito.

And how freely their nicotine dialect had spouted from her pristine mouth when she left last night. *"FIX IT, Will. And stay the fuck away from me until you do."* Stupidly, Will assumed Tessa meant the news article, the muddled engagement. Wounded and furious as he was, it went without saying that of course he would fix it! He only went to the shop to say how sorry he was, that he'd make everything right somehow.

On pulling up to the Blue Iris and finding no sign of her, it dawned on him what she really wanted him to fix. Not their relationship, bleeding at her feet. Not the ticking clock on their future home, her family's welfare. *Still,* all she could think about was that filthy fucking garden store.

Will had run title searches on Rowan Miller weeks ago; he knew where to look next. Sure enough, there was her car, in the third driveway along the back of the block. *Luke.* A thousand horses reared under his ribs, rocking him onto his edges.

He waited. The need to catch her coming out of that flophouse, to watch her clamor to explain why she'd run straight to that lowlife, after flat-out denying there was anything between them, was insatiable. But four-thirty came and went, and the compulsively punctual Tessa never emerged.

Will's thoughts turned radioactive; Tessa wasn't going to work after all. She'd be spending the whole day in there, wrapped in those *big rig* arms, writhing breathless in his bed. Had she ever even *been* to the terminal?

It was enough to make his teeth chatter, how love so pure could spawn such blinding hate.

Will set down the photo, smearing his cheeks dry. Last night, Tessa accused him of using her "fear of skydiving" as an excuse to hijack the plane, whatever that meant. The point was, she'd forgotten *it was his plane.* Plucked from a basement party at seventeen, never knowing differently, had she ever fully grasped what he brought to the table?

She wanted space? He'd give it to her. Once it sank in how much she took for granted, how dark and lonely the world was without Will Westlake, Tessa Lewis would fall on her knees and beg him to make her his wife.

Crown Vetch / *Securigera Varia*

"I surrender."

◄○►

TESSA

NANO WORRIEDLY added another casserole to the stack in Tessa's fridge. Tessa, discharged from the hospital yesterday, looked longingly at the untouched food from the couch. Her cheek was a purple football, jagged nylon stitches tight across the wreckage. Her eye was a mottled slit in an eggplant pouch. Worst, the shattered bone along her temple—the *zygomatic*—made chewing feel like her skull was being pried with a crowbar.

"He's not going down for this, you watch," Pop was saying, eyes trained on the news channel. "Cameras every ten feet my arse. Protecting who, that's what I'd like to know."

Tessa had briefly considered not even filing the police report. She'd helped Will prep enough cases to know her half-recollection would barely hold up against a random stranger, much less the attorney general. If anything, she risked facing charges herself after admitting she went at him like a rabid wolf, scalded him with coffee. *Bit* him.

The last thing Tessa remembered before waking in the laneway, her temple chewed to the bone and ambulance lights bouncing off Newspaper Norm and Darryl's horrified faces, was that pompous Rolex coming straight at her.

Will would have figured out how to access the report. Would he concoct a way to hold Thornton accountable?

"He'll never let him get away with it," Nano said, reading Tessa's mind.

Pop ranted on. "Crows don't fly with robins, you know. That Peter Wetflake knows exactly who he's in bed with, or he can't tell shit from Shinola."

Tessa squeezed her grandmother's hand. "You two go home, get some rest." The pain meds were hitting again, affixing tiny weights to Tessa's eyelids. "Sorry again I didn't tell you about the proposal. I just . . . I couldn't take him up on it yet. Not until I found my *big*."

Pop turned to look at her. "Your big what?"

"You used to tell everyone I'd be something *big*, remember? And I will. I'll make all your sacrifices worthwhile." Her eyes drifted closed. "But what if Will's *big* is as big as mine is ever going to get?"

Pop's voice drew near, the skin of his hand rough over hers. "You listen to me. You go anywhere—*anywhere*—you're already the biggest thing there. Just like your mother." His voice broke. "She was so goddamn *big*, it scared the shit out of me." He cleared his throat. "I never wanted you thinking you had to pull that back, like she did. And you weren't *sacrifice,* you were pure joy. If you decide to run a self-automated car wash, because you *want* to, not because your mother dying left you without choices, then I did my job."

Tessa smiled, tears slipping from her closed eyelids, pulling at her sutures.

Pop kissed her forehead. "Holding out on a guy like Will? Calling

303

out that sonofabitch Thornton?" He chuckled. "You're even *bigger* than I thought."

Tessa pumped her fist weakly, chin wobbling. "Yay, me. I let him drive away."

"Never mind." Her grandfather's voice moved closer. "You're going to wear that scar like a goddamn Star of Courage, you hear me? You're going to look at it every single day and remember that you don't make yourself smaller for anybody."

Tessa was hard asleep when the phone buzzed. She frowned, her groggy brain fumbling to understand. It was the shop's number, but Ainsley's voice in her ear.

"He's on his way!"

"What? Who?"

"Luke!"

Tessa shot up, then hissed in pain and sank slowly back into bed. "You're joking."

"Tony said he just left."

"I thought you told them no visitors!"

"I *did!*"

"Put him on."

Tony's voice was soft, like he was waking a sleeping baby. "Hey, Tee, how you feeling?"

"WHY-DIDN'T-YOU-STOP-HIM?"

Tony sighed. "He took all the Sterlings. Two full pails. Pulled them straight off the truck and bolted in the middle of Friday rush. *Selects,* Tee. Told Rowan to take them off his pay."

Shit.

Tessa's pulse quickened, setting the side of her head throbbing anew.

She'd forcibly kept herself from *oooh*-ing like a tween at a Bieber concert whenever Sterling roses came off the truck, even after buying them at auction herself. The silver-purple petals curled as they opened, like they'd been moulded by hand from baker's fondant. Tessa was enraptured, even before discovering they had no thorns. Running an ungloved hand along the slippery stems, after fistfuls of prickly foliage all day, had bordered on seductive.

Select was the highest grade, probably twenty-four-inch stems or longer. Two pails would hold around twenty dozen or more. Even at cost, it was . . .

"Maybe it's that girl from the bar," Tessa said.

Tony scoffed.

She exhaled slowly. "He doesn't even know where I live!"

Tessa *really* wished Luke hadn't taken them. Electric French carnations, maybe. Even painted double lisianthus would have left some interpretive wiggle room. But two hundred and forty long-stemmed Sterling roses had only one statement to make.

"Listen, Tee, I need to get back. Charlie had an appointment, Ainsley's helping me cover inside. Get better soon, okay? We all miss you."

Tessa heard the clap of heavy floral wrap being torn off the roller as he hung up, the tinny squeal of the tape dispenser. The *shhh-thunk* of the cash drawer. The intensity with which she missed all of it swirled in her throat, tugging at her sutures. She tilted her head against the headboard, trying to ease the throbbing. Her heart wasn't ready to acknowledge the Luke situation as real. She needed all thoughts of him to remain confined to her *head,* abstract and pliable, until she'd had time to properly sort through them.

Luke's pickup grumbled down the driveway. She flung her phone onto the mattress, cringing at her ratty pajamas until she remembered with fresh horror the crash scene that was her face. He took the steps two at a time, a traveling wall of forearms and floral wrap.

Shit, shit, shit!

Tessa tucked behind the door. Jumped when he rapped against it.

"Come on, Tess. I know Ainsley tipped you off."

Tessa peered through the sidelight. Already, she could smell the flowers.

"Fine, don't let me in. I'll just keep working on my tan."

She pressed her palm against the door. "Luke, I—"

"I know. You don't want visitors. But here's the thing . . . I don't believe you."

Tessa's mouth closed. These past three summer days were tundra without Charlie's meme-worthy cracks, no hushed rounds of What-did-Darryl-eat-for-breakfast-using-clues-on-his-shirt with Rowan, the only uncle she'd ever known. No spelling contests across the aisles with Luke, Tony shouting random car names from behind the fence. Without these routines, Tessa was unmoored, and while it was true she didn't want Luke seeing *her*, she found she very much wanted to see him.

"Tony can't cover all day," Luke called.

She lay a hand gingerly to her face and stayed silent.

Luke tried again. "I've seen you covered in sheep shit, remember?"

"It's a lot worse than sheep shit."

"My arms are about to fall off."

Eyes downcast, she swung the door open, waiting for Luke to flinch or suck in his breath, somehow affirm the spectacle. Instead, he tilted his head sideways, craning around the mass of blooms towards the floor until he captured her gaze. With their eyes in lopsided embrace, Tessa broke into laughter, prompting Luke's firework smile. Relief flooded the furrows in his forehead.

She glanced at the roses. "Leave any for the customers?"

"Actually, since we seem to be short-staffed, we've decided to start sending the customers here. Think these will get you through the five-thirty rush?"

She waved him in. "You're hilarious."

"H-I-L-A-R-I-O-U-S. What else you got, Spellcheck?"

"Seriously, Luke. They're beautiful. But I can't—"

Luke set the flowers on the counter, his expression turning pained. "Just hear me out, okay?"

He wandered to the window, taking in the cards, bouquets and plush bears holding little mylar balloons. He lingered over the dozen red roses, suffocating in baby's breath, necks already folded. Love, Will on the enclosure card in cold, block type. "I started opening up, like any other day. I thought it was one of Darryl's fucked-up pranks until I saw—" Luke's every muscle tensed, like his own words were trying to shove him through the glass. "It knocked the wind out of me. For real. Every time I picture—"

"I'm sure it was a shock for everyone."

"Yeah, and they're all torn up, but they're still going about their *day,* you know?" He stared outside. "Meanwhile, I keep coming around that fence expecting that look you get when the customer changes her mind for the hundredth time. I catch myself standing there like a tool, listening for the off-key pop solo that tells me which aisle you're in."

"Hey. I nailed that Black Eyed Peas one."

Luke smiled, but the pain in it made her eyes burn. He nodded at the Sterlings. "When I saw these on the truck, it was like every last one of them already belonged to you. Like it would be wrong for anybody else to have them." He stepped towards her. "Tessa, I—"

She looked at him, silently begging. *Please. Stop.* Every word, every inch closed between them, made pretending more impossible.

Luke stopped short, caught on her invisible string. Sighing, he pulled a hand through his mop of curls. "I'll take them back. I just needed you to know it's not business as usual without you. Not for anyone, but especially not for me."

At hearing they hadn't reverted to however things were before she showed up, that there was a hole on that windswept corner only she could fill, Tessa had to press her feet into the floor to keep from rushing him.

"Tess, this whole thing made me realize—"

"Luke—"

"That place was everything for me. And I don't know how to be there without you anymore."

They looked at each other. Again, Luke appeared both agonized by, and oblivious to, the carnage on her face.

Tessa walked to the counter. Wordlessly, she tore the paper from the roses, fluffing apart the stems, fanning them with practiced precision. With a jerk of her chin, she directed him to join her. They worked in silence, her movements swift and deliberate as she modeled how to slice the ends on an angle, swirling the preservative into tepid water.

There was no vase big enough, in the apartment or anywhere. They filled every glass, pitcher and mason jar in her cupboard. Still, more roses remained. They floated blooms in mixing bowls. Baking pans. The crispers from her fridge. When they'd finished, lavender blossoms hovered on every surface high and low. It was like sinking into a giant, scented bubble bath. Tessa's words popped the silence, melting Luke into laughter.

"I'm *so* glad we didn't let things get weird."

Baby's Breath / *Gypsophila Paniculata*

"Breathe."

---<◇>---

ELEANOR

"**H**AVE THEY set a date yet?"

"Would I know? He's still ducking my calls!"

Someone at the front of the studio shushed them. The instructor cajoled them to return to their stupid breath.

The nugget about Tessa's coworker was meant to widen the fracture between Will and Tessa, not accelerate their *engagement!* Peter insisted it was just a campaign strategy, but it sure seemed to Eleanor like a convenient antidote for Will's unholy jealous streak.

"That's boys for you," said Moira, who never missed an opportunity to point out how superior an experience it was parenting a daughter. "My Portia checks in every day."

The instructor glared. Eleanor yanked her mat from the floor, letting it flounce like a cape as she stalked through the sweaty patch of downward dogs and out the door, Moira clamoring to collect their sandals. *Screw hot yoga.* Eleanor's nerves were whistling louder than all the teakettles in England; she needed to let off real steam.

Tony would have been her first text. A gorgeously uncomplicated creature, his pleasure drive unrelenting. He never demanded anything more than a premium lay on a summer morning. But the risk was too high now, with the campaign, and Eleanor accepted that—though Peter would surely continue managing *his* risks perfectly well. For her family, she was what Teddy called "ride or die." But with Will already shutting her out, presumably over the planted Tessa-Luke rumor, she could do without him learning the truth about how she came to learn of Tessa's birthmark in the first place.

No, it wouldn't come to that. Eleanor was almost completely sure Tony wasn't the type to make trouble.

Then again, she never pegged him as a reader of newspapers.

Sweet Chestnut / *Castanea*

"Do me justice."

LUKE

THE GLASS DOOR looked heavier than it was, flinging open with a clang as Luke stumbled into the whitewashed entry, work boots thunking against the travertine. If law firm receptionists had silent alarm buttons, this one was definitely pressing hers.

"Do you have an appointment?"

"Just tell him it's Luke."

Luke waited, pulse trekking uphill. He'd crossed a line with the roses. He understood this even before taking them, then wrapped them up anyway. Like it was reflex, not volition.

Luke had no clue how he came to know Sterlings were her favorite, or when he started scanning the back of the cube truck for their lightning storm hue, angling to be the one who offloaded them so she'd brighten at the sight of him. Other boggling revelations of the day:

Tessa looked like a welterweight nine rounds into a heavyweight bout, and somehow, she was more beautiful than before.

Luke had spent two hours in another man's couch dent and left her apartment with zero self-reproach.

The only weirdness between them, even now, was how *not* weird it still was.

Luke was led through a padded ecru maze. An unseen army of keyboards *tickety-tickety-ticked.* Outside the corner office, he swallowed hard. *Nothing happened.* He'd simply been to check on a friend. Talked to her, got her to laugh; *fuck,* he missed that laugh.

Except, by the time he left her rose-scented apartment, the place was so hotboxed with intimacy anyone would have guessed they'd been naked.

The receptionist swung the door open, then took off as a waft of takeout leftovers and stale breath smacked Luke in the face. He found himself dialing back much of the hostility he'd preloaded on the drive down. Will, the airy Adonis he'd squared off with at the shop, had shriveled to scruff, his bloodshot gaze lost behind his own desk. Suit like Sunday morning bedsheets.

Westlake, too, tried glowering, but gave up halfway. "What do you want?"

"I, uh—" *I heard you two aren't speaking, so why not unfold this here triangle we've been ignoring into a straight line, with myself as the midpoint?* "We want to help."

Will spat a laugh. "Haven't you done enough?"

And there was that tone again. The one that made Luke's fists ball up. "Excuse me?"

"You just kept leaning on her. Longer days, earlier hours. Starting her shifts in the dark!"

"Save the mindfuck for someone else, Westlake, it was her day off. She was trying to fix a mess *you* created, and she went early to get away

312

from *you*. The only part that's unclear is why you haven't made that piece of shit Thornton pay for what he did yet."

"What do you think I'm sleeping at my desk trying to do?"

Now they were getting somewhere. If whatshisname was to get a jump on the necessary lawyering or whatever, he needed full information. And if Tessa wasn't feeding it to him, *someone* had to. "There's no question it was Thornton," Luke offered. "They were the only two there."

"It doesn't matter."

"My buddy heard the Bentley. He's willing to testify or whatever."

"Really? Well, that makes all the difference."

Luke wanted to pull him from behind that desk and smack the sarcasm off him. "It's . . . you haven't—" *You haven't seen her face.* He leaned down, bringing his eyes level with Will's. "She's practically got the word ROLEX stamped into her head."

Will averted his face, then sank forward, pressing his palms to his eyes. "It doesn't matter!"

Luke squinted. "What do you mean, it doesn't *matter?*"

Will continued speaking through his hands. "There's no case."

Luke's voice was a needle hovering at threat level red. "Then *make one.* I'm pretty sure I'm standing in a fucking law firm with your name on it."

Will stood. "You think any prosecutor in Ontario is taking on the *attorney general* based on . . . what? Ainsley Murphy's flavor of the month *heard* a Bentley? Where was neighborhood watch when Tessa pulled in his own driveway a half-hour too early?"

"A CRV doesn't exactly break the sound barrier, even a lawyer should understand that."

Will pinched the bridge of his nose. "It's Tessa's word against Thornton's. End of story."

"And Thornton was shitfaced, and Tessa remembers everything, right up until he *knocked her out,* then *left her lying there.* I still don't see the problem."

Will huffed, his tone impatient but the words slow, like he was explaining brain surgery to preschoolers. "First off, there's no breathalyzer on Thornton. Second, Tessa's what you call an unreliable witness. She has a head injury! She's already on record admitting to memory gaps!"

"You don't believe her?"

"Thornton's team will ensure *no one* believes her. It was dark, no lights or cameras, thanks to your idiot boss. She'd been awake more than twenty-four hours. She was exhausted, hadn't eaten. On top of that, she was highly distressed because—" he turned, stared out the window.

"Because she was fighting with you," Luke finished. "Because life stopped going your way for five minutes, and you lost your shit." He yanked open the door. "Never mind, I understand now. Thornton's not the only one who needs this to go away."

Luke was nearly gone when Will's words stopped him in his tracks.

"Watch it, asshole."

Luke turned, his silence daring Will to say more.

"You. You're a fucking *blip*. Do you hear me? *I'm the love of her life*. If I thought there was any chance, I'd go after Bradley with everything I have. But I refuse to drag her through the mud for nothing!"

Luke had no reason to doubt him, much less Tessa, who'd spent years entwining her future with his. But up close, the guy was off. "So…that's it? She's supposed to carry on like it never happened?"

"You have no idea how this plays out!" He paced the length of his desk, hands flinging. "People of the jury, what *was* Ms. Lewis doing alone in the street at that hour without her phone? Who was she *really* meeting, and why did that meeting go so terribly south? Given her mother's tragic death, which we'll now examine in lengthy, unnecessarily graphic detail, was a psychotic break inevitable the whole time?"

Luke swallowed.

"Or, they'll round up a hundred high-profile witnesses who saw Thornton flirting with her at the gala. Turn her into a disgruntled mistress, or a gold-digger squeezing a payoff. Tess *already admitted to starting it.*

They'll paint her as a violent, scheming liar with no conscience. Believe me, there's no limit to how low these people will go!"

Luke turned in the doorway. "Oh, I believe you. Listen to yourself. You're one of them." He stormed from the building, hands shaking as he fired a text to let Tony know he'd be longer still.

The second Luke learned Tessa had been injured, his lungs crumpled in on themselves like an empty baby food pouch. For three days, he'd stumbled around airless, trying to mind his business. Kept his distance. Until not seeing her smiling face tucked under its ball cap, her ears globbed with sunblock—until not doing *something*—wasn't survivable another second. Whatever this was, it wasn't a blip.

And Luke was done pushing it down.

After what happened to Tess in his own backyard, Luke was done with rules and lanes and coloring between the lines. Most of all, he was done giving two shits about William Fucking Westlake.

Mr. Prettyboy couldn't nail Thornton with a sledgehammer; whatever the guy had in means, he was sorely lacking in balls. Luke threw the truck in reverse, then pointed it towards the one person he knew who had plenty of both.

Wisteria / *Wisteria Sinensis*

"Welcome fair stranger."

———◀◯▶———

TESSA

L UKE MAY as well have announced there was a giant sinkhole under her porch.

"You want me to go out *there?*" Tessa asked.

"Tess. It's time."

Tessa flopped back on her couch; no way she was going anyplace. The last of the Sterlings, brown along the edges, scowled in agreement.

Outside that door waited a world where people like Thornton drove drunk and smacked people unconscious. One where people would congratulate her on being engaged to a man she no longer recognized.

Ten days had passed in this rose-scented bubble, sutures and prescription labels exempting her from the realities piling at her doorstep like online purchases she couldn't afford. As her wine-colored bruises faded, a fresh dread reared; summer was nearly over, and she still had no idea why her mother wanted all that bittersweet. Worse, she was more confused than in the spring about Will's proposal, her career plan, even her future address.

Luke called from the open doorway, grease blackening his fingers and one stubbled cheek, August glory beckoning behind him. "How many days like this are left before we're shoveling snow?" His grin tugged at her like a kite on a string.

There was also that.

An hour ago, Tessa had watched him roll to a stop halfway down the driveway, where Pop stood cursing at the lawnmower. Her heart hammered so hard it all but cracked a rib.

Her grandfather had seen the riot of roses, and surely, Luke's truck in the days that followed, sprawled on the diagonal across a fading set of ruts the width of Porsche tires. Nano, too. They didn't ask, and Tessa couldn't bring herself to explain. What could she say? That whenever her head met the pillow now, Luke—the rousing smell of him, that smile that felt exclusively her own—was waiting right there behind her eyelids?

She thought constantly of that morning in Charlie's dark hallway. How close she'd come to feeling his roughed-up hands over her, his perfectly unkempt hair through her fingers. Ever since, they'd gone to near-laughable lengths to avoid physical touch, but with Luke's every flimsy excuse to visit—the outstanding pay Rowan could have e-transferred, the forgotten tube of sunblock—they waded deeper into territory far more dangerous than sex.

Only her mother's photograph witnessed Tessa's SWAT-like movements as she monitored Luke and Pop's encounter in flash-glimpses through the window. Moments later, they moved to the workshop on the level below her. Metal clanged. Tessa heard the *zzz-zzzz* of power tools, then Pop declaring the mower in better shape than the day he bought it. Bellowing laughter. The *sssss-thwack* of beer cans opening, then—she groaned—the familiar strains of Pop's heyday stories.

These past days on her couch beside Luke, at the heart of all these lavender roses, should have felt illicit. Like a morally bankrupt betrayal. Instead, it was a bucket-list trip to someplace where even the signposts carried the thrill of discovery, with Will as the pang of homesickness throughout. Tessa never wanted it to end, nor could she handle it lasting any longer.

She pulled her eyes from Luke and looked back at her phone. On the home screen, Will grinned inside his fleece-lined hood, her lips and the cold tip of her nose pressed into his ruddy cheek, the Rideau canal a jubilant slur of ice skaters behind them. It was her favorite photo of them, taken a few hours before Will stood barefoot in their Ottawa hotel room, hair dryer in hand, heating his socks to pull over her frostbitten toes. She'd been psyching herself up to call him when Luke knocked. She didn't know what to say, or whether Will would even pick up, but she had to try. For the man holding that hotel hair dryer.

If only Tessa had said goodbye to the drunken attorney general, then run to the cube and called the police. Kept her emotions in check for once. What exactly was she waiting on Will to do next, when she couldn't recall Thornton hitting her, only his arm lifting then a searing white light? Derail his father's campaign, and his own career, for an unwinnable fight? Backtrack on his efforts to force the sale of the Blue Iris, when the shop was on the brink of collapse regardless?

A cardinal's song floated on the breeze. Luke waited, golden arms folded, the day bright with possibility. He was a friend. They'd done nothing wrong. Would it be so awful to be out in public, with a friend, doing nothing wrong?

She stood with a sigh. "Where are we going?"

"Wherever you want, I'm free all day. But first, the shop."

"Hah. No chance."

Luke jingled her keys, and she remembered. He'd brought her car back from the Lodge, where it had been parked since that awful morning.

Tessa groaned. "I'll drop you, but that's it."

Luke shook his head. "Tessa Lewis, there is a mandatory staff meeting in half an hour. Rowan's orders."

Tessa's expression said she knew as well as he did that Rowan didn't give orders.

"No, seriously. We have to be there."

She made a face. "It's the middle of shift, and I don't work there anymore." With so few days left in the season, Tessa told Rowan not to bother putting her back on the schedule. She couldn't bring herself to walk past that laneway, and besides, she was too ashamed of her unwitting role in helping Will make trouble for the shop.

"Don't be an idiot. He specifically told me to bring you."

Tessa chewed at her lip. She really believed Will would have fixed it by now, found some loophole to stop the shutdown of Trucks. For her. "Then it's bad news. It must be, right?"

Luke lifted his hands, exasperated. "Go get dressed, and we'll find out."

Tessa would face the music in person, find out whether Will had accelerated the shop's demise or harnessed his power to save it—as a step towards saving them. *Then,* she would call him.

Luke eyed her thoughtfully from the passenger seat as she drove. "You doing okay, Princess?"

Behind her ballcap and largest pair of sunglasses, she flicked her eyes at him. "Do I look okay, jackass?"

"Would you stop? It's barely noticeable. And besides, scars are sexy."

Tessa swiped him on the arm.

His deep laugh filled the car. "What? It's a thing. Seriously, look it up."

"Whatever."

"It's still you, Tess. Not to downplay it, but all that scar does is tell the world you're cute *and* a badass."

Tessa flushed at the cute part. "You called me Lewis."

"Huh?"

"Back there, at my door. You called me Tessa Lewis."

"That's your name, right?"

For all the intimate conversations they'd shared, the hours spent side by side every day, their last names had never come up. "How did you know?"

"That newspaper article, I guess."

"Oh," she said. "Because I realized I don't know yours. How weird is that?"

Luke nodded. "When I found out what happened with Thornton, I wanted to text but I didn't have you in my phone."

"I guess it didn't matter before." They always knew they'd see each other the next day, at work.

Luke stared out the window. "It's Dunn."

Tessa frowned. "What's done?"

"My name. It's Luke Dunn."

She breathed a smile, extending her hand. Puzzled, Luke took it and they shook.

"Nice to finally meet you, Luke Dunn."

Phlox / *Phlox*

Unanimity.

———◀◎▶———

ROWAN

H E'D CONSIDERED waiting until after closing to tell them, but his fingernails were frayed stumps. He needed it over.

Rowan felt the sting of tears as he watched Luke prod a paler, slightly gaunt Tessa up the sidewalk. From the first day she'd wandered in for a bouquet, well before declaring herself the honorary niece he never knew he wanted, the girl unlocked a kindred place in Rowan's heart. He'd never forgive himself for what happened to her here. But, he could ensure nothing like it happened on his property again.

For fifty years, a seven-dollar padlock and some flimsy snow fencing had proved enough to secure inventory in this neighborhood. But hadn't he told Tessa only weeks ago to cut through the yard on buying days, because the idea of her alone in the street at that hour made him uneasy? It was the sort of instinct his father would have followed through on.

They were mobbing her now. Charlie, Tony, Flash. Even Darryl was pile-driving affection. Tessa extracted herself and charged towards Rowan. In a mix of surrender and protest, his hands flew up like stop signs. She blew through them, sniffling apologies into his shoulder. Blaming herself for the shop's demise.

Rowan shushed her. He folded his arms over her like she might break. "None of this is your fault. It was happening, anyway."

Tessa pulled back. The room squinted at him.

"I . . . there's—" Rowan had been trying on phrasing all morning, but none fit. Everyone's questioning eyes pierced like blow darts, seizing his muscle groups one at a time. "The thing is, I . . . we need to—" His jaw locked up.

"Jeezus fuck," Darryl said, "spit it out!"

Rowan lifted the fold of papers like a flashcard. Tessa plucked them with the care of a bomb-handler and read silently, face scrunched.

Her voice broke, and she was sobbing into his chest again. "I'm so sorry. I really thought he would fix it."

Darryl snatched up the papers. Ran his hand over his face and down the back of his neck, his eyes wet cement. "You're really doing it. You're selling off my mother's legacy. Her *house?*"

"I bought as much time as I could!" Rowan said. "We won't get a better deal!"

Darryl was behind the counter in one step, sending the air in the shop atwirl. Luke and Tony mobilized. Tessa leaped protectively in front of Rowan.

"They're giving us five more years," Rowan pleaded. "You'll get a condo in the new development, free and clear. Charlie and the guys, too!"

"You money-grubbing sellout son-of-a-*BITCH!*"

A stadium yell tore from Charlie, rattling the windows. *"Enough!"*

Everyone froze.

"We get it, Darryl," she said, "your parents opened a flower shop. A lovely one. And they worked very hard. But *Simon* turned it into an asset. Took away their mortgage, made them boatloads of cash. *Rowan* stepped up, kept that vision going all these years." She waved her hand wildly. "You think you and your alcoholic brother would have pulled all this off by yourselves?"

Rowan focused on the ragged fray around his nails as Charlie pressed on. "You ever stop to think of the overhead? The taxes, utilities, insurance? Your rent that hasn't increased in *thirty years?* The solid business decisions he lets you override *because* of your mother? How about a little respect? How about *thank you, Rowan?*"

Charlie crossed the floor to stand beside Rowan. "He doesn't owe you shit, Brick."

Darryl stared, jaw quivering. Finally, he walked out of the store, pausing only to smash his palm against the door frame.

Charlie turned to Rowan. "I should have said all that years ago. You made it look easy, just like Simon. But I should have asked more questions." She picked up the offer, signed and ready to send to EnvidaCorp, and tore it in half. "Nobody's taking you for granted anymore."

Rowan shook his head helplessly. "We'll never get a better deal than that."

Charlie waved away the paper bits. "Forget it. I want in."

He looked at her, confused.

"I went to the bank. I've got preapproval for a mortgage, and a loan."

"Okay."

"Sell me the house. And an equal stake in the shop."

It pained Rowan to look at his friend. In a few minutes, when he printed off a fresh copy of that offer, there would be no house to buy. No business to invest in. Without permission from the city to use the back half of the property for business, Trucks had to close by tomorrow.

The Blue Iris would live out its final five years in its humble, small-scale beginnings, before giving way to condo towers.

Charlie's determined gaze sent goosebumps down his arms. "We can do this, Rowan. Whatever it takes, I'm with you."

He couldn't say the words. He simply shook his head. *It's too late.*

Tony chimed in. "I could buy the Lodge." All heads swiveled towards him. He shrugged. "I started cutting lawns when I was nine. Probably have more saved than half the fake-ass posers who shop here."

Charlie darted around the counter, grabbing him by the shoulders. "Enough for a down payment?" She began throwing numbers at him, based on the market assessment of her own place.

Tony nodded. "Like my dad says, if you're busy making money, you're not spending it."

Rowan blinked. His thoughts *zizzed* like fingertips on a calculator. Would it be enough to get back in the black? If so, how long could he stay there with a crumbling storefront and no Trucks?

Darryl filled the doorway again, two red milk crates stacked in his arms. Tessa, looking on in rueful silence, peeked inside the crates and gasped.

"Holy shit." Luke waved Darryl inside, locking the door behind him.

Darryl stacked the boxes next to the pail of alstroemeria at Rowan's feet, each one filled with tidy bundles of cash. He looked at Rowan. "Dad's never money. Thought you could renovate the place or something."

Rowan reeled. Blobs of light floated through his field of vision. "But Trucks . . . the fines."

"We could start a petition," Tessa said. "I'm sure the local residents would prefer a beautifully renovated flower market over condo towers. The landscapers and their crews would definitely be on board. Peter would push the variance through if enough votes depended on it."

Charlie lifted her eyebrows, offering Rowan her hand. "Partners?"

Rowan took it, grinning. The dingy room exhaled. Only one cloud remained—that reptile Thornton walking the streets, Tessa's scars unanswered. But that, too, would come to a head. Tessa had, against all reason, seen the beauty in this tangled heap and fought for it. Now, with the same solvency it had shown the rest of them, the Blue Iris would do the same for her. It always did.

Darryl swallowed Rowan's clammy hand in his. The others closed in around them, hollering. Rowan lifted his eyes to Darryl's. "There's going to be changes. Lots of them."

Darryl shrugged. "Could probably use a few."

Charged with enthusiasm, the group set about brainstorming. All agreed the counter and basic inside layout should be preserved. The building itself would be structurally updated, expanded, and extensively redecorated. Powder-coated aluminum shelving would replace the rusted setup, with formal space carved out for Tessa's redesigned front display. Cameras, security lights and a powered gate system would go along the entire perimeter.

For the rest of the afternoon, customers were treated to free flowers and slices of the cake that had somehow materialized in the staff room. Charlie and Tony placed calls to the bank. Rowan instructed Bobby to draw up the paperwork, then informed his crew that effective tomorrow, a stop-credit would be issued on all overdue accounts, with penalty interest accumulating until the balance was paid. Going forward, legitimate wholesale clients had thirty days to settle up. All other customers had to, quite simply, *pay for their stuff.*

Darryl offered to help enforce the new protocol, but it all seemed so reasonable now. Rowan said to send anyone with a problem directly to him. The Blue Iris was his family, and it was home. All the more reason he had to start treating it like a business.

Customers poured merrily in. Inexplicably, cheap plastic leis and party hats with elastic strings were now being passed around along with the cake. Everyone was pulling them over each other's heads, giggling and crowding into selfies when the icy shatter of glass meeting concrete brought the festivities to a halt. Rowan gasped.

Charlie.

She stood paralyzed behind the counter, jaw a heavy noose. Hands still clutching the nineteen-dollar hourglass vase that was no longer there. Rowan tracked her gaze through the crowd to where a figure stooped near the door, plucking a honeycomb of her favorite dahlias from their pail.

The room plunged underwater in a myopic slur. Rowan took in the customer's hair, the silhouette that rounded at the shoulders, as if carrying an invisible backpack full of rocks. The stranger straightened, his twilight eyes clear as a church bell and fixed—impossibly—on Charlie, the bouquet a Hail Mary at his chest. Rowan could no longer breathe.

It was Sam.

King Protea (Honeypot) / *Protea Cynaroides*

Earth's oldest flower.

———◄○►———

LUKE

THEY STOOD THERE, every leaf and bloom trembling. Sam stepped forward, Charlie backwards. More silence. Next, it was Charlie plunging ahead, dodging limbs and flowering buckets until only a sheet of air hung between them. No one breathed as she pressed a chlorophyll-stained finger to Sam's cheek.

He was real.

Then, she slapped him so hard, Luke felt the breeze of it. Shoved him with a wrangled cry. Volumes passed in the silence, until Charlie took off. Sam followed her. Down the sidewalk, out of sight.

After awhile, everyone quietly dispersed. Tessa practically skipped alongside Luke all the way back to the Lodge like a child on Christmas

Eve, full of questions he had no answers for. *"But how is it possible? Where did he stay? Why didn't he call?"*

Luke walked in stunned silence. *Sam was back.* They would laugh and joke and smoke again. Charlie's heart and conscience would mend. The shop would be whole. It was a miracle, and Luke was grateful beyond words, yet his own predicament weighed heavier by the minute.

Tessa must have felt it, because as they reached the Lodge she stopped talking and turned to him in the driveway, blue eyes full of worry. Luke nearly reached for her. But after staff night, he vowed never to lay another finger on her again. It would be too much.

"Luke," she said as he wriggled under her gaze.

It hurt to look at her.

It hurt not to look at her.

With a weary sigh, he drew her into him. What did it matter anymore? He'd be gone soon enough.

A lock of her hair fell into the crook of his arm. Her cheek found the dip in his sternum. "What are we doing?" she whispered to his heartbeat.

He drew in her scent. Exhaled it into the crown of her head. "I wish I knew."

"I can't stand it anymore. I've never been so confused."

Luke couldn't take much more, either. He needed it to end, for her sake as much as his. "Tess, listen. I'm leaving." She pulled her head back, looking up at him. "The co-op credit I missed? Because of Sam? I'm doing it over the winter."

"But . . . how?"

"Frank knows a crew in San Diego. A spot opened up, and I took it."

Her expression was unreadable. "When do you leave?"

Luke swallowed. "Training starts Monday."

Labor Day. Three days away.

He had to take the job. He'd worked too hard to come this far. He couldn't put everything on pause, upend his life again, set himself back further. This way, he could start taking his own landscape clients in the spring as planned, no matter what.

No matter *who*.

Tessa looked at the ground, emotions billowing.

"Hey," Luke cradled her jaw with both hands. "It's only a few months. And I'm not *going* anywhere. We'll still be us, Princess Pain-in-the-Ass and her Super Hot Best Guy Friend."

She pretend scowled.

"Super Hot Jackass and his Royal Pain-in-the-Ass?"

A smile broke through, but she still wouldn't look at him.

"For real, Tess. No matter what happens, you've got me. I've *got* you. Okay?"

Luke meant it. His heart would limp battered and bruised across that airport finish line, knowing Tessa and Westlake might very well rebuild bigger and stronger while he was gone. She could be married by the time he got back. But their friendship was everything, and he'd have her back, always. He just couldn't be anybody's blip ever again.

Then, somehow, they were kissing. More accurately, it was Tessa kissing him, though his lips more than accommodated as she drank from him like a flask that wouldn't flow quick enough.

Reason rocketed swiftly downstream, and Luke started thinking that given the circumstances, maybe he was fine being a blip after all. He let his arms fall tightly around her, pulling her in.

Just then, Tessa emitted a sound into his mouth. An anguished sort of hiccup. With violent force, she stepped back, one hand clapping over her wet lips as her eyes, still on him, snapped wide in a mix of shock and horror. His chest sank, because she looked like she'd been stabbed.

And then, she was gone.

Jacob's Ladder / *Polemonium Caerulium*

Rupture.

◄◦►

TESSA

H EADLIGHTS.

Had her subconscious withheld this memory on purpose, waiting for full-blown flames in the cockpit before triggering her ejector seat?

The penthouse elevator slid open, and the first thing she saw was Will's face, like he'd been standing there ever since that black morning she left.

A shaving nick by his Adam's apple looked freshly clotted. His eyes jumped to the puckered grape line along her temple. He touched it lightly, like she was a bubble he was afraid of popping. "Does it still—"

"*Shhh.*" Tessa pressed her lips to his, her thoughts a hot heap— their fight; Thornton; Will's jarring show of force against the shop; the newspaper article; his proposal-turned-ultimatum, set to expire in three days.

Before they began unpacking any of it, she needed to let herself feel, just for a moment, how deeply she loved this man in front of her. How intensely she still wanted him, despite everything. Will pulled back, affirming the lust in her eyes, then pressed her to the wall in a hard gush and kissed her again. For a brief moment, Tessa had the whole mess in hand. They would figure all this out. Everything would be fine. Until Will's mouth, the lips she knew more intimately than her own, proved jarringly naked. Devoid of dark stubble.

She stopped cold. Her insides carved themselves down the middle like the thin spine between yin and yang, each half containing a glaring dollop of the other. These past few days, whenever her thoughts found Luke, there was also Will. Now, she was sure, there could never again be Will without Luke right there between them.

Tessa had long struggled with indecision, but there was no choice here. Will was a favorite movie, watched for the hundredth time. Luke was a symphony, exploding in deaf ears. She needed both. Somehow, whatever it took, she would have *both*.

Her gaze ran wild over Will. She pushed her hands into his hair, one flip-flop slapping to the floor as she pulled her legs up, around him, his hand fumbling below as he shoved aside her running shorts. The shorts she'd thrown on in haste mere hours ago, while Luke waited on the other side of the door.

One thrust was all it took to send her conscience spurting everywhere. Tessa fled across the room with a muffled cry. Will stared after her, his pants around his ankles.

He was her happily ever after; she had never wanted more.

Luke was her friend; they never meant for it to catch fire.

"Thornton didn't hit me," Tessa blurted.

Will didn't answer, just joined her at the window. They stared over downtown. "I've been out of my mind," he said. "Wondering if you were okay. If you were ever coming back to me."

"Someone else was there. I remember now. There were headlights, and I stumbled off the curb."

"I should have been there. By your side, through every second of this."

Tessa wandered aimlessly. "I looked straight into them. That's why I couldn't see—"

Behind her, Will's tone pinged off the vaulted ceiling. "You shouldn't have been out there alone at that hour, *period!*"

Her head snapped back. "It was *my fault?*"

"I didn't mean—" He stepped closer. "What made you think it was a good idea to take a run at the attorney general in a dark alley?"

Tessa held up one hand to stop him moving any closer. How smug of her, expecting all along Will would choose her. Thornton couldn't go after Tessa for assaulting him without implicating himself as an impaired driver who fled the scene, the same way Will couldn't press him without risking the brassy alliance his family needed. With these people, it always came down to the win. "You're protecting him," she breathed, "over me."

"You *attacked* him. Just once, you couldn't stop to think before flying off the handle? Or were you purposely trying to ruin me?"

"He was DRUNK, Will! I was supposed to let him drive away? For your father's stupid election?"

"You realize this dead guy Sam you rave about had *three* DUIs, right?" Will started pacing. "You'd have me turn my back on all of it . . . family, career. Our future." His face twisted. "For a *flower market?*" He looked at her. "You want to talk choices? Look me in the face and tell me you didn't leave here and run straight to him."

Tessa hurled a ragged breath at the ceiling. *"Why* are you so bent on punishing me for something I haven't even *done* yet?" The last word scurried out before she could stomp it.

Will's eyes were green baseballs. *"Yet?"*

Tessa studied the carpet pattern, gnawing her lip. His gaze revved around her like a chainsaw.

"Just say it. You're dying to sleep with him."

"*What?* No!" But as fiercely as she denied it, she knew in another life, another world, the answer would be different.

Will stopped circling. "What, then? Are you in love with him or something?"

Tessa stayed silent. The plush rug began to swim.

"*ANSWER ME!*"

"I don't *KNOW,* okay?"

Will sank into the couch, staring numbly at her knees until the shards in his mouth dissolved, his next words trickling. "Do you still love me?"

Tessa sank to the floor in front of him, absently rubbing her arms and thighs, a full-body shiver mounting, the warning kind that typically reared before she threw up. She ignored it. "More than I could ever love anyone."

Will let out a shaky gust. "Then we can still fix it."

Tessa glanced around, as if he had some magic wand lying around. "How?"

Will slid from the leather, half-crawling to her. "Whatever it takes. I'll make it happen, you know I will. Tell me what I'm missing, Tess. Just tell me what you need and it's yours."

"It's not some sort of checklist, Will."

But Winning Westlake was already off, doing what he did best. "We start over. Right now. Clean slate, for both of us. I take back the ring, make the paper run a retraction. And obviously I'll call the bank, cancel the instructions for Monday. The offer on the house stands indefinitely."

"Will."

"I'll move to the coach house. We've got people commuting from Cambridge, for God's sake. I can make it work. Guaranteed."

"Will, that's—"

"And I swear to God, Tessa, Thornton won't get away with it. I just need your patience on that part, okay? We have to play the long game there, wait until after the election. Let dad make the right inroads with cabinet and then, when the timing is right—"

Tessa hugged herself. The cold shakes were overpowering her, injecting a stagger into her words. She shoved the feeling aside, determined to press on. "It's always going to be like this, isn't it? Strategizing. Power plays. The almighty Westlake agenda."

Will shook his head helplessly. "I'm still figuring it all out. But I *will* figure it out. It won't be this way forever, I promise."

"You can't make that promise."

"I just did!"

"You *can't*. It's way bigger than you, and you know it."

He clasped her hand between his like rosary beads. "It's not bigger than us." His voice caught. "Tessa, please. I need you. *I need you.* Please, I'll do anything."

Tessa looked at him—really looked, for the first time in weeks. Sadness struck her bones. He was sunken, faded. A castle with no keep. She pencilled the finer details into memory, eyes pressing like carbon copy over his hand-painted pores. The delicate line of his brow. The supple curve of his Adam's apple. Finally, her cross-hatching complete and safely stowed, she spoke. "I'm not good for you."

Will sighed. "That's Eleanor talking. But all that's going to be different now, too, because if she can't see you're more than good enough—"

"That's not what I meant." Tessa, her insides in full spasm, considered whether it wasn't what Eleanor meant, either. Maybe Will's mother had seen all along that being with Tessa, needing Tessa in order to feel himself, was reshaping her son into something else. Something less. "I'm *no good* for you. As in, I don't know . . . unhealthy."

Will's face blanked. "You're the best part of my life. I told you—I'll fix it."

"You can't spend your life fixing what you've already done!" She touched his cheek. "And I can't spend mine trying to keep you from breaking. We each have to be enough on our own."

Alarm crept into Will's features. "We are. I know it. I've known it since the second I saw you. I'm in love with you, Tessa Lewis. With us. I always will be."

By now, even Tessa's fingertips were quaking. It was physically rupturing her, this sudden and violent clarity, the way a seed coat cracks and splits in the soil, dying as its center finds light. She pulled her hand away. "No. You're in love with an idea, a picture you landed on at seventeen years old. That girl doesn't exist, Will. Not anymore."

Will clutched her shoulders. "She does! You're right here!"

Tessa stood, lifting her shirt to expose the jewel in her navel. "Staff night."

Will forced his brow flat. "It's nice. I like it."

He hated it. Next, she tossed a pack of cigarettes on the table. "All summer."

This time, he made no effort to disguise the horror. "How is that possible?"

"I lied."

He heaved a sigh. "Fine. Now I know. These aren't big things, Tessa."

"No, they're not. And still, I didn't tell you." She blinked, remembering how their conversations once flowed completely unfiltered. "And you didn't notice, because you've been not-telling me things, too."

Will looked like she'd pressed a gun to his forehead, and he was deciding whether it was loaded. Tessa knew then what her gut hinted at weeks ago, about Muskoka. And strangely, that was enough; she didn't want to *know*. She hadn't told him everything, either.

She drew close, tilting her forehead to his. Above her, his face drowned to a pale slur of tears. Uselessly, she tried blinking him back into view. "The idea of hurting you—" Her jaw steeled against the heaving in her chest, her throat. Her stomach roiled. "I can't—"

"Then don't," he rasped, breath minty on her cupid's bow. His tears came tumbling, splattering hot onto her cheeks. "You just finished saying you still love me."

Tessa pressed her lips to his, their grief mixing salty on her tongue. He was right; she still loved him. Way too much to walk away.

Then, just as suddenly as when her mouth was on Luke's, it happened again. Every synapse fired at once, unseen memories rushing like floodlights over a football field.

No . . . Tessa scuttled backwards, toppling a side table. The lamp smashed to the floor. *No-no-no-no-no-no . . .* The tremors erupted into heaves, her body desperate to evacuate the realization.

Then again, hadn't her subconscious known the whole time? Kept the truth circling someplace overhead like a plane waiting for a runway?

"There's not a luxury car in this neighborhood I can't pick out of a lineup blindfolded."

How many times had Tony said it? Yet, when Ainsley relayed Tony's pillow confession to her days ago, that he'd heard not only a Bentley that morning, but a Porsche 9-11, Tessa dismissed it straightaway. The idea of Will anywhere near that corner, that he saw or heard anything at all and drove away? Left her lying there? It was absurd!

Instead, she had simply un-remembered that conversation. Locked the coach house door, sank deeper into couch-oblivion with Luke. Strung up silvery roses to ward off the truth. But now, Will's guilt was sucking the air from this room. Physically choking her.

"I didn't know," he said. He inched towards her and she screamed, loud and curdling. "Tessa, you have to believe me. *I didn't know.* It was so dark. I was driving too fast. I didn't see you, or Bradley. I didn't see anything!"

The penthouse swirled. The headlights glowed in Tessa's memory, their oval shape horrifyingly familiar. Her temple throbbed where, she was now sure, the cold metal tip of the Porsche's rear passenger side had clipped it ten days ago as she'd stumbled off the curb. The same car Will had pulled off the highway and under the trees after Drew and Daniella's wedding, their hands ravenous, the tossing bouquet squished flat as they reclined the seatback. Afterwards, the car was stuck, its tires sunken in the boggy ground. Will got out, pushed the vehicle and, on his signal, Tessa gunned the engine, underestimating its pull. Mud everywhere. Tessa, laughing hysterically, kissed his soiled face, then tore his suit off all over again.

Right now, down in the parking garage, Tessa knew she'd find no dent or scratch on that car, no miniscule bit of hair or skin or blood. Nothing to suggest anything but a misguided hunch. Still, she couldn't believe him.

There was simply no guessing what he was capable of anymore.

"Tess." His footsteps shuffled close behind her. "*Tessa,* please. I had *no clue* you were out there! If I'd had any idea, I would've . . . but I didn't—"

By the time the elevator doors slid closed, there were no more words, only anguished noises that would keep Tessa up at night.

Peruvian Lily / *Alstroemeria*

Abundance.

◄━━◄○►━━►

TESSA

WHATEVER SHE was expecting when Luke opened the door, his expression fell dramatically short. "Tess, hey." He glanced past her into the street. "What are you . . .?"

Tessa had been driving for hours, with no idea where she'd been. She recalled only broken lines and bright smudges beyond the open windows, the late summer air wicking her tears, until the car rolled to a stop in front of the Lodge.

Her smile was sheepish and starchy against her cheeks as she slipped past Luke inside; it was late. He had work tomorrow. But she was desperate to lean against the solid oak of him on the screened porch, let the tide of blossoms lull the dust whirls inside her before they swelled into a raging cyclone. Tessa kicked off her flip flops, plodding into the kitchen. "We're definitely going to need that—"

Jameson. Tessa was about to say, *we're definitely going to need that Jameson,* when the words fell away like space junk. Sitting at the kitchen table, turning a butter yellow tracksuit into bedroom couture, her strawberry locks shining like Eve's apple, was Olivia Thornton. Tessa recalled the gunmetal Mercedes she'd nearly sideswiped by the curb when she pulled in, and humiliation squashed her like an anvil.

Olivia's head cocked in pity. "Tessa, hi. Listen, Luke told me everything. I just want—"

Tessa stopped listening at *"Luke told me everything."* She met his eyes. *Of course you did. People tell things to the people they're fucking.*

Luke shook his head. *Slow down, Princess.*

Mumbling an excuse, she made for the door. This was the karmic bitch-slap Tessa had coming to her after stringing Luke along, relegating Will's diamond to her panty drawer, waffling between two men and offering promises to neither.

Luke caught up to her in the hallway. "Tess, wait up. Olivia's—"

Tessa gave a jerky laugh, waving over her shoulder. "You don't owe me an explanation." Even though an explanation was exactly what she wanted. Had he been screwing Olivia the whole time, and flat-out lying to her about it? Was he trying to even the score?

Or maybe, Tessa really *was* his friend. Someone he flirted with to pass time at work, nothing more. Which would have been fine, except kissing him had pried something free, poured it into the open like a new can of paint, turning *years* with Will into . . . an approximation. A splattered attempt to hammer the lid back on.

She yanked the door open. "I have to go."

Rowan, on the other side of the door, practically fell on top of her. "You're . . . here?" He lifted his eyebrows at Luke. "You finally told her."

Tessa shuffled past. "Oh, I'm all up to speed."

"Wait, you're leaving?" Rowan frowned. *"Now?"*

Tessa let the screen door rest against her hip, considerably less willing to storm off in front of her boss.

Luke tried again. "Tess, hold up, would you? You don't understand."

"No, I think I do."

"You *don't*."

The door swung away again as Tony bounced into the crowded entry. Like Rowan's, his eyes flicked to Luke's, his smile wary at finding Tessa. "Hey, Tee. Are you coming or going?"

"*Going.* If I could make it to the damn car."

"Dude, I still say tell her," Tony said to Luke.

"I'm trying!"

Tessa turned with an impatient sigh. "What is it?"

Tony checked his phone. "Hurry, bro. She's five minutes out."

Tessa threw up her hands, annoyed to still be standing there. "*Who?*"

All three men looked at each other.

"Eleanor," Tony said. "Eleanor Westlake."

Rowan had prepared an envelope with Eleanor's name on it, which contained Olivia's sworn affidavit attesting to Bradley's drunken, agitated state when he arrived home around the same time Tessa was carted to hospital. The document was accompanied by security camera images of Bradley in a wainscoted room, a towel around his waist and an angry welt down his back, along with a pair of scarlet parentheses on his right trapezius.

Coffee burns and a bite mark.

"Nanny-cam footage," Olivia explained, "not that we have a nanny, or kids. Just an attractive housekeeper."

Tessa looked at Luke, stunned. He lifted one shoulder. "The guy's a fortress," he said. "The only way at him was from the inside."

"It might not be enough to arrest him," Rowan said, "but it backs up your story big time."

Olivia turned to Tessa, full of apology. "Somewhere along the line, it became easier to just look the other way, you know? He's everywhere, controlling everything. But when Luke showed me that pic . . ." For a second, Olivia looked like she might be sick. "It was right there, all the stuff I've been looking away from the whole time." She cleared her throat. "I'll help any way I can."

Tessa looked back at Luke. Reluctantly, he pulled up the photo Olivia had referenced on his phone: Tessa, asleep, her freshly-stitched orbital wound screaming. A collective draw of air sliced through the kitchen, Tessa's included. Already, the memory of it had started to fade.

"Your Pop," Luke explained, a grin creeping in. "He said, *I keep my own goddamn medical records. You know they like to bury—*"

"Their mistakes," Tessa finished. Pop meant doctors, but wasn't anyone capable of digging a grave, when the shuffling of dirt took place in slow, spaced increments, each one presenting as the last? She looked at Olivia, worried. "What happens when Bradley finds out?"

Olivia smiled sadly. "I'm filing for divorce in the morning. If anybody can get me out of this marriage quickly and painlessly, it's Peter Westlake."

That explained why Eleanor was on her way. Olivia was going to appeal for Peter's help, one beautiful, suffocated housewife to another. Tessa frowned. "Eleanor wants that election more than Peter. They need Bradley in their corner."

Tony glanced at Luke, who nodded. Tony handed Tessa his phone. "Then we'll have to convince her."

The text thread was a thousand lightning rods at once. Breasts that defied gravity, a signature blond shade falling around them. Bare thighs spread over familiar quartz like hot casseroles on Boxing Day. Dialogue that could have been from a porn movie transcript, set into throbbing word-bubbles. Hogg's Hollow Tina was *Eleanor.*

Tessa's stomach heaved again. "Seriously, Tony? *Eleanor?*"

"Tessa." Will's mother stood in the doorway, looking her age for once, her eyes round with fear.

Tessa scooped up the paperwork along with Luke's phone, still open to the gruesome photo of her face. "Thank you," she told the group. "All of you. I'll never forget it. But I've got this from here."

Every light in the Lodge was on. The old bottle of Jameson sat empty on the counter.

"If we don't hear from her by mid-week, I say we go to the media with all of it," Tony said.

"They'll kill the story," Rowan said. "But I could post it at the shop, get the landscapers talking at every jobsite. All their friends and neighbors would hear. Everyone in Westlake's voting district would still *know.*"

"It won't come to that," Tessa said. "Eleanor's smart, and relentless. She'll pull this off."

It proved less enjoyable than expected, watching Will's mother all but sink to her knees outside the Lodge, knowing Tessa had all she needed to destroy Eleanor's reputation where it mattered most—inside her own house. Tessa couldn't do it; Will had a mother who loved him, and right now, he needed her more than ever.

"Or," Luke said, "they'll come at us harder than before."

Rowan shrugged. "Everything we have is true. We're only asking Peter to uphold the oath he took before the bar. They can't come after us for libel, or even extortion."

Olivia looked surprised. "You're a lawyer, too?"

Rowan tucked his chin. "I came close once."

Olivia's lips pulled together like a pink waxflower bloom. "Came to your senses just in time, then."

Rowan's complexion ripened.

Her boss rendered immobile, Tessa saw Olivia to the door. "Are you sure you'll be okay?"

Olivia wafted a reassuring hand. "He's in Vegas until tomorrow. I'm already checked into the Sutton under a fake name, and Rowan's offered to store my stuff in his garage until I find a place. The only thing I'll miss about that big, drafty house is the backyard."

Tessa smiled. "I'm sure Luke will gladly design your new one."

"You know something? I think I want to tackle it myself."

The women hugged. "Thank you, Olivia. I mean it."

"It's Luke you should thank. He never stopped fighting for you, none of them did. No matter what it might end up costing them. You have great friends, Tessa."

Tessa smiled towards the kitchen. "I'd say they're your friends, now, too."

Olivia winked, the woman she was before Bradley already coming unburied like daffodil shoots. "Lucky us."

With Olivia gone, Rowan came off pause. "I'd better hit the road, too."

Tessa squeezed him until the still-tender side of her face ballooned. "How can I ever thank you enough, Uncle Row?"

"*Pffft*, that's easy. Come work for me full-time."

Tessa laughed, though his face stayed serious. "But, Sam's back?"

"Something tells me he'll be taking it slow for a while."

"Not to mention," Luke said, "a spot just opened up in Trucks."

Rowan looked at him. "You've decided, then?"

Luke nodded.

Rowan's hand disappeared in his. "The corner won't be the same, but I'm *so* proud of you. Don't be a stranger, okay?"

Luke's glance flicked ever so briefly to Tessa. "Like you could keep me away."

Across the hall, Ainsley beckoned Tessa into Tony's bedroom. She closed the door and pulled Tessa to her fiercely. "I'm sorry Will didn't step up."

Tessa's tears welled anew. "Me, too."

"I wanted *so bad* for Tony to be wrong."

"Me, too."

Ainsley wriggled from her jeans and jewelry, pulling Tony's faded Raptors tee over her head. It was a backwards homecoming, her friend happily coupled off, Tessa flailing unattached.

"You want to hang awhile just us?" Ainsley asked. "Talk about it?"

Tessa shook her head. Ainsley, aware by now of Tony's leverage against Eleanor, had endured more than enough Westlake talk for tonight. Besides, Tessa was still furiously outrunning the train; she couldn't stop to examine it yet. "We'll catch up later."

Ainsley leaned in. "You sure?" she said, studying Tessa's expression.

Tony opened the door to find them by his bed, Ainsley in her underwear, her hands cupping Tessa's face. He tipped his face upward in a show of heavenly praise. "Oh, *hell* yes. I am SO down!" He yanked feverishly at his work boots. "Sam's going to die for real when he hears about this!" Ainsley lobbed a pair of socks at him.

Tessa left them play-wrestling, pulling the door closed behind her as she stepped into hallway and felt her stomach dip.

With that, it was down to her and Luke.

Catchfly / *Viscaria Oculata*

"Dance with me?"

CHARLIE

SEPTEMBER CREPT in hot and cloudless and summer-brilliant overnight. Sunshine blasted past the open curtains, seizing Charlie with panic. She tunneled under the covers, her fingers closing over Sam's arm, his bare chest, the achingly familiar curve of his ear.

"You're really here," she managed, her vocal cords still raw.

She'd spent most of yesterday screaming. Then, the wee hours of today using no words as Charlie grew reacquainted with the man she'd loved more than half her life. The man who made her curse the gardenia-scented morning they met, and ugly-laugh herself breathless. And also, an entirely new man. One who called time to check in with his sponsor and pray beside her bed. A man with rules and hard limits, which seemed, ironically, to unchain him; no booze, no drugs, not even a lotto ticket. Not ever.

Charlie would be stupid if not skeptical, but they had to at least try, didn't they? Clearly, the only way out was through. Groggily, he pulled her to him. As always, he smelled like fireflies and woodsmoke. She settled against his chest and let her eyes fall closed again, permitting her thoughts to drift two doors away to the Lodge. "I hope it's all going according to plan over there."

Sam opened one eye. The skin around it had creases now, a few new spots, but the same schoolyard mischief teemed. He peered down at her. "Would that be their plan, or yours?"

Charlie pinched his nipple between her teeth until he howled. "I have no idea what you're talking about."

Sam chuckled. "Okay, Spider. But trust fund or not, my money's on Lukey-boy."

Charlie frowned. "What if he's not back to fighting weight?"

"You still think it's too soon?"

All summer, Charlie had watched flirty banter evolve into easy contentment as the hot sun and high pressure melded Luke and Tessa into left and right hands of one being. But Luke had been so low, *so scary low,* for so long. This must be how it felt watching your kid zip around one of those sadistic skate parks, determined to break himself in two.

Watching Luke try to process the news that Tessa had been taken to hospital was like replaying the moment Darryl told her Sam was gone. Everything inside him clawed to the surface, trying to get to her, and then it hit him; he couldn't. The shop pulled its own in so fast and close, it never occurred to anybody to swap numbers or handles.

Charlie stood behind the counter wringing her hands for an hour afterwards. *Oh, fuck it.* She wrapped a brick of floral foam in banana leaves and fit it into a glass square the perfect width for a nightstand. She stuffed in sweet pea blossoms delicate as duckling fluff, anemones you had to touch to prove they weren't paper, lily of the valley like faeries in chapel. Because two things could be true at once.

Because Charlie of all people knew too well the sorts of spells a little loose earth could shake free.

She waited, pen in hand, as Rowan went through his personnel file, scribbling Tessa's address on a corner of newspaper when he recited it to the courier. Then, she marched to the laneway and slipped her sweet, surrogate boy the permission he so obviously needed.

What business was it of Charlie's to decide when Luke was ready? Were any of us ever truly *ready*, anyway? Seeing him crushed again would be unbearable, but not nearly as much as watching him spend the next thirty years wondering.

Sam looked at her, still waiting for an answer. She swirled her fingers through his chest hair and sighed. "I think, if there's peonies, there's peonies."

He laughed, easing back on top of her. His purple-blue eyes held a clear view for miles, and it stole Charlie's breath away. He lowered his mouth to hers. "Good old Martha Lavery . . ."

Mountain Ash / *Sorbus Americana*

"With me you are safe."

———◀◉▶———

TESSA

T ESSA PULLED herself to sitting, head like wet paper mâché, and squinted into the day. The screened porch was empty.

Out here last night, he was a flaring orange dot in the dark. The air was body temperature, undetectable against her skin. Luke offered a drag, but she didn't want it, nor the Jameson anymore. Her thoughts were speeding like a race car; she needed to feel every rumble and shudder to keep from flipping over completely.

He stubbed out the cigarette. "I've smoked more this summer than in my whole life."

"Me too. You really stress me out, Dunn."

His laugh rolled like thunder.

"Any word from the others?"

Luke shook his head. Sam's arrest warrant for disappearing while on probation was still active; no one was sure what happened next. "Darryl was over here wearing tracks in the floor before you came, then decided to barge in on them. Guess he's still there."

"You're being so *chill*. Aren't you dying to find out what's happening?"

Even in the dark, his expression was unmistakeable. "I know how to wait my turn."

"So. Olivia Thornton . . . you were making big moves. How come you didn't say anything?"

"I wasn't sure she'd come through, or if Tony could really get Eleanor on board. Then I thought, maybe you'd rather not know. In case you end up . . ." He sighed. "I didn't want to let you down."

She looked at him, doubtful he'd ever let anyone down. "You know, when I first saw Olivia here I thought—"

"I know what you thought."

"You did all that. For me, her. For anyone Thornton might hurt next time he's driving around drunk." She sank quietly into the couch.

"Anytime, Princess. Hope I didn't overstep."

They stared into the shadowed yard. Then she said it aloud for the first time.

"Will and I are done."

Luke shifted almost imperceptibly beside her. "Are you . . . okay?"

The heaving started up again as it all washed back over her. Tessa squeezed her lips together, determined to weep undetected. Trying to shove it down only made her gasp louder. Luke sat next to her. She buried herself in him, her body a convulsion of grief and betrayal. "He really believes it was all for me," she croaked. "He thinks he can still turn it around."

Again, Luke seemed to weigh every syllable. "Can he?"

"If you knew him before . . ." Tessa shook her head, wiping her nose on her sleeve. "Even now, I still love him. I'll never *not* love him." Her face crumpled. "He was right, it was too much. I never should've pushed him.

But now, I'll never know for sure. I'll never really trust him!"

Luke had both arms around her now, his stubble brushing against her scalp. She held tight, waiting for the crashing to slow. Next thing she knew, her cheeks were dry under the blinding shaft of morning, a stash of pillows and a cotton blanket where his post-and-beam body had been.

Cauliflower / *Brassica Oleracea*

Water magic.

———◀◯▶———

TESSA

"ARE YOU TRYING to wear out my buttons or what?"

Tessa abandoned the controls, leaving the radio on "Desperado" by The Eagles and forcing her hands to her lap.

The Porsche's leather would have been glued to her thighs by now, but the truck's upholstery was soft. She'd have a twinge of carsickness, too, from the push-pull of the twin-turbo, but Luke's Dodge had comparatively little to prove. How long before Tessa stopped sorting every data point into *Will* and *After Will?* Would she ever reach for her phone without the fleeting expectation of his seeing his name, *I love you* or *thanks again for last night* with heart-eyes lighting up the screen?

Luke's arm rested on the wheel, thick veins like highways on a map. Beyond him, cornfields streaked past in a continuous wall. He sent a spine-trickling smile her way. "My sisters and I used to hate when the corn got this tall. It meant summer was over."

"If my family owned a cabin on a lake, I'd never want summer to end, either."

Luke looked offended. "It's not a *lake*. It's Georgian Bay."

"Sor-*ry*. What's the difference?"

A smirk played at his eyes. "You'll see."

An hour ago, Tessa had ambled inside the Lodge and found him dressed for work, ball cap backwards, sunglasses at the ready. But there was a cooler by the door, and his shorts looked suspiciously like swim trunks. "Wheels up in ten, Lewis. You coming or what?"

Luke had switched shifts with Tony and was seeking a co-pilot in charge of playlists and snacks on a mini-road trip. But Tessa couldn't match his enthusiasm.

"I can't leave you moping all day by yourself," he said.

It seemed she *should* spend the day moping. Compulsively replaying yesterday's scene at the penthouse until it felt real. Then again, there would be plenty of time for that on Monday, when Luke was on a plane.

Now, in his truck, it seemed she'd forgotten how to have *hands*. She opened the small duffel at her feet, uselessly fumbling her swimsuit and towel. She reached in the backseat to confirm, again, that Nano's frozen strawberry rhubarb pie hadn't shifted. "How many people are going to be there, exactly?"

Luke shrugged. "Everyone, probably. The annual corn roast is kind of a big deal."

Her stomach fluttered. She wished he'd mentioned earlier it wouldn't be the two of them.

"Would you relax? It'll be fine."

The truck turned down a dirt driveway tunneled by cedars. A slew of kids ranging in age from pull-ups to training bras came charging. A chorus of "Uncle Luuuuke!" rang out, and he sank into a flurry of wrestles and hugs. In the distance, the woody earth dropped into a glittering panorama, vast and thrumming and virtually horizonless, water unrolling into sky like a runaway bolt of satin. No, Georgian Bay was not the sleepy tea-stained bog Tessa had been picturing at all.

"Mom said you weren't coming," the tallest girl said as Luke climbed to his feet and they executed a practiced greeting of knuckle slaps, fist-bumps and finger waggles.

"Didn't know I was until this morning, Cara-bear. Guess I get to see that no-handed cartwheel in person now, huh?"

The littlest child, late to the ruckus, unplugged a soother with a plush lamb sewn to the handle and pointed it at Luke. *"Lu-Lu."*

"Aww, hey Squeaker." Luke plucked the toddler from the ground and smothered her in loud, squishy kisses. Tessa watched as the child both delighted in, and squirmed from, the stubble on his face.

You and me both, kid.

A boy wearing knee-scrapes and Superman underwear eyed Tessa like moon rock. "Is she your girlfriend?"

Luke ruffled the boy's sun-streaked head, smiling. "No, Geoffy. This is—"

"Hey everybody! Uncle Luke has a girlfriend!" another boy sang. Two more erupted into kissing noises that quickly devolved into farting sounds.

"What's her name?"

"She's pretty."

"Are you going to marry her?"

"Is she staying for corn?"

"Ohmygod," a tween said through braces and sparkly lip gloss, *"so embarrassing!"*

A girl in light-up heels and Disney tulle curtseyed before Tessa. *"Bonjour."* She unfolded her hand. "I'm Georgia." Tessa bowed with a flourish. Georgia lit up.

Grown-ups flocked over in droves as Tessa surfed through clapping embraces and double-cheek kisses. She met Luke's dad, sister after sister—

five in total, all older than him—a slew of relatives and neighbors. Inside the vintage cabin, brunch was being plated with factory efficiency. Celery appliances flung open, toast stacked into Pyrex and scrambled eggs into chafing dishes. Across a long pine table, electric griddles sizzled with bacon, sausage and pancake batter.

The woman in charge handed off her spatula, tearing away her apron. "What a wonderful surprise!" She squeezed Luke, then Tessa. Her eyes were ringed in gold. "I'm Audrey, Luke's mom. And *you* must be Tessa."

Tessa threw Luke a surprised look. *You told your mom about me?*

Luke looked away, no longer fluent in telepathy.

The day was a hedonistic highlights tour—great food, cocktails poured from the blender, tunes and views on the ambling dock. Laughter skimmed the lazy swells. An impromptu Super Soaker shootout, instigated by the children and escalated by Luke, drove shy Tessa to abandon her cover-up and dive underwater for cover. A washer toss tournament afforded a leisurely view of Luke's rippling upper half. As the sun melted like a pat of butter, CorningWare filled the picnic tables and the air squeaked with the sound of corn being shucked. By dark, a tent village dotted the treeline and children reappeared with comb-lines in their hair, smelling of Ivory soap.

Tessa and Luke sat by the firelight, arms an agonized distance apart on the joint armrest. His pinky found the delicate bump at her wrist, grazing it up and down, the tiny shaft of friction shooting through her body like quicksilver. Georgia's head popped up between them, and Tessa pulled her arm away with a start.

The child waved a stick loaded with marshmallows. "Aww, for me?" Luke said, mouth widening. "Thanks, Peach!"

Georgia's face fell.

He laughed. "Kidding. You want extra toasty or medium toasty?"

Georgia, grinning now, replied in a posh accent. "Extra toasty, please."

"Right away, your ladyship."

Georgia settled into his chair to wait, auburn curls bouncing as her feet paddled. "Uncle Luke toasts them the best," she whispered. "*And,* he hides extra chocolate in the s'mores—don't tell my mom."

Tessa zipped her lips, then tossed a pretend key over her shoulder.

The little girl leaned in, her rich brown eyes thoughtful. "How can mommies be babies?"

Tessa shook her head, bewildered.

"Auntie Lynne said Uncle Luke never even brought the *baby-mommy* to the corn roast."

"Oh-wow."

Georgia shrugged. "I guess only grown-up mommies are allowed."

"That seems to make sense," Tessa offered.

Luke shifted his weight from foot to foot, imploring the flames to work faster.

"And *then,*" Georgia continued, "Auntie Lynne bet Auntie Marie a *hundred bucks* that you and Uncle Luke are going to—"

Luke blew frantically on the s'more, then gently corked Georgia's mouth with it. "Okay Peach, there you go. Hey, can you go find Auntie Lynne and tell her I'll fix her broken filter first thing tomorrow?"

Georgia skipped off, licking the side of her hand. Luke reclaimed his seat, wincing. "That one might be a little too quick."

Tessa laughed. "She's great. They're all great." She looked away, the urge to cry rearing again. She loved everything about this place, this day. Being with Luke. And already, it was ending. "I can't believe you're leaving in two days."

He looked her straight in the eyes. "I told you. I'll be in California a few months, but I'm not going anywhere."

On the way home, the city's skyglow shone like a flashlight under a bedsheet. It occurred to Tessa if she let things go no further, if she left this truck and drove straight to the penthouse, she and Will could probably get back to where they were. In her heart, she knew what happened in the street that night was an accident.

One he could have told her about eleven days ago.

Back at the Lodge, she and Luke loitered in the hall, awkward as a blind date. He glanced around the empty house. "They're probably at Ainsley's."

"Mm-hmm." Tessa had never seen him so nervous.

"Are you hungry? Who knows what's in the—"

"I'm okay, thanks." She tried pinning his gaze, but it kept darting away.

"A drink, maybe?"

"Luke. I'm good." Tessa bit her lip, drawing closer until the heat of him warmed her face. His scent hit on a primal level, and she ached to swim in it. She lay a hand on his chest, felt it heaving like a smart car over speedbumps.

He looked at her. "Suddenly you're all about skydiving?"

She shook her head. "Nope. Still as terrified as you."

He closed his eyes. "Last night, on the porch. You said you still, that you'd always—" He let out a shaky breath. "I can't be second choice, Tess."

How could she explain? Yesterday, in the Lodge driveway, moments before she understood the true source of her injury and life with Will cracked irreparably open, Luke's lips on hers were already the steady current of a gold-flecked waterslide, his arms the impossible blue of Endless Summer hydrangeas.

"I won't pretend he's not still in my heart, maybe forever. But I can promise to be completely honest with you. Always."

He slid a hand behind her ear, tracing her jaw with his thumb. "You've spent a long time being somebody's girl. Don't you want to go . . . be Tessa for a while?"

"Maybe. I might." She lifted her hand to her cheek, closing it over his. "Look, if not knowing the ending up front is a dealbreaker, I get it. I just didn't want to spend the next four months wondering what the beginning looked like."

His voice was hoarse. "I've wanted to kiss you for so long."

She smiled. "And?"

Confusion crossed his face.

Tessa giggled. "You kissed me yesterday, jackass."

"Not the way I would have. I thought we were kissing goodbye."

Tessa sank her fingers into his wavy hair, locking her eyes on his. "Kiss me hello, then."

Luke looked at her another second before his lips emptied into her with a steady pour. She swallowed him greedily, clutching at his face, his hair. Desire migrated south in a heavy swoop. Tessa felt herself sinking away, too consumed to bear her own weight. As her legs abandoned her, his calloused hands lifted her clean from the floor, a rough cry turning in his throat.

He had her to his bedroom in what felt like two strides, like she weighed no more than his clothes. Tessa took over, yanking wildly at his shirt, then her own, pressing her every surface fiercely to his as he fell backwards on the bed, grinning in surprised surrender. Her hair fell in a curtain, the spaces between them fusing into a knot of giggles and whispers as together, over and over again, they tumbled out of the plane.

White Violet / *Viola Albus*

"Take a chance on happy."

◄○►

SAM

H E PATTED the old mini fridge in apology for its new contents. Darryl meant well, but why call it *beer* at all? Alcohol-free booze was like Russian roulette with foam bullets, or fucking without penetration. It only fooled the onlookers.

Sam leaned back in his chair, surveying the rainbow-lit festivities. Offing himself had prompted widespread improvement around here—*in as little as eight months!* He was a bloody Hair Club for Men commercial.

Two days ago, the whole crew celebrating in the middle of the day, he'd nearly booked it all over again. Was he still so hopped up on his own bullshit to think Charlie would be sitting around waiting? That she hadn't found herself a nice dentist, maybe an accountant, someone without priors who came home to grill lean meat for dinner and swirl wine in one of those idiotically huge glasses? Sam had no business showing up now, killing off new growth like a rogue frost in June.

He turned to leave, then he heard his mother's voice, clear as the clink of a bottlecap. *Buck up, Sammy-Baby. Did you come this far to only come this far?* Then, his father's. *Quit being a little bitch.* If Charlie wanted to tear out his heart and piss on it, well, she'd earned her due. What he hadn't properly considered was how holes-in-his-chest-with-her-eyes *fuming* she'd be, like his disappearance was some deliberate, all-time dick move.

But then, they always were spectacularly good at assuming the worst in each other.

When Sam disappeared from her porch on New Year's, he *was* dead, and had every intention of staying that way. For her. Darryl, too. They'd turned saving him into a lifestyle, but it was no use. The Sam who dove headfirst into the kitchen that night Iris died was never coming back.

Maybe the coke had gone off the night he went to the cabin, or maybe he really was a little bitch. He'd dipped south towards Manitoulin by snowmobile countless times in the dark; he should have made it.

Clef, ex-military, was ice fishing in the frostbitten dawn when he spotted Sam sputtering a hundred yards off the tip of Drummond Island, just inside the Michigan border. Sam, long flipped-off by gods of every denomination, took in the whitewashed sheets of rock all around him, the icy guillotine edges sparkling along the surface, and found no earthly explanation for how he was still breathing. His resolve teetered.

He opened his bag and tossed Clef twenty grand in exchange for food and a place to hide while he worked up the nerve again, even though Clef's handshake said he'd have done it for free. For eleven weeks, Clef fed him vegetable soup and bottled water by the caseload, didn't leave so much as a sip of rum extract lying around. Sam screamed until his larynx emptied of sound and the hallucinatory carpet of spiders around his cot had dissolved into the floorboards. Then, he waited, but for what he wasn't sure. Scent-tracking dogs? A SWAT team to blow Clef's rough-hewn door off its hinges?

Turns out, a fortysomething not-so-recovered addict of no fixed address doesn't command much search-and-rescue.

Weeks passed. Months. Sam was clean for the longest stretch in memory, jogging six miles a day through the woods, fitter than he was in his twenties. His thoughts, never more than a tangled fishing line begging to be snipped, began to flow with unprecedented clarity.

What could his life be if he were to finally let it all . . . *be?* What if his young daughters overseas could still grow up knowing more of their father than the bitter slices fed by their mother? What if he could be the man Charlie once hoped for? But he'd be dead to them by now. Until he was absolutely sure, he had to stay that way. He wouldn't put them through it twice.

Back on the corner, Sam had done a double take; a flourishing parkette had sprung from the rot of tears and rust. The Darryl he'd left behind would have just as soon blown up the place. If only Sam and his brother talked years ago, instead of just the other night at Charlie's. To think Darryl blamed himself all this time, as if a different song that New Year's would've changed their parents' dance? No wonder the kid turned into such a powder keg.

Tonight, though, Brick was *laughing.* Charlie's glow under these trees was an aurora, calling him a fucking slob for the beer foam spouting down his shirt. It was magic, all of it. Rowan, who really packed a smile when he stopped chewing those nails, had claimed a chair instead of a bucket. Antonio Suave had a girl in his lap, which spelled actual relationship, *no-grenades-in-the-beer-garden* being Sam's number one rule. And Luke, his beautiful Lukey-boy, had finally dropped the vendetta against womankind.

Indeed, Sam's favorite apprentice was grinning electrically, no doubt thanks to Tessa, over there giving him enough fire-eye to melt a candle.

Any second, he'd be making some lame excuse to sneak her back to Sam's old room, and Charlie would be gloating for weeks.

As for the newbie with the smart mouth and tumbling hair, something wouldn't quit tugging. The way she talked? Her facial expressions? Like one of those snotty bits in the egg white, Sam couldn't grab hold of it. He took another phony swig and quit trying; after abusing his brain like a rented mule for decades, it was riddled with fugue patches.

Right on cue, Luke gave Tessa the nod, signaling they'd put in an acceptably long appearance at Sam's Not-Dead shindig. *And now, back to our regularly scheduled programming of screwing each other's brains out.* They stood to leave.

"Going so soon?" Sam teased.

"My flight leaves first thing," Luke said. "Tess is . . . helping me pack."

"You'd better hit the road then, son. Be sure to leave extra time getting to the airport." Sam grinned; twenty minutes ago, he'd slipped away and chalked everyone's tires with bruised apples from the cooler. He pulled Luke into a near headlock. "Leafs game after I'm out of the slammer, yeah?"

Sam had stolen twenty-four unbroken, unbreaking hours with Charlie, then called his probation officer. The emergency hearing was scheduled for tomorrow, and while the judge would look favorably on his progress, his failure to submit to random alcohol testing all these months guaranteed some amount of jail time.

"Goodnight, Tessa," he said. "And hey, thanks for helping hold down the fort. Sounds like my brother would've melted the Clock without you."

Tessa waved off the accolades. "Sure thing, chicken wing. We had a blast, right Darryl?"

Sam looked at her, his brow a progress tab during a very large download as Tessa said her goodbyes, pressing her cheeks to theirs like royalty in running shorts.

Sure thing, chicken wing.

The red shirt in Charlie's bedroom.

No. It wasn't possible.

Was it?

Sam had been with more women than he could ballpark, and truthfully, few besides Charlie stood out. But there *was* one whose translucent image had passed through his mind on occasion like a porcelain ghost-doll, part déjà vu, part hallucination. He'd never been able to forget her, exactly, nor place her. Until right now.

Holy fuck.

Sobriety had finally lifted the fog.

Instantly, he smelled the chives on the potato skins, floating in grease. Overhead, Don and Ron were duking it out over a bad icing call during the penalty kill. Charlie had been away at university over a month, no guarantee she'd return. Sam, miserable and sick of Darryl chucking shit about it, started hanging out at a dive on Morrow after work, where the bartender broke more glasses than she filled, but with a breezy resignation, like the objects themselves were being unruly. He remembered thinking Charlie would like her; she was also a wiseass, and her pastel gaze was this giant opposing magnet; when it landed on you, all your inner black filings shoved aside.

One night, her heel caught in a floor plank, and she dumped a full tray of chicken wings on herself. The only spare uniform shirt was a triple-XL that hung like a red barrel past her knees, the bar's wacky logo vanishing into her armpit. But in a classic stroke of female ingenuity, she used her ponytail elastic to cinch the waist, cuffed the sleeves, and *POW*—crotch-socking minidress. The patrons cheered their slurry approval as she twirled self-mockingly, head thrown back in laughter, hair falling in chestnut waves.

Sam decided to stay until closing.

"Rough day?" she asked as he helped her flip up the chairs.

"Yeah. Unless by chance you'd like to buy six carts of fresh-cut American bittersweet at triple the market price?"

She leaned on the broom handle. *"Again?"*

"It is shockingly easy to bid on the wrong clock. Someone should really look into it."

"Well, I'd take them off your hands, but I left all my money in Europe."

So that's what she was doing here. Paying for a past adventure. She asked if wiping down her bar top was some kind of community service requirement, or was he going to buy her a drink already. Sam teased in reply, "Sure thing, chicken wing."

She swatted him with the bar towel, then fetched two lowballs and shimmied onto the stool beside him. On this, the sad side of the counter, smoke-filmed potlights and the TV gone black, Sam saw a loneliness that rivalled his own. But then her gaze met his and set off the most wonderfully naked feeling, like she was painting the best parts of him into a much bigger installation.

"This is going to sound like a line," she said, tipping her glass, "but I never do this."

"Then you should know up front . . . I do."

"Does it help?"

He shrugged. "For as long as it lasts."

She bit her lip. The pinch landed square in his own gut, followed by a spreading of heat down his legs as she threw back her whisky. "In that case, I should probably get your name."

Sam introduced himself, chuckling when she did the same, as if the letters on her nametag weren't already etched into every wretched soul to set foot in that bar.

"Good to meet you, Sam. I'm Beth."

EPILOGUE

——◀◦▶——

WINTER

Snowdrop / *Galanthus Nivalis*

Hope.

OUTSIDE THE WINDOW, row upon row of white-capped evergreens were lined up according to size and species, and snow was a meandering waterfall against the pewter sky. Along the curb, wooded heaps tingled the sinuses: gold-studded British Columbian cedar dripping like chandeliers, pine boughs oozing sap, prickled blue fingers of Douglas Fir.

"Hello?"

(TAP-TAP-TAP)

"HELLO?"

(Deafening microphone clatter)

"It's not working."

"Give it a second."

"What the . . . ? I can't see a goddamn thing!"

"Turn the camera around."

"I don't . . . how the hell? For fuck's sake, Spider, can't we use the phone like normal people?"

"Just give me that thing, please . . ."

(More muffles)

Charlie's face, stamped with the red outline of a snorkel mask, filled the screen. "Merry Christmas everybody! Whoa, look at the snow!"

"Hasn't let up since we left for the terminal," Tessa said.

"Calling for another ten to twenty overnight," Rowan added.

The door crashed open. Darryl rushed a tray of poinsettias in from the cold like he was transporting a trauma victim.

"I kind of miss it," Charlie said. She and Sam had jetted off shortly after he completed his sixty-day sentence, before the snow began to fly.

Sam's face squeezed in beside hers. "Says the woman with a grand total of two Canadian winters under her belt."

"Seriously," said Ainsley, climbing the stepladder, canvas in hand. "I'd trade a white Christmas for the Seychelles with Tony any day."

Darryl dropped the tray, sending half the poinsettias crashing to the floor.

"Jeez, Brick," Sam said. "Would you like a hammer?"

Darryl flipped his middle finger at the screen. That Toronto's most sought-after holiday plant detested cold weather summed up everything he'd never wanted to know about indoor stock. "I thought you were in Kenya?"

"That's next week. Sam wants to have breakfast with the giraffes."

"Who doesn't?" Sam said with a wink. "How did auction go today, Tess?"

Tessa sighed. "Ask your brother."

"A know-it-all, this one, just like her old man," Darryl said. "Sitting pretty with her lightning fingers, acting like I can't spot a decent poinsettia."

Tessa's hands flew up. "The one time he's supposed to load up on red, and he's all about salmon!"

Sam's laugh crackled through the speaker.

"Forget it, girlie. He's color blind, I've been saying it for years."

"That explains a lot about his kitchen reno," Rowan teased.

"You keep yukking it up in here," Darryl said. "Some of us have work to do. *Mele Kalikimaka,* lovebirds. Try not to get eaten by sharks or lions or whatever the hell you're spying on today."

"Same to you, brother. See you in a few weeks."

"Love you, Brickie!" Charlie sang.

"Yeah," Darryl mumbled as he headed for the door.

"I should get out there, too, Tony's probably . . ." Tessa trailed off, distracted by an incoming call. She flashed her phone at Ainsley, who arched one eyebrow at the sight of Will's name. Tessa blew a kiss at the tablet, heading for the door. "I'd better take this. Have a blast, you two. Merry Christmas!"

"I'll call you tomorrow, hon," Sam called after her. Tomorrow, she would be with her grandparents, who had warmed to Sam considerably since Tessa introduced him, if confused at first by the missing Greek accent. "Don't forget to send pics from tonight!"

Olivia scuttled in from the cold. She'd left the last of the holiday hampers with Eleanor to distribute so she could swing by the shop on her way to check on the caterers; she needed a few more boughs. Tonight had to be perfect.

Tessa, on a call, waved as she passed. Olivia watched from the doorway as Rowan panned his tablet over the latest phase of renos; a new washroom and storage closet. He caught her eye, looking almost relieved to see her as usual. And happy. For the first time in ages, Olivia was starting to feel the same.

The women's outreach center, founded with the gluttonous divorce settlement Peter Westlake quietly secured, was already impacting more clients than imagined, thanks to Olivia's silent partner. By fronting the operation as an upscale wellness spa, they'd been able to usher it into their own ritzy postal code without the usual not-in-my-backyard objections, ensuring even women like Olivia could access help if needed. Eleanor showed up daily and rolled up her sleeves, but mayoral photo ops were strictly forbidden. She'd refused even to put her name on the door. At the end of the day, what Mrs. Westlake really needed was someone to fight for.

Olivia smiled back at Rowan, eyeballs floating in watery bliss as they so often did lately. Finally, she'd gotten it right. Rowan was a good man, and he'd unearthed the good in herself.

That's why it had to be tonight, at dinner. Technically, it was a touch too soon, but he'd want everyone there, and what better way to mark their first Christmas together? Besides, she wasn't sure she could hide it much longer. She'd read it was still only a tiny cluster of cells, barely bigger than a poppy seed, yet somehow, her insides already felt so different.

Will took a long look out the window as the cabin pressurized, committing snow to memory. He pulled out his phone, open to the same thread all morning.

In a few hours, he'd step off this plane a different man entirely; it felt wrong to leave without saying something. The engines below him grew louder. With eyes squeezed shut, he tapped the call button, stomach lurching with every ring.

She'd texted a few times after he was conspicuously absent from the mayoral swearing-in. Then, a few weeks later, when he dropped from the firm's website. To date, Will hadn't responded; he was too angry. At her, himself.

The Will-and-Tessa-shaped hole in the campaign plan triggered a fair bit of panic in Peter's war room, until Eleanor tabled the masterful pivot no one could oppose—an end to drunk driving. Peter took a hard line out of the gate, pledging a wall-to-wall crackdown within city limits for as long as he was in office. Support among the coveted low-to-middle income demographic pushed through the roof, and no one cared what the mayor-elect's family got up to, least of all his friend Bradley Thornton, now under permanent, legally-binding contract with a chauffer company, purportedly on account of his packed schedule.

"Merry Christmas, Will." Her voice was a song lyric you strained to recall, until those first notes brought every word back.

"Merry Christmas, Tessa."

"Is everything okay?"

"It wasn't. But yeah, I think now it will be."

She exhaled. "I'm glad."

"Thanks, for . . . you know."

In her last voicemail, she'd complained that she still couldn't recall how she ended up with the scar on her face. Will understood; she'd never tell a soul. She felt the weight of his guilt, his shattered heart. A lesser burden than he deserved, but more than she wished him to carry.

"You're welcome."

A pause.

"Rowan's lawyer found a missing file. Copies of all the paperwork we needed to keep Trucks open."

"Oh, yeah?"

"Turned up out of nowhere. All the fines have been dropped."

"Wow. Lucky break."

Will heard the soft click of her lips and knew she was grinning. An overhead voice instructed him to power down his device. "I have to go." *Love you,* he started to add, purely out of habit, before ending the call on a garbled syllable instead.

Her words the day she left crippled him for weeks. If they were true, that she still loved him, that she always would, why didn't it change anything? Now, he understood; he'd love her always, too. But some love curdled like sour milk when you stayed too long, snapped like the tip of a pencil if you pressed too hard.

Sometimes, letting go was the only way.

Will leaned back and closed his eyes as the ground dropped away, lifting him off into the sweet relief of not having to be anybody else.

Tessa slipped her phone back into her pocket and looked up at Charlie's window, framed by seeded eucalyptus the color of ripe figs and magnolia spears that shone like emerald leather, their undersides like camel suede. At the laneway, Tony stood half-inside a Q-8, a cord of sisal between his teeth, securing a Fraser fir to the roof rack.

"Hey, Tee. How were the roads?"

"Pretty bad, but I took it slow, let Darryl grab some extra sleep. What's next up here?"

"Could use a few balsams. I sold the last ten-footer a few minutes ago."

"On it. Oh, and heads up. Ainsley wants you to take her to the Seychelles."

Tony chuckled. "That stuff she's been hanging behind the counter keeps selling, she'll be taking me."

Tessa kept an even, casual pace all the way to the yard, then sprinted through the snow-capped gate. She scanned the aisles, deflating. In the corner, Darryl was hammering a wooden *X* into the bottom of a Scotch pine. Her uncle saw her and rolled his eyes, then jerked his head towards the sold area. Tessa dashed off, ducking under the yellow rope into the dense green thicket flecked with red tags. She shrieked as two gloved hands slipped over her eyes.

"Excuse me, Ma'am, this is a restricted area."

"Let go of me!"

"I'm afraid I am going to have to cuff you."

Tessa wriggled, laughing. "I'm serious!"

"Hmm, you do sound serious. What's the secret password?"

"Shut up and let me look at you, jackass!"

Luke spun her around, the evergreens forming a low-lit cove around them. He wore one of the novelty hats sold at the shop, *I Believe in Santa Claus* stitched across the front. Tessa slid her mittens inside his coat and sank her lips into his. Wet, chunky snowflakes collected on their eyelashes.

"Finally," he said hoarsely, thumbing her cheek.

"No stupid screen in the way for two whole weeks."

Luke lifted one heavy eyebrow and kissed her again. "No stupid clothes in the way would be better."

Tessa laughed. "Might make dinner at Uncle Row's a bit awkward. Pop would come over the table at you, walker and all."

"Nah, Jimbo would fall back. Who else is going to plow that long-ass driveway tonight?"

On Labor Day, Luke had kissed Tessa's every tear before they could slide back to her ears. "You have to go," she'd whispered as he moved inside her once more. "You'll be late."

His thick lashes grew darker as they wettened. "I can't. I don't even want to anymore."

Tessa nearly let him abandon all his plans. Finally, she understood how *certain* felt; it took everything she had to turn it away. "Hey, look at me. *Go.* Do what you need to do. We've got this."

One winter apart wouldn't make any difference. The life her mother had nudged her towards wasn't some showy bloom, dying on-peak in a vase. Like those peonies her father described, it would survive the frost and come back bigger, hardier. All on its own, in the place it had chosen from seed.

ACKNOWLEDGMENTS

To become an author is to decide every day to keep going in the face of a million reasons to quit. I'm deeply grateful to all whose advice or encouragement spoke louder than those reasons:

The mighty and wonderful team at Koehler Books, especially Greg Fields, who saw these characters in every light I'd hoped to paint them and Christine Kettner, who brought my dream layout to life.

Grace O'Connell, who helped me dig up the courage to begin this book, and moreover, to finish it. Gina Frangello, Stacy Bierlein and Anna Barrett, who helped me break it open, locate the heart, then safeguard that above all else. Thorne Ryan, whose invaluable insight and guidance crystallized my goals as a writer. Credit goes to Catherine Cho for the idea to name the chapters after flowers, and Cheralyn Darcey and S. Theresa Dietz, whose respective books *Flowerpaedia* and *The Complete Language of Flowers: A Definitive and Illustrated History* were most helpful in this regard.

The brilliant and beautiful tribe that is the Women's Fiction Writers Association, several of whom read early drafts of this book, and in particular my write-in sisters who inform, inspire and uplift me daily: you changed the whole game for me. Jen "Mission Control" Sinclair, you have pulled me and these pages back to standing more times than I can count. I'm grateful beyond words.

Immense gratitude also to the wise and wickedly funny Joey Boltin, mentor and cherished friend whose family founded the "Very Long Market," which inspired the setting of this story. Jo, you taught this girlie so much about life while I thought I was learning about the flowers, and you nurtured the writer in me long before she was ready to bloom. Everything Tessa finds in Charlie, I've found in you and then some.

Heartfelt thanks to my mother, Catherine, for always encouraging me to be *bigger* while believing me perfect enough as I am, my father,

Martin, for my dogged insistence on running my own race, members of my extended family for a lifetime of unwavering support, and my cottage family for your faith and unparalleled fellowship.

To my sweet girl with the glittering aura, Leah: being your mother is my highest honor, humblest privilege, and deepest joy. You make me better every day. I pray that somewhere between all my navel- and ceiling-gazing these past years, you've learned it's okay to fail (repeatedly), to cry until you can't help but laugh, to recalibrate and start all over again—but never to abandon what lights you up inside.

Finally, to my coworker-turned-everything, Mike: it's been twenty-four years since I first saw you on an overturned bucket at the back of a flower market, and you still make me cry all the good tears. You are my first reader, my fiercest believer, and when I said I wanted to abandon my career to write stories on the fragile hope someone might want to read them someday, you didn't even blink. You've walked every step of this journey with me, carried me for much of it, told me over and over *"you got this"* when I most certainly did not, and asked me time and again *"what do you need?"* when all I've ever needed is you. A finer man could only be fiction; thank you for doing real life with me.

Printed in the USA
CPSIA information can be obtained
at www.ICGtesting.com
JSHW022356221023
50468JS00002B/15

9 798888 240093